The Sirdar Ikbal Ali Shah

MUHAMMED: THE PROPHET

MUHAMMED:
THE PROPHET

by

SIRDAR IKBAL ALI SHAH

TRACTUS BOOKS

MUHAMMED: THE PROPHET

Copyright 1996 for republication © by the Estate of Ikbal Ali Shah & Tractus

All rights reserved. No part of this book may be utilised in any form or by any means, electronic or mechanical, including photocopying, or by any information retrieval or transmission system, without permission in writing from the author's estate or the publisher.

La loi du 11 mars 1957 n'autorisant, au termes des alinéas 2 et 3 de l'article 41, d'une part, que les «copies ou reproductions strictement reservées à l'usage privée du copiste et non destinées à une utilisation collective» et, d'autre part, que les analyses et les courtes citations dans un but d'exemple et d'illustration, «toute représentation ou reproduction intégrale ou partielle fait sans le consentement de l'auteur ou de ses ayants droits ou ayant cause, est illicite» (alinéa 1er de l'article 40). Cette représentation ou reproduction, par quelque procédé que ce soit, constituerait une contrefaçon sanctionnée par les articles 425 et suivants du Code Pénal.»

The publishers gratefully acknowledge the help of Omar Ali-Shah in re-editing the text of his father.

Original Edition published by Wright & Brown, London, 1932

Cover by Alain Jacob

Printed by Graphics Group/France with thanks to Larry Larson

ISBN 2-909347-04-4
TRACTUS
P.O. Box 6777
Reno, Nevada 89513 USA
phone/fax (702) 345-7585
TRACTUS BOOKS
43 rue de la Gaîté
75014 Paris FRANCE
fax (33) 01 44 07 12 07 phone (33) 01 40 47 63 63

DEDICATION

In token of high esteem and admiration,
this book is respectfully dedicated by a
humble Afghan to that great Afghan—

HIS LATE MAJESTY
ALLA HAZRAT GHAZI MUHAMMED NADIR SHAH,
The Monarch of Afghanistan

who, by his redeeming efforts in the cause of peace, has so
nobly upheld the teachings of the Prophet.

CONTENTS

FOREWORD by Omar Ali-Shah   8
INTRODUCTION by Ikbal Ali Shah   9

1. PRE-ISLAMIC ARABIA   11
2. THE MIND AND PRACTICES OF PRE-ISLAMIC ARABIA   31
3. THE LAND AND THE PEOPLE   43
4. THE PROPHET'S ISHMAELITE CONNECTION   49
   THE BUILDING OF THE KAABA   54
5. THE GOVERNMENT OF PRE-ISLAMIC MECCA   57
6. THE BIRTH OF THE PROPHET   75
   EARLY CHILDHOOD OF THE PROPHET   78
   THE CHRISTIAN MONK AND THE PROPHET   83
7. THE PROPHET AS A MERCHANT AND CITIZEN   91
8. THE FIRST VOICE OF TRUTH   99
   THE BEGINNING OF THE PREACHING—EARLY CONVERTS   103
9. REASON FOR THE ENMITY OF THE QUREISH   106
10. THE PERSECUTION: AND ASCENSION   117
11. HIJRA, OR THE FLIGHT   131

12.	ENTRY INTO MEDINA	149
	SETTLING DOWN IN MEDINA	151
	INTERNAL TROUBLE IN MEDINA	155
13.	ESTABLISHMENT OF OTHER ISLAMIC INJUNCTIONS	161
14.	THE BATTLE OF BADR	165
15.	BATTLE OF OHUD.	171
16.	THE JEWISH REACTION	179
17.	THE ARMISTICE OF HUDAIBIYYA	191
18.	THE FALL OF KHAIBER	197
19.	THE EXPANSION OF ISLAM	201
20.	THE MOSLEMS VISIT MECCA	209
21.	THE CONQUEST OF MECCA	215
22.	THE BATTLE OF HUNAIN AND AFTER	219
	THE ISLAMIC PILGRIMAGE	225
23.	THE HOME LIFE OF THE PROPHET	227
24.	THE PROPHET: THE LAST PHASE	237
25.	THE CARDINAL PRACTICES OF ISLAM	243
26.	SLAVERY AND MARRIAGE IN ISLAM	253
27.	THE INTERNATIONAL SPIRIT OF ISLAM	261
28.	THE SPIRIT OF ISLAMIC IDEALS	269
	INDEX	278

FOREWORD

by Omar Ali-Shah

It is with considerable trepidation mixed with enthusiasm that I write this foreword to my father's book. Trepidation as, inevitably, my few faltering words will be judged against themajesty of his style, and enthusiasm because I believe, not just out of filial piety, that the life of the Prophet should reach a wider readership than it did when originally published.

There can be few informed persons who have not followed the life of Muhammed without being impressed, and motivated, by his character as the Perfect Man, military commander, politician and humanitarian who bought peace to Arabia and an end to the barbaric practices in vogue in the Peninsula.

I write these few words in humility and gratitude to the author.

Omar Ali-Shah Hashemi

In the name of Allah, the Compassionate, the Merciful.

INTRODUCTION

In the world of today, when rank, ancestry, race, ascendance, and above all desire of material wellbeing have swept over the nations of the earth and are precipitating crisis after crisis in the life of mankind; when individually or collectively the entire Adam's family is in a sad way; when men's lives are in the swirl of a giant machine-age; when they dare not tarry, but must eternally, as it seems, be moving onwards and onwards to an uncertain and unknown destination; when remedies for the ills of "civilised man" are suggested, only to be found unspecific; and when humanity—if humanity has the courage to own to it—is distracted, and stands as a man lost in a fog, not knowing which way to turn: let me perform my humble duty towards humanity!

I shall not deliver a sermon nor yet write a pious treatise as if begotten of me; and say "do not act thuswise, but do thus and benefit thereby, for I am doing better".

I am simply placing before you the life story of a Perfect Man; aye, man is the word, not God: for the Prophet Muhammed was made of flesh and bone, even like you and I; and yet he was a model.

This was possible, for he was an ideal Personality. And it is in the study of the life work of this timely wondrous man that the whole drama of Islam is cast.

MUHAMMED: THE PROPHET

Read, therefore, in this book about the remarkable method by which success was so permanently attained, that the world has ceased to be what it was, before the sixth century. There is no achievement like it in the known history of man.

In writing this book, I have consulted the works of many Moslem scholars. Especially I am indebted to the researches of Maulana Shibli Nomani, Syed Amir Ali, Bin Ibrahim and Ibn Hisham; and, being a Moslem, as I do not owe allegiance to non-Moslem writers in the matters of Islamic religious history, I had to shun much which otherwise might have been of some interest. I hope that this story of the Prophet might act as a mirror transmitting to others the way of supreme and ever shining benevolence, as it has done to me.

In conclusion, I record my gratitude for encouragement and help of Sir Akbar Hydari, His Highness the Agha Khan, Maulana Abdul Majid and my wife. Allah alone can reward them.

Al Faqir.

Syed Ikbal.

London
1st Ramadanul Mubarik. 1350 A.H.
10th January, 1932, A.D.

Chapter 1

PRE-ISLAMIC ARABIA

You may know of Imra ul-Qais, or on the other hand, you may not. Suffice to add here that few ranked higher than he in the Dark Ages of Arabia, both as a poet and as a warrior-prince.

Recollecting the desert escapades and song of that pre-Islamic singer, the Prophet Muhammed himself described him as *'their leader to Hellfire.'*

Far it is from what is related of him and others; in the scenes of battles, poetical contests, gala fairs and revelry, that you can correctly comprehend as to what hedonistic state society had reached, before and during the early period when the Moslem drama was cast upon the stage of humanity.

The day was hotter than other days in the parched valleys of Arabia of which I speak.

As related, when Imra raced on and onward through the stunted thorny bushes, his heart was sinking with fear, for although he loved his father as little as was his father's affection for him, the murder or burning at the stake of his parent by the rival tribe meant an inter-clan war, a war perchance to last for generations.

Especially at that time of the year it was most inconvenient to him, for the day of the annual fair was nigh and the gallant lads of the clans had many allurements there, amidst song, wine and dancing.

MUHAMMED: THE PROPHET

Presently a rider climbed the edge of a sand dune. *'Ya' Imra ul-Qais!'* he called to the racing poet, *'What hastens thy steps; and where thy train of retainers?'*

Imra, however, was too wrath to reply. He continued his journey towards where they were reported to have slain his father.

But the camel rider questioned again, for prince though that hastening man was, the desert scouts must know the reason, for raiders were many in Arabia, and the safety of the tribes was their first consideration.

'My father wasted my youth,' he tarried to reply, *'and now that I am old he has laid upon me the burden of blood-revenge'*: and he tore his way through the thorny bushes.

Alighting from his mount, the scout sat chewing some dried berries. In his narrowed eyes lurked the suspicion of the desert, as he saw the swiftly disappearing figure of the poet dip and rise between the sand dunes far off.

For long he sat thus scanning the horizon, then his gaze floated northward. Little clouds of dust were now seen arising in the distance, gradually they became larger as white-clad riders were kicking the bellies of their she-camels.

The scout had no doubt that the best part of valour was now to get out of the way of Imra's hordes. He leapt to his saddle and was swathed by those mysterious vastness, where sand seems to stretch to the other end of the world.

Imra in the meantime, so says the narrative, was nearing the gully where his father was reported to have been ambushed.

At the distance he could hear, now faint, now slightly louder, those plaintive notes which only the reed flutes can make. Their notes beat and rose through the gullies. A sinister meaning there was to that flute playing. And he rode on towards them with

PRE-ISLAMIC ARABIA

the fury of a maddened man.

The warmth of the afternoon sun was disappearing with the waning sunshine. Before he could travel another five hundred yards, the twilight had come and had gone.

A blood-red glow lit the little pocket of the rocky defile, as he reached the opening which led to the pass.

Hearing boughs crackling like muffled drums as flames went up and down, he thought that he was seeing the blaze of a giant bonfire.

Presently, he was standing beside his father's mutilated form.

Those who had killed him had celebrated the event by a feast, and had gone. Those free lawless sons of Arabia had a grudge against Imra's father and his class.

That he was a harmless wayfarer did not matter. Had not more than five of them cut their arms and collected their blood in one common bowl, and then, dipping their fingers in it before their clan, sworn to kill at least one man from Imra's tribe? For the sheer devilry of it, in order to prove that the savagery of the desert can always conquer.

'Bah,' they drank the date wine, saying *'Whosoever heard of taming the desert-born.'* Every man was a law unto himself.

Upon the arrival of Imra's men on the scene of the outrage, a war council was held. Revenge burnt in their hearts. Was there going to be another Forty Years' War of tribal revenge, as raged between Bakr and Taghlib?

Are they to accept so many camels or coins as Diya, or blood-money, and would warriors like them then suffer the jeering of tribes by owning *'that they preferred milk of she-camels to blood'*?

> 'With the sword will I wash my shame away,
> Let God's doom bring on me what it may!'

MUHAMMED: THE PROPHET

shouted a warrior. *'Aye, aye!'* the chorus rose, as a hundred spearheads shot up in the air, *'We shall fight.'*

But valiant though he was, at any other time but just then Imra would have ridden ahead of his men, and slain even the children of the rival tribe.

At that time, however, it did not suit him. It meant his taking an oath not to touch wine till the murder was avenged; it meant also non-participation in the gala fair *'where merrymakers will see paradise on earth at gambling tables'*; it meant his not seeing the whirling dancers of Greece and Rome and not hearing the lilting lays that gladden the heart of youth wedded to incarnate love.

> *'Could the taking of revenge not tarry a while?'*

asked Imra.

> *'Besides, would it not be all the greater punishment to the offenders to know that they will be slain by our hands, yes slain, even their wives and children!'*

Those of sensual mind amongst his men appeared to be weakening, even at a time when an Arab should banish everything from his heart and proceed to the business of killing as a point of honour.

The affair, after all, in the first instance concerned Imra; and if he was prepared to swallow the insult, they were surely not going to urge him. There was of course the fair, the merrymaking, the gambling tables and the women: but of this they said nothing to Imra.

But one, bolder than the rest, eyed his companions darkly:

> *'Nay, nay,'* his voice rose. *'Mine ears have heard the hooting of Nama (owl), perched as it was on the tomb of my relation, whose blood revenge I had delayed in taking. Even now, by the spirits of the four winds, can I tell that*

PRE-ISLAMIC ARABIA

the soul of my murdered kinsman had entered that owl. 'Thou shalt hear the spirit of thy father,'

he pointed to Imra,

'and hear the bird cry and hoot for water to drink.'

And although nothing was dearer to the mind of Imra than to postpone going on the warpath at that time, yet he was over-careful not to give a definite order to his clansmen, lest he lose control over his bloodthirsty followers.

At last, one of the younger men reading what was in the mind of their Chief, reminded them that at a moment of grave importance, when significant issues were involved and opinions were divided, the only plan to adopt is to beg guidance from their idol.

To the valley of Tabala, north of Najran, they hied forth, as an idol by the name of Dhul Khalasa stood there. *'That oracle will give the answer.'*

Three arrows, marked the *'Commanding'*, *'Forbidding'* and the *'Waiting'*, lay in a case.

In the usual manner of seeking the answer, he drew an arrow. The reply was the second arrow, *'Forbidding.'*

Inwardly, Imra rejoiced, but to show his faith in bloodthirstiness, he assumed a wrathful attitude to show his men. Breaking the arrow in two, he threw the parts before the idol, exclaiming in apparent anger to the deity: *'If thy father had been slain, thou would'st not have hindered me.'*

Some further particulars about this prince-poet, which I give below, are calculated to show how, even the best specimen of Arab rulers, as he was of his time, inclined towards pleasure, superstition and savagery of the most sordid type; and how the rendezvous of unspeakable vice at the fair of Ukaz, near Mecca, fascinated *'the best princes of their line.'*

MUHAMMED: THE PROPHET

The ebb and flow of that society can be gauged by knowing what great importance Imra ul-Qais possesses. This is my only excuse for giving any account of him here.

When his father, Hajr, was assassinated, Imra shouldered the task of punishing Banu Asad, the rebels, aided by Mudhir. But he failed. He then went to the court of Justinian at Constantinople, from where he received a high appointment and was to be installed as Phylarch of Palestine, but before reaching his destination he died at Angora,

> *'by putting on a poisoned shirt—a gift from Justinian.'*

The Ukaz fair, however, rivalled the scenes of Rome's greatest glory in gaiety and all that enthroned debauchery and licentiousness. Warriors of all tribes, sworn blood enemies for generations, sat in open-air cafes. In taverns, wine goblets were filled and emptied with alarming rapidity.

Hundreds had set out in a gay cavalcade of mules, camels, or on foot. Ribbons flirted from their hair, bells tinkled in their toes as dancing, prancing, women and girls walked alongside their menfolk. Gay Lotharios rode back and forth, round and about on their prize mares, proud of their horsemanship. Every heart beat with the joy of amusement unrestrained *'where shame had left the eyes of women.'*

As caravan after caravan of merrymakers flocked to the fair from every corner of the desert, the plain of Ukaz was filled to overflowing; it stretched to Mecca and beyond. The streets of Mecca, too, were a surging sea of humanity. In the heart of the city lay the Shrine of Idols. Lat, Minat and Uza were the stone representation of the three daughters of their god.

Sword-dancers twirled and twisted to the music of the flute. Girls clad in scanty dresses danced and hopped in the street. Storytellers and soothsayers rubbed shoulders with beggars displaying their sores, and, last of all, the poets were seen

PRE-ISLAMIC ARABIA

hastening to the poetical contests.

Singers of renown assembled before the shrine of Mecca, each poet recited his poem, and the most celebrated ones—at least those which appealed to the sensual side of a debased society, or which excited revenge and warfare, or extolled the vain glories of tribal rivalry—were suspended at the door of the Kaaba.

But the places where people thronged most were the winebibbing booths, converted into sorts of gambling dens.

Beside the many murderous-looking nomads of the desert who had come *'to drink the purest wine of date and millet,'* play dice, and watch the dancing girls, lay a kind of low divan on which the woman proprietress of the tavern displayed her charm by inviting first one, then another man from amongst her customers to share the wine with her.

In the centre of the gathering, the hired dancer whirled and danced to the amusement of rival tribesmen. Other girls sat around with men they had never seen before.

One of the girls of a particular tribe is now pushed on the floor to perform an intricate dance. Her performance is loudly applauded, and they rise and take her forcibly into their arms. Another girl of a rival clan jumps now onto the floor, and the taunting and jeering of the rival men is only drowned by the drawling and drunken voices of newly arriving men of the desert.

Wine having gone to their heads, men and women, quite strangers to each other, throw the dice upon the floor; the whole gathering shouts, roars, even passes unseemly remarks about the comeliness of one and another. One more sober than the rest, rising to her feet, taut as a bowstring and quivering like a thrown dagger, dances amidst the hilarity of men reeling in the dust from the strong date wine.

MUHAMMED: THE PROPHET

The dance gets wilder and wilder. They clap hands; they extol her beauty, the music wells up loud and confident, the dancer whirls, throws her dagger high into the air and then catches it in her teeth. The savage passions of the spectators are let loose; they run to clasp her in their arms. She may be a chief's daughter, but what does it matter in that night of revelry —the three daughters, whose idols are even then watching them from the Kaaba, have sanctioned it all, all: winebibbing, gambling, licentiousness; for they owed no allegiance to a god which prohibited the full play of their animal appetites. They hungered to satisfy nothing but lust.

Raids and blood feuds having been prohibited during those four months of feasting and riotous orgies, clan after clan gathered, not at their places of worship—idol adoration though it was—but betook themselves from tavern to tavern, drinking, singing, dancing and making beasts of themselves generally: for whether men of the desert or the town, love of gambling, the pleasure of romantic song was all they cared for: beyond that lay the grave, as the following in *Hamasa* shows:

> *Roast meat and wine: the swinging ride*
> *On a camel sure and tried,*
> *Which her master speeds amain*
> *O'er low dale and level plain:*
> *Women marble—white and fair*
> *Trailing gold-fringed raiment rare:*
> *Opulence, luxurious ease,*
> *With the lute's soft melodies—*
> *Such delights, hath their brief span;*
> *Time is Change, Time's fool is Man.*
> *Wealth or want, great store or small,*
> *All is one since Death's are all.*

Occasionally, however, young and old gathered at the steps of the shrine of Kaaba to hear the poems of the great singers. Long robed, or almost naked, they encircled the Kaaba, the former being the Qureish, the custodians of the shrine, and those who circumvented without any clothes at all were non-Qureish tribes.

Then human sacrifice was offered to the idols; cases were decided when, according to their accepted traditions, one's widowed stepmother was forthwith wedded to one.

Even real sisters were given in marriage to brothers, so says Nomani; there was no limit to the number of wives that a man might have, and the custom of polyandry was celebrated at such gatherings.

It was at meetings like these, at the shrine too, when the aforementioned Imra ul-Qais, read his *Qasida*, a poem, before a crowded audience with gusto, and described in the most obscene language his adulterous behaviour towards his cousin.

The relish with which he paused after each stanza of that notorious poem thrilled his hearers, but even in the most debauched society of the world today, its recitation could not be tolerated. Withal, the poem was so highly commended by those who heard it that they immediately voted for the excellence of this creation of the poet-prince. It was forthwith exalted to the rank of *Muallaqat*, was written on finest Egyptian linen with gold, and suspended at the door of the shrine as the choicest gem of poetical work; so true was it to the mind of men and women of Arabia of that period.

A little too outspoken though such poetical compositions of the pre-Islamic Arabs may be to us, or obnoxious as they certainly were to the Prophet Muhammed—who, as will be shown later, rigorously stamped out licentiousness—it must be admitted that in the desert regions, the art of poesy was much coveted.

A poet was as great a personality as a conquering hero of many battles. The popularity of such singers, as can be judged, was due to the fact that they produced none other than those compositions which appealed to the people of their age. They let people have what people wanted. Consequently, you may find an Arab woman pray that she may be blessed with a son who should become a poet, and a she-camel to feed such a renowned poet, whose Qasida might hang over the door of the holy Kaaba.

Such being the case, it is permissible to conclude that those giants of pre-Islamic poetical literature, whose works flirted over the shrine and were included in *Muallaqat* were symptomatic of a period which we Moslems now call the Dark Ages of Arabia: so that when we quote from the life and work of any of these poets, we are fairly close to a correct criterion and data with which to judge the society in Arabia before the advent of Islam.

At that period we know that pleasure reigned supreme; and whosoever spoke of it in such fashion as to draw people near any aspect of that pleasure was a favourite bard and singer.

And whereas I quote from Lyall's *Ten Ancient Arabic Poems* in testimony of what is stated above, the following extract from Asha's works should not be confused with the outpouring of later singers like Omar Khayyam or Maulana Rumi, whose mystic meaning, couched in terms of wine and flowers and beauty, has no counterpart in Asha's pure and unadulterated reference to naked vice, with no trace of allusion to the Divine, but mere camel love and depravity of manners.

In the description of gatherings of winebibbers, Asha has no rival.

The following lines from his most celebrated poem is interesting, especially when it is added that his devotion to earth's good things was so great that, when midnight wine-drinking orgies took place at his tomb, as a tribute to his genius, it was the custom to pour the unconsumed wine over his grave.

PRE-ISLAMIC ARABIA

Here is what he says in *Asha and Alqama:*

> *Many a time I hastened early to the tavern—*
>   *while there ran*
> *At my heels a ready cook,*
>   *a nimble, active serving-man—*
> *'Midst a gallant troop, like Indian scimitars,*
>   *of mettle high;*
> *Well they know that every mortal,*
>   *shod and bare alike, must die.*
> *Propped at ease I greet them gaily,*
>   *then with myrtle-boughs I greet,*
> *Pass amongst them wine that gushes*
>   *from the jar's mouth, bittersweet.*
> *Emptying goblet after goblet—*
>   *but the source may no man drain—*
> *Never cease they from carousing save to cry:*
>   *'Fill up again!'*
> *Briskly runs the page to serve them:*
>   *on his ears hang pearls: below,*
> *Tight the girdle draws his doublet*
>   *as he bustles to and fro.*
> *'Twas the harp, thou mightest fancy,*
>   *waked the lute's responsive note.*
> *Here and there among the party,*
>   *damsels fair superbly glide:*
> *Each her long white skirt lets trail*
>   *and swings a wineskin at her side.*

Considering the state of society in which the poet lived, and the many ceremonies which were held in Arabia over his grave, it is impossible to escape the conclusion that Asha meant literally every word that he wrote.

There were no allusions, nothing whatever of the gorgeous

imagery which characterised the later mystics of Islam.

In Asha's poems dwelt no deep significance of hidden instructions, in which he who seeks may, indeed shall, find if he be eager enough or ardent enough. It was a plain tale of riotous living; no more, no less.

Asha's or Imra's *'wine,'* for example, did not signify devotion, any more than *'sleep'* meant meditation of the Divine perfection; or *'perfume,'* the hope of the Divine afflatus.

In the songs of these spokesmen of pre-Islamic Arabia, zephyrs did not signify the gift of godly grace, and kisses, the transports of devotion and piety. With them, the keeper of the tavern was no hierophant.

Compare these materialistic poems with what was sung in the Masnavi centuries afterwards: the song is there, the flute and all the elements of passion, but cast in a different mould. The Maulana sings:

> *Oh! hear the flute's sad tale again:*
> *Of Separation I complain:*
> *E'er since it was my fate to be*
> *Thus cut off from my parent tree,*
> *Sweet moan I've made with pensive sigh,*
> *While men and women join my cry.*
> *Man's life is like this hollow rod;*
> *One end is in the lips of God,*
> *And from the other sweet notes fall*
> *That to the mind the spirit call*
> *And join us with the All in All.*

Whatever disparity may exist between these two classes of poets, no one can deny that each class was a mouthpiece of its epoch; and it is my purpose to show how the poet's art in both cases brings the contrast vividly before us, as a result of the preaching of Islam.

PRE-ISLAMIC ARABIA

Here again, we have Omar Khayyam singing:

And lately by the Tavern Door agape,
Came stealing through the Dusk an Angel Shape
  Bearing a Vessel on his Shoulder; and
He bid me taste of it; and 'twas—the Grape!

The Grape that can with Logic absolute
The Two-and-Seventy jarring Sects confute:
  The Subtle Alchemist that in a trice
Life's leaden metal into Gold transmute:

In this, like Rumi's work, you have the imagery *par excellence,* for these men acquired the state of initiation of the self.

The term *'beauty'* is used to denote the perfection of God, and *'lovelocks and the tresses'* the infinitude of His Glory. *'Down on the cheeks'* is symbolic of the multitudinous spirits which serve Him. *'Inebriation and dalliance'* typify that abstraction of soul which shows contempt of mundane affairs.

The reason of it is, as I have said before, to be found in the initiation of the self, which the authors of *Muallaqat* sadly lacked, even though their poems were hung at the shrine in Mecca. The moral glow and warmth which you find in Islamic poets was not due entirely to their devotion to the rites and ceremonies of the religion, it was on account of their attuning to a state of spirituality as well.

Ritual of itself is naught compared with this spiritual knowledge. They no doubt symbolise the process and lend dignity to it, but that is all: for rite and symbols, apart from high intentions and spiritual significance, can even be degrading if performed for show.

Yet they express much more than mere words: that is, they are efficacious in supplementing the imperfect medium of human speech in the conveyance of subliminal ideas.

And whereas it is entirely by virtue of that initiation of the self which exalts the Islamic poets above those of the Dark Ages, yet initiation itself can never reveal the truth in its entirety. The degree of truth unveiled is in ratio to the seeker's own potentialities.

Of such potentialities, those who sang at Mecca before their idols were singularly barren. Their society, vitiated as it was, did not demand anything other than what they were.

Here, however, we must see how that initiation of the self worked in the minds of men, which characterises their Islamic poetry.

The nature of the doctrine revealed to their initiates is assuredly capable of expression in one formula:

It is the entrance into a new life, or rather, the return to an old and real one; that is, to that *'paradise'* from which man fell, to that divine communion from which he, by his own acts, has been excluded.

Initiation is the instinctive as well as intellectual aspiration of the higher man towards restoration to the divine communion, unity with, or absorption in, the divine. The initiate is equipped with the knowledge of how he came into the material world, and how he must re-ascend.

The several grades of initiation, although they differ considerably in respect of the various orders which have existed in the history of mankind, may actually be reduced to three, or perhaps four.

The first is the nascent grade or *'rebirth'*; but not in the Hindu or Buddhist sense, however.

The second is the stationary, or that of spiritual *'hovering'*, or juvenility.

PRE-ISLAMIC ARABIA

The third is the new life proper, and lastly and more occasionally, its sequel, which is symbolical of the experience of the new condition.

It is only when material life is left behind and *'supernatural rebirth'* is achieved, that initiation has taken place.

The three great degrees may roughly be described as purification, consecration, and illumination.

Does initiation, in itself, suffice for actual illumination?

That actual spiritual knowledge was passed on to the epopts, we cannot doubt. Even so, it must have been insufficient of itself, without a spiritual transformation in the soul of the neophyte.

Indeed, the genuine neophyte is himself the true hierophant, nor can the official hierophant be other than a demonstrator, adviser and inspiring force. He cannot by any word or act transform the neophyte into the perfected initiate unless there be already, in the heart of the latter, a supreme intention and responsive desire.

Initiation is, indeed, an inward act of the soul, a supernatural act of the psychic entity in man: free, unfettered, determined, responsive, yet with the self wholly inspired in the ultimate.

But it may well be said, that, having accomplished initiation, it is impossible for the epopt to convey its full significance to those outside of the portals, even if he would.

Words and forms he can reveal, if he be so minded, but these would hold no meaning for the uninitiated; simply because such a person would be confronted with matters unterrestrial, and outside the scope and vocabulary of mundane knowledge and apprehension.

Indeed, such secrets as are unveiled to him are, and were, conveyed to his spirit through the voiceless message of symbols and not through words. And they are actually apprehended as often as not through subsequent reflection and contemplation, rather than through immediate illumination.

There is, to be sure, nothing in the mysteries which the born mystic may not excogitate for himself by dint of his own genius, just as the born poet invariably discovers for himself those fundamental truths regarding his inspirational art which appear almost as of a semi-supernatural order to workaday men.

He will quickly find for example that, of itself, the human soul is imperfect; that, lacking the quality of receptivity, the spirit is powerless—and other and equally cogent illuminations will rapidly present themselves to the veridical mystic. It follows that the initiation of the self is perfectly possible, that it has been attained in hundreds of instances, and not only by the exceptional.

The descent of the soul into matter is one of the most profound mysteries of human existence, as is its converse, the ascent of the spirit into the realms immaterial. These twain constitute symbolic death and 'rebirth'; and were bodied forth in the Mysteries.

It is a legend of ages untold, embraced by all the mystical orders. It is, indeed, the intellectual and psychic discernment of the divine, when the soul, making not a mythos for herself, but through sheer sleight of awakened and instinctive spirituality, arrives at a knowledge of the truth concerning her actual origin and the 'realities' of her existence.

It is a novel, or rather, a reawakened sense of perception, and initiation is merely its drama, the symbolic gesture of its aroused consciousness of the need for reunion with divinity.

By initiation, nothing can be gained except that which has to be gained.

The seeming crudity of such a statement includes a truth so

PRE-ISLAMIC ARABIA

obvious, and yet so deep, as to appear as needless as profundity frequently appears to persons of material tendency—for there is but one way which God opens into the temple which was founded before the beginning of the world.

The way is well trodden, the stones are deeply worn. There are no unessentials of power, of mere romantic potentialities won for the adept—like wealth, charm, long life, or the ability to wield occult powers.

These are, indeed, the insignia of the slight and fatuous soul dallying in the purlieus of the temple, vain and degenerate in essence.

The true secrets are those of grace, understanding, perfect apprehension, and joy in the knowledge of the abounding life unrolled before the spirit; rhythmic delight: the sovereign poise of certainty.

The core of the revelation in the Greater Mysteries lay in intellection, in which the archetypal image of universal nature was revealed. The contemplation and union with the Highest supervened.

Thus it will be seen that the ritual and drama had little to do with the higher stages, which were almost purely of a supernormal and spiritual character. But to express this adequately, mere language fails. These things are apprehended, neither seen nor heard.

What is there to learn in this apprenticeship of life, other than the essential poise necessary to the approach towards Otherwhere?

This world is, indeed, an aerodrome, in which man is building, fitting and testing those winged pinnaces which shall bear him to immortality. If he fail in his 'prentice task, then must he assuredly lose and suffer accordingly.

It is merely the self discipline of the Divine, endeavouring

MUHAMMED: THE PROPHET

at great distances to justify itself through various experiments in the depths of time and space, sending out its colonist particles to replenish the spheres, and to triumph, ere they return to the Fatherland, to gain new strength from the sources of the Ultimate, and answer for what they have done.

This means that, toward this end, it becomes essential to cultivate a particular psychic state through steady contemplation of the divine; the afar—that distance, that wonder of aloofness—which is the heart of Paradise.

Intellection, introspection, the reduction of mental and psychic chaos, of the worldly confusion of the heart, mind, and soul, towards the orderly though rapt comprehension of the one simple truth and necessity—'union with God.'

Moreover, the true significance of the divine union is too frequently misapprehended, especially by those who dread it as being peradventure of the nature of individual psychic extinction.

In one sense, the human soul is never entirely out of communication with the divine, indeed its native character renders it more easy to aspire than to grovel—the doctrine of its native wickedness notwithstanding.

The wretched and truly damnable doctrine which says that the heart of man is 'desperately wicked' has, I contend, wrought mischief untold, and has probably wrecked more lives than it has helped to ways of grace. It is a dark saying of hierophantic superiority, based on a degenerate assumption of universal and widespread human depravity, which could only have been engendered in some hypersensitive and cloistered mentality, unused to human converse and aloof from the true nobility and divineness of the common mind, which shows visibly in the neighbourhood of each and every one of us.

The soul of man is tired of being told it is wicked, when, on the whole, it is good; and is essaying most admirably to find its way through the fogs of sin to the sun.

And who can blame it if it is equally tired of religions, in which the truth that eternal life must inevitably not end in spiritual ecstasy (if its laws be adequately fulfilled), and is somewhat occluded by a ministry, which, with all its virtues, is prone to lay stress on the gloomy side of things, and is most certainly unvisited by the spirit of rapture in things divine, devoting all its song and poem to love of this world, as did the authors of intellectual outpourings in pre-Islamic Arabia?

The consciousness of fellowship with God is the First significant token that the process of union with the divine has commenced.

But of this I am very sure: that it does not imply the full achievement of unity.

It is, I believe, an expression prior and preparatory to, initiation, for union with God grows and advances as comprehension and expression and intuition grow through successive acts of the spirit.

The wings strengthen and the flight grows longer. The lamp is constantly burning and it behoves man to make use of the light.

The neophyte, however, understands that the Mysteries, as we know them, must assuredly be described as the Mysteries of Earth. Their whole intent is a stepping from this mortality to immortality, consequently they cannot in any way be related to the Mysteries of the Divine, of which man has rumours, but cannot even conceive the nature or the felicity thereof.

The Prophets alone have that honour.

Mystery, in short, reveals, on its unveiling, fresh mystery: and so must the progression proceed far past the human ken.

MUHAMMED: THE PROPHET

The peculiarly insensible attitude of the greater part of the pre-Islamic Arabs toward the deeper mysteries of spiritual existence constituted a grave danger to humanity.

Avidly seizing upon the husks of the material, it had permitted itself to forget the inestimable treasures of the spirit. Its attitude of impatience with affairs spiritual and of granting the utmost importance to its own racial and individual welfare ought undoubtedly to have aroused the gravest unrest in men and women of serious and exalted character.

A country like pre-Islamic Arabia, which could not afford to examine and grapple with the great problems of psychic existence, and which was wrapped up in things material and pleasurable, and which was not established on the rock of indubitable truth; whose people believed all wisdom to be based on material fact—which had, in short, no strain or desire towards spiritual ascension—was indeed in a perilous position.

Just as I am well assured that no individual can lead a life of psychic security without at least a minimum of contemplation upon things hidden and divine, so am I equally persuaded that no nation which, in the main, ignores them, can be secure in justice and in loftiness of ideal if it lives only according to a passion-exhausting programme of life—as did the people of Arabia before the advent of the Prophet Muhammed

Chapter 2

THE MIND AND PRACTICES OF PRE-ISLAMIC ARABIA

So far I have said little of the savagery which these pre-Islamic Arabs showed in war, and in other customs of their everyday life. Those facets of their behaviour can also be depicted by their poetry.

Reading the passages of their early literature, one notices a most extraordinarily complex mentality of savagery mixed with cowardice.

It was a common custom with them to bury their female children. Proverbs of that time have it that

'The despatch of daughters is a kindness'

and

'The burial of daughters is a noble deed.'

In contrast to what I have already explained about the idea of life-after-death, and the conception of the Day of Judgement, the pagan Arab's afterlife counted for naught.

There was only a primitive idea of ancestral affection, brotherhood in arms and common love of pleasure, with which life ended for them.

They will give no quarter to their enemies, and often show ruthless behaviour in battle, whether in provoked attack or revenge, and will gloat over the miseries of their enemies.

A warrior sings about a battle:

MUHAMMED: THE PROPHET

> *Oh, the warriors girt with swords good for slashing,*
> *Like the levin, when they drew them, outflashing!*
> *Through the noonday heat they fared: then, benighted,*
> *Farther fared, till at dawning they alighted.*
> *Breaths of sleep they sipped; and then, while they nodded,*
> *Thou didst scare them: lo, they scattered and scudded.*
> *Vengeance wreaked we upon them, unforgiving:*
> *Of the two clans scarce was left a soul living.*

In his exaltation he proclaims in glee; for no longer need he keep away from his beloved wine cup, which he had forsworn whilst his enemies lived:

> *Lawful now to me is wine, long forbidden:*
> *Sore my struggle ere the ban was o'erridden.*
> *Pour me wine, O son of 'Amr! I would taste it,*
> *Since with grief for mine uncle I am wasted.*
> *O'er the fallers of Hudhayl stand screaming*
> *The hyena; see the wolf's teeth, will discover*
> *Vultures treading corpses, too gorged to hover.*

Bravery may sound through all of this, but it was always so when in number the victors were superior.

They were also not averse to resorting to cowardly tactics, as shown in *Hamasa*:

Humble him who humbles thee, close tho' be your kindredship:
If thou canst not humble him, wait till he is in thy grip.
Friend him while thou must; strike hard when thou hast him
    on the hip.

Are these the traits of brave warriors, to strike a man when he is not looking, or who considers one a friend?

Such, however, were the Arab clansmen of the pre-Islamic era.

MIND AND PRACTICES OF PRE-ISLAMIC ARABIA

Worse than that is the unchivalrous character of another chieftain who thirsted for revenge. It is the story of the treachery of Qays b. al-Khatim.

I cannot do better than let it be related in the words of Aghani, which shows how one Qays, after slaying his father's murderer, is befriended by one Khidash.

Both set out to satisfy another blood vengeance on account of Khidash.

> 'Then Khidash called for one of his camels,' says Aghani, 'and mounted it, and started with Qays to find the Abdite who killed his father. And when they were near Hajar, Khidash advised him to go and inquire after this man, and to say to him when he discovered him: 'I encountered a brigand of thy people who robbed me of some articles, and on asking who was the chieftain of his people, I was directed to thee. Go with me then, that thou mayst take from him my property.'

> 'If,' Khidash continued, 'he follows thee unattended, thou wilt gain thy desire of him; but should he bid the others go with thee, laugh, and if he ask why thou laughest, say 'With us, the noble does not as thou dost, but when he is called to a brigand of his people, he goes forth alone with his whip, not with his sword; and the brigand, when he sees him, gives him everything that he took, in awe of him' ... If he shall dismiss his friends, thy course is clear, but if he shall refuse to go without them, bring him to me nevertheless, for I hope that thou wilt slay him and them.'

It will be seen from the story how a treachery was being planned, firstly by harping on the valour of the desert-born—if indeed they had any—by way of a taunt to lure a man away unarmed; and secondly that a second man was being made the cat's-paw for this nefarious act; whilst the avenger himself would not come out in the open.

MUHAMMED: THE PROPHET

But to proceed:

> 'So Khidash stationed himself under the shade of a tree, while Qays went to the Abdite, and addressed him as Khidash had prompted; and the man's sense of honour was touched to the quick, so that he sent away his friends and went with Qays. And when Qays came back to Khidash, the latter said to him, 'Choose, O Qays! Shall I help thee or shall I take thy place?' Qays answered, 'I desire neither of these alternatives, but if he slays me, let him not slay thee!' Then he rushed upon him, and wounded him in the flank and drove his lance through the other's side, and he fell dead on the spot ...'

After reading about such deeds of utter cowardice, it is really begging the question to ask whether these pre-Islamic Arabs had any noble characteristics left at all.

And yet we had much of valour described in *Muallaqat*, in the war-poem of Tayyi.

It is hard to imagine an Arab warrior in a battle scene as depicted by that wonder-poet of Pagan times.

But I must let you judge its truth from what is related above regarding the unchivalrous actions of their Chieftains.

Tayyi sings:

> Full-armed against me stood
> One feared of fighting men:
> He fled not oversoon
> Nor let himself be ta'en.
>
> With straight hard-shafted spear
> I dealt him in his side
> A sudden thrust which opened
> Two streaming gashes wide,

MIND AND PRACTICES OF PRE-ISLAMIC ARABIA

Two gashes whence outgurgled
His lifeblood: at the sound
Night-roaming ravenous wolves
Flock eagerly around.

So with my doughty spear
I trussed his coat of mail—
For truly, when the spear strikes,
The noblest man is frail—

And left him low to banquet
The wild beasts gathering there,
They have torn off his fingers,
His wrist and fingers fair!

Let us know these people of Arabia a little more, by examining their general way of living, and in regard to their own beliefs, we find that those who were at all attracted by the ideas of spirituality fell into three categories.

There was a section which thought that all the panorama of life is nothing but nature—mother nature, a biological phenomenon.

No controlling power guided the growth and decay. Man was evolved out of the interplay of vegetating manifestation, it grew, it thrived and it withered and died, just like a tree, and when reduced to dust, it remained. That God had no place in their imagination was patent.

A second section, however, believed in the existence of a Divinity, but did not tolerate the conception of retribution, which meant that they owed no allegiance to the idea that every human being is answerable for his actions.

Yet there was a third section which believed in God and His reward and punishment, but denied the fact that, through

MUHAMMED: THE PROPHET

Divine Will, man can be charged with a Mission and be styled as the Prophet of Allah.

There were sun and star-worshippers amongst them, others offered prayers to the moon; but by far the largest number were idolaters.

Altogether three hundred and sixty idols reposed in the Kaaba. Various other idols such as Lat, Uza, Minat, Dadd, Sowaa, Yaghwas, and Yawaq were worshipped at Taif, Mecca, Medina, Domatul Jindal, and in Yemen respectively. But the largest idol, known as Hobal, was built in the roof of the shrine of the Kaaba.

Hobal's aid was sought in war cries, and thus he may be termed as the war-god of the Qureish tribe.

> *It was not necessary,* says Mohammed Ali, *for the pagan Arabs to have the stones even properly shaped, any rude image was installed as a deity.*

When they went on a journey, their stone gods travelled with them. The method of carrying these idols was, however, peculiar.

> *They carried four pieces of stone: three were used to make a hearth for resting their cooking pots on, and the fourth was placed as an object of worship in a hurriedly erected shrine. At times, even those very stones on which cooking had been done previously, were used for worship.*

Over and above the three hundred and sixty idols set up in the Kaaba, every clan had his own stone god and even every individual carried an image of sorts. Their prayers consisted in offering sacrifices before these idols; they circumambulated around them and knelt before them.

But whereas they thus did honour to these idols, I am inclined to believe that these idols were rather the medium

MIND AND PRACTICES OF PRE-ISLAMIC ARABIA

through which supplications were made to a godhead—whatever that be—probably an indefinable idea involving something that had reposed in these stones in the form of some sort of benign and holy attributes, and that through the agency of such, the worshippers could propitiate for rain for their crops, victory in battle, and childless women pray to be blessed with children.

An interesting proof of this contention may be given by quoting the instance when Umru Bin Lahi, whose real name is Rabeayta Bin Harsa, once went to a Syrian city and found the people of the town there bending low before an idol.

'To what purpose do you kneel?'

he asked the head priest.

'Knowst thou not, this idol answers our prayers.'

Umru, who was destined to be the introducer of idol worship in Arabia proper, felt frankly perplexed; and asked to be enlightened further. Then he was told of the Syrian belief in the idol, how the stone image sent rain to them when drought set in, how it blessed them with victory in battle, how their crops were protected by him.

Umru also took a few idols from that shrine, and having brought them to his native country, set them up near the Kaaba.

As Mecca then lay on the trade route where many Arab tribes paid regular visits, and took their cue, both in worship and in social custom, mostly from that cradle of Arab culture-mixing, idol worship forthwith spread far and wide into every nook and corner of Arabia. The oldest idol was, of course, Minat, which was set up at a place called Qadid on the seashore, where the people of Medina took their offerings. This was also the spot where the pagan pilgrims of Mecca, on their return, discarded their holy garb.

MUHAMMED: THE PROPHET

A remarkable fact, however, emerges out of more profound reasoning about the idol-worshipping of pre-Islamic Arabia. The people, to all intents and purposes, were idol-worshippers as we commonly understand the term today; they considered their stone deities to be mediums of the acceptance of the worshipper's prayers and wishes.

It was the only centralised mode of worship for the majority of the Arabs.

In battle they fought in the name of Hobal; in victory, they made sacrifices at thanksgiving services before these idols: and yet side by side with this, you have the idea of rank insubordination, even of sacrilege, towards their idols: such as is related in the case of Imra ul-Qais, who broke the spear and threw it in the face of his idol because the oracle would not allow him to wage war: or, on other occasions, using their gods so perfunctorily as to rest their cooking pots upon them.

And what may be said of those cave dwellers, who inhabited the rock-city on the north of Medina? Their cult was associated almost entirely with the making of rain. In their naive philosophy, only one thing could conjure down the amount of moisture necessary to the growth of the millet and dates on which they frugally lived in their stony valley, and for the sustenance of their flocks and herds—and that was human blood.

Unless the thunder-god of Sinai was frequently refreshed with draughts of the vital essence of humanity, he would grow old and wither away, and the millet and date crops would fail. Rain was indeed blood, magically transformed into fructifying moisture, and the Rain-maker on the mountain-peak must be kept in life.

> 'And mark you,' said Abu-Zeitun, 'How those Unbelievers had a reasoning of their own. For they

MIND AND PRACTICES OF PRE-ISLAMIC ARABIA

thought, benighted folk, that the Efreet they called their god would not be contented with the blood of slaves or fellaheen, but required that of the noblest in the land, of men with many fathers. And with their foolish faith they mingled the government of their city, which Allah in his good time laid low, as you perceive, and gave to the vultures, the bats and the hyenas, as He will assuredly give the other cities of the pagan to his creatures of ruin in His own good time.'

And on a day in the early spring while yet there was no sign of rain they brought the hereditary princess of the city and the man her husband, who was not really her husband at all, but a fair youth selected for the rite, and they filled the red valley with banners and the sound of trumpets, making a great procession in honour of the false demon they called their god, whose image they bore in a chest on stretchers. And with shoutings and hymns they came to the spot at the head of the valley yonder where the cliffs meet, and they bound the pair separately to the twin pillars, the bases of which you may still behold there.

And the whole multitude of the people, every man, woman and child in the valley, gathered round the pair, howling and calling on their god to send them the rain they desired for their crops and herds, saying that without his aid the date-tree would wither, and the millet fail, and the cattle and sheep perish for want of water, and even they and their little ones be without drink and sustenance.

Then, when their prayers and hymns and shoutings had died down for very want of more vigour in their lungs and throats, the horrible priest of their mystery came forward with a great knife in his hand, dressed in striped garments, the stones of witchcraft sparkling upon his breast.

MUHAMMED: THE PROPHET

And, having made his false prayers to the demon, he spoke to the young man, telling him that on that day he would be wedded to the woman bound to the other pillar, who was veiled, and whose face he had never seen.

Having adjured him to be a good husband—frightful mockery,—he raised his hideous knife, and with all his strength brought it down on the bowed neck of the ill-starred wretch. With one or two strokes he severed the head from the body, tearing it from the trunk, and when the welling blood fell on the sand which drank it up, the multitude cried out that the god of thunder was appeased, and that they should have rain.

Then, taking the ghastly head in his hands, the priest carried it to the Princess where she stood, bound to the pillar, telling her that this was her husband, and that she should love and cherish him. And she, on her part, entering into the heathenish business, took the head between her hands, calling it her husband and her lover, kissing the purple lips and cherishing it to her bosom, at which the people set up revived shouts of joy."

Do you marvel, that this valley is as you see it, its pillars the haunt of wild beasts and its images cast to the ground?

Among many other sordid practices of theirs, their superstitions may be noted. The sacrificing of camels and leaving the carcasses by the side of the grave till they were decomposed and nothing but the skeleton remained, was a common practice. The idea was that the deceased could thereby continue his journey—to wherever he went after death—on that very same camel.

As often as not the best camel of the family herd was tied to a peg near the grave to starve and die in order to serve the abovementioned purpose.

MIND AND PRACTICES OF PRE-ISLAMIC ARABIA

The reading of Oracles by means of pointless arrow, called Kidah, was rife.

Belief in incantations and charms was universal, women were mere chattels, and treated with utmost barbarity. Prostitution was an accepted profession.

> '*Over and above the plurality of wives,*' says Mohammed Ali, '*a man could have illicit intercourse with any number.*'

Captive women, kept as hand-maidens, were forced to earn money by questionable means for their captors.

Married vows were not binding, for such were permitted to conjugate with others for the sake of offspring. This barbarous practice was called Istibza, a similar practice obtaining amongst the Hindus styled as Niyoga.

A man could divorce his wife a hundred times and then could take her back.

The art of reading and writing was limited to a very few.

Concurrently with the worship of idols, their belief in divination, witchcraft and omens was steadfast.

Little bits of hay were tied to the tail of a cow, and then the tuft set on fire as the animal was driven across to the rocky defiles. That totem was believed to act act an express message to whosoever sent rain, to end the drought.

In case of a reverse in battle, the vanquished warriors entered their houses by the back doors so as not to bring bad luck into the house. Should a bird cross their path from left to right, success lay in their errand that day.

Solitary places, according to their belief, were peopled by evil spirits.

Man's soul, they thought was born with the child in equal

proportion to the newborn: as the body grew in size, so did the soul.

The entire extent of Arabia was split into factions, tribes and clans: warring against each other, blood forays and battles of revenge were the order of the day, even amongst the various units of a clan.

Every man had his own code of laws, no one could control lawlessness, there was no central government of any sort. The chief of the clan, too, was obeyed if it was convenient to his followers, especially if there was a prospect of loot and rapine in the wake of a battle call.

There was neither law nor unity, sense of morality, nor even decent citizenship. All was a chaos.

'The first peculiarity, then, which attracts our attention,'

says Sir William Muir—who does not love the Prophet Muhammed overmuch—

> *'is the subdivision of the Arabs into innumerable bodies, governed by the same code of honour and morals, and exhibiting the same manners, speaking for the most part the same language, but each independent of the others; restless and often at war amongst themselves; and even where united by blood or by interest, ever ready on some insignificant cause to separate and give way to an implacable hostility.*
>
> *Thus, at the era of Islam, the retrospect of Arabian history exhibits, as in the Kaleidoscope, an ever-varying state of combination and repulsion, such as had hitherto rendered abortive any attempt at a general union'* ...
>
> *The problem had yet to be solved, by what force these tribes could be subdued or drawn to one common centre; and it was solved by Muhammed.*

Chapter 3

THE LAND AND THE PEOPLE

It now behoves us to know something of the geographical and tribal history and distribution of the country where the early Arabian drama was enacted.

The country of Arabia usually styled as Jazirah, or the island, is bounded on the east by the Persian Gulf, in the south by the Arabian Sea and the Gulf of Aden, and on the west the Red Sea separates it from Egypt, whilst on the north an imaginary line, drawn across the Syrian desert from Basra to Jerusalem, marked its extent and separated it from the warring hordes of Chosroes and the Caesars.

This vast region, which embraces an area twice the size of France, is, geographically speaking, a plateau. Down practically the entire western border runs a wall of mountains from north to south, as I have described it in one of my earlier works on Arabia. All along the Red Sea, from ten to fifteen miles eastwards of the shore, one finds it rising to varying heights of several thousand feet above sea level. Gradually, however, the wall of these mountains merges into the plateau, and these slope eastwards in the direction of the central areas of the sandy desert.

The plains, whether on the western, southern or eastern shores, are scarcely broader than thirty miles. The western face of the mountain attains its highest point at its southern extremity, where an altitude of ten thousand feet is reached.

MUHAMMED: THE PROPHET

The slopes of the plateau too, show a difference as they plunge into the central and northern Arabian sandy wastes, for there are two of these slopes, the one dropping away north-eastwards into the sandy tracts of the Syrian desert, and the other southeastwards into the Arabian no-man's land of Rubi-el-Khali.

In the peninsula itself we find three distinct regions. There is a middle portion of hard boulder-strewn sand with a very considerable number of oases, which maintain a large population. Around this hard sand, in both the south and the north, lie hundreds of mere waste tracts of the desert, where there is almost complete absence of life. The plateau or highlands of Nejd are mostly composed of areas as described in the first of the three above-mentioned divisions, Rubi-el-Khali is an area of the second type, and the mountain regions of Asir and Yemen fall into the third category.

Nejd and Yemen are separated by a mountainous province known as Yamama which figures very prominently in the Islamic history. Northeast of Nejd lie the deserts of Iraq bordering on the fertile regions of the Chaldaeans, more easterly again is Al-Ahsa. It is, however, in the barrier-land on the eastern shores of the Red Sea that the Hijaz lies, in whose lap repose the holy cities of Mecca and Medina, and around which Islam battled with paganism. Mecca has the honour of being the birthplace of the Prophet Muhammed, and it was to Yathrab or Medina he was forced to flee from his people when they menaced him on his proclaiming himself the Messenger carrying Allah's word.

The climatic conditions vary too in Arabia with the characteristic geographical change of the land. In Nejd the temperature is hardly ever below 102° in the shade, and in Mecca a degree of 133° has been recorded: and yet at night keen frost is experienced in the desert. The central portion of

THE LAND AND THE PEOPLE

the country has probably the healthiest climate. Dry conditions of heat or cold are to be met there. So refreshing is the morning breeze of Nejd that the fame of its zephyrs, or Nasim, has passed into poetry. It is then the coastal regions of Arabia which have given a bad name to the country as far as its climate is concerned. There is no bracing atmosphere, there is a closeness near the coast, the air is humid and the damp heat is most oppresssive. The Red Sea coast is notorious for its unhealthyness for this reason.

Because of its mountains, the province of Yemen in the sothernmost corner of the peninsula receives more rain than other regions. As much as sixteen inches of rain are said to have fallen in Yemen; and Aden, for instance, which adjoins it, has received only a degree less than Hodada. At Oman on the Eastern coast, not only a good rainfall is registered but snowfalls have also been experienced: the rest is arid, and, at times, very severe on human endurance, especially during the daytime.

The interplay of events which followed the advent of the Prophet Mohammed, cannot be followed without an adequate knowledge of that historical background which alone can show the transformation that the ministry of the Great Arabian wrought in the minds of an ancient people. For this, we will have to go to the original sources of Arab historians.

The Arabs divide the people who inhabited their country, as early as can be comprehended, into three classes. The first were the Arab ul Baidah, traces of whom vanished almost completely before Islam, although the Hamitic colonies which came slightly prior to the Semites were included amongst this section. The section subdivision were termed as Arab ul Aariba, the original Arabs believed themselves to be descended from Kohtun, and are supposed to have extirpated or absorbed the native elements of astra-worshippers. A third, the so-called Arab ul-Mustaariba or the naturalised Arabs, the Abrahamitic Semites, however, were the most important.

From the fold of the second section, namely Arab ul Aariba, rose the four powerful clans of Bani Aad, the Amalika, the Bani Thamud and Bani Jadis. The first-named covered the whole of Central Arabia with their settlements, and by dint of desert hardiness and colonisation skill, these people soon grew in power and set up principalities.

One of their kings, Shaddad, is spoken of in the Koran, and is believed to have carried his victorious armies up to the borders of India on one side, and to Egypt and beyond on the other. Whether this Arab invasion of Babylonia more than two thousand years before Christ is the same as that with which Shaddad is credited may remain a moot point, but, regarding his march towards Egypt and the check placed in the way of the Eastern invaders there by the princes of Thebaid in alliance with the Ethiopians, admits of a measure of credence.

The second clan, that of Banu-Amalika, entering Arabia by way of Yemen, spread all along the coast right up to the confines of Syria, thus embracing modern Yemen, Asir, the Hejaz and Palestine.

There is evidence to show that several Egyptian Pharaohs originally belonged to this clan but that they were overthrown by a branch of Banu Kohtun, who had settled in the south of Arabia. These were called Banu-Jurhum.

The third section, the Banu Thamud, populated the country between the Hejaz and Syria. These people were cave-dwellers, but as they lay on the trade routes and provided both shelter and guards for the passing caravans, their prosperity increased enormously, but they were rooted out by Khozar al Ahmar, the Elamite conqueror. The Koran also made an allusion to the terrible fate which befell these troglodytes.

THE LAND AND THE PEOPLE

One fact of interest to note here is that when the southern hordes of Banu-Jurhum—who, as we have seen above, exterminated Amalika—settled down and consolidated their position in Yemen, they showed tolerance towards the Ishmaelites and allowed them to live in peace amongst them.

These Ishmaelites were destined to play a great part in Islamic history, as the foundation of Mecca, attests Amir Ali, was apparently coeval with the establishment of the Abrahamite Arabs in the peninsula; for according to the Arab traditions, a Jurhumite chief named Meghass-ibn-Amr, whose daughter was married to the progenitor of the 'naturalised Arabs,' Ismail or Ishmael, was the founder of the city.

It was, too, Abraham who erected the Temple of Kaaba; and it was the line of descent from which the Prophet Muhammad's ancestry is traced. We will now examine these points before going any further into the history of the Arabs of those times.

Chapter 4

THE PROPHET'S ISHMAELITE CONNECTION
AND
THE BUILDING OF THE KAABA

We have seen that three sections of peoples inhabited Arabia, and the Moslems claim that the Prophet Muhammed belonged to the Ishmaelites.

A little discussion is needed here to show further that both Abraham and Ishmael, having migrated into Arabia, built the shrine of Kabaat Mecca, and that the Prophet Muhammed is not only descended from them but also received the ministry of Abraham.

Regarding the last statement, the *Koran* says in the tenth section of *Al Haj:*

> The faith of your father Ibrahim, who it was that named you Muslim first of all.

For had Abraham not prayed that his progeny should be of those who had complete submission to the will of Allah—the true spirit of the meaning of the term Muslim—and according to the Sura *Baqara,* had recited as follows?

> Our Lord! and make us both submissive to thee (Muslimeen is the word used),
> and raise from our offspring a nation submilling to Thee...

I especially make those points here because non-Moslem writers deny all these statements.

MUHAMMED: THE PROPHET

Now first of all, let us endeavour to determine whether Hagar and Ishmael came to live in Arabia or not, and secondly, who was it that Abraham wished to offer in sacrifice to his God, whether it was Isaac or Ishmael.

According to the Hebrew traditions, we are told that it was Isaac who was sacrificed, and on that contention, the sacrificial spot is pointed out in Syria. But if it could be proved that it was Ishmael and not Isaac who was to be sacrificed, then not only the entire chain of evidence can be linked; but also regarding the scene of sacrifice, we will have to own to the authenticity of the Arab writers.

In the Sacred Book of the Jews, we read that the first child of Abraham was the son of Hagar, and the boy was named Ishmael. Isaac was the second son of Abraham from his other wife Sarah.

When the two boys grew up, Sarah persuaded her husband to have Hagar and Ishmael banished.

After that, in the twenty-first chapter of *Pentateuch* where it speaks of the *Journey Of Birth*, we are told the following in the *Old Testament*:

> 'And Abraham rose up early in the morning, and took bread, and a bottle of water, and gave it unto Hagar, (putting it on her shoulder) and the Child, and sent her away: and she departed, and wandered in the wilderness of Beersheba.
>
> And the water was spent in the bottle, and she cast the child under one of the shrubs.
>
> And she went, and sat her down over against him a good way off, as it were a bowshot: for she said, Let me not see the death of the child.
>
> And she sat over against him, and lift up her voice, and wept.
>
> And God heard the voice of the lad; and the angel of God

THE PROPHET'S ISHMAELITE CONNECTION

> *called to Hagar out of heaven, and said unto her, What aileth thee, Hagar? fear not; for God hath heard the voice of the lad where he is.*
>
> *Arise, lift up the lad, and hold him in thine hand: for I will make him a great nation.*
>
> *And God opened her eyes, and she saw a well of water: and she went, and filled the bottle of water, and gave the lad drink.*
>
> *And God was with the lad, and he grew, and dwelt in the wilderness, and became an archer.*
>
> *And he dwelt in the wilderness of Paran: and his mother took him a wife out of the land of Egypt.'*

Although the *Torah* of the Jews insists upon the fact that it was Isaac and not Ishmael who was *'offered for Sacrifice'* by Abraham, other proof points to the fact that the reverse was the case.

It was, for instance, the rule in the earlier ministries that only the first-born was to be thus sacrificed. Abraham proposed to execute that command of God literally and not metaphorically, inasmuch as, by the sacrifice, no actual shedding of blood was intended, but of deputing the first-born to serve the shrine and the cause of Allah.

In any case, when Abraham proceeded to slay his son in the cause of God, so to speak, *'at His behest'*; and if that son happened to be Isaac, then it was tantamount to discrediting another command of God in which He had pronounced in the *Book of Genesis xvii, 19*, thus:

> *'And God said, Sarah thy wife shall bear thee a son, indeed; thou shalt call his name Isaac; and I will establish my Covenant with him for an everlasting covenant, and with his seed after him.'*

It is obvious from this that God could not issue two orders so diametrically opposed to each other about one and the same

MUHAMMED: THE PROPHET

man. The real misunderstanding, of course, is in assuming that Isaac and not Ishmael was the elder brother. Ishmael, indeed was thirteen years of age when his father attained the age of one hundred, when Abraham is believed to have

> *'fallen upon his face and laughed, and said in his heart, Shall a child be born unto him that is an hundred years old? And shall Sarah that is ninety years old, bear?'*

And thus we found him saying to God *'O that Ishmael might live before thee!'* This term really means that Abraham meant to *sacrifice* and *offer* his elder son, the first-born, to the service of Allah, and not Isaac, whom he made his heir in worldly affairs. All these facts prove that the *sacrificed* person was Ishmael and not Isaac.

As regards the place of Sacrifice, we must note the Jewish belief which is pointed to be at Marya, situated at Solomon's Temple. A Christian belief has it that the place is no other than where Jesus was crucified. Both of these places are discredited by later researches.

This Moriah, Marya, Moarya or Moreh, is definitely indicated to be within the provinces of Arabia.

In the *Book of Judges vii. 1*, we find ...

> *'the host of Midianites were on the north side of them, by the hill of Moreh, in the valley';*

and, of course, Midyan is in Arabia.

This, then, unquestionably fixes the position of Moreh as being in Arabia; but we might go a step further and quite legitimately assume that the common usage of the word Moreh assumed the form of Marveh, which is no other place than the hillock near the Kaaba shrine in Mecca, where Moslem pilgrims perform the rite of *Saey* during the pilgrimage season.

Imam Malik relates that the Prophet Muhammed, pointing towards Marveh said:

THE PROPHET'S ISHMAELITE CONNECTION

'All the valleys and hills of Mecca are places of sacrifice.'

Enough has been said to substantiate the belief that it was the eldest son of Abraham—who was Ishmael—that was taken to the land of Moreh or Moriah, to be given as a burnt offering, and that Moriah was in Arabia, and at no other spot than the hills of Mecca.

Indeed, so patent is the proof of this that the entire collection of rites and ceremonies which are enjoined upon the Moslem pilgrims are in strict commemoration of that event of the sacrifice of Ishmael by Abraham.

Let us see how the two approximate. When Abraham had laid the wood near the altar and bound his son, as in *Genesis xxii, 10:*

> *'And Abraham stretched forth his hand and took the knife to slay his son. And the angel of the Lord called unto him out of heaven, and said, Abraham, Abraham: and he said, here am I.'*

To this day in the long history of Islam the pilgrims' call is:

> *'Labaik—Labaik—here I am in Thy Presence, here I am in Thy Presence.'*

In the ministry of Abraham, it was enjoined that during the sacrifice, a several times circumvolution had to be performed.

During the ceremonies of Moslem pilgrimage, the seven rounds of the space of Marvah is the prototype of the same idea.

No hair was cut till the pilgrimage was over, and this is still the fact in Islamic pilgrimage practices.

Also, of course, the cardinal injunction of actual sacrifice is carried out annually during the Haj at Mecca.

Do they all not point to the similarity of the two conceptions?

THE BUILDING OF THE KAABA

It is sometimes assumed that the city of Mecca and the birth of its ancient history is really imaginary, thrust upon it by the Moslems. The facts, however, are different. The true name of Mecca was Bakka, and it is styled so in the *Koran* in *Al Imran section 4*:

> 'Most surely the first house appointed for men is the one at Bakka, blessed and a guidance for the nations.'

In *Tafsir-i-Kahir* it is spoken of as *Tebak*, meaning *the crowding together of men*, obviously merchants and pilgrims or a meeting place. Also a further reference in the *Koran* when Abraham and Ishmael were enjoined to clean up and purify *'My House'* must necessarily mean that the House—the Shrine of worship—did not exist before Abraham. These two, the father and the son, according to the *Koran*, 'raised the foundation of the House.'

Even such a great sceptic of all matters Islamic as Sir William Muir, testifies to the hoary age of Mecca.

> 'A very high antiquity,' he says, 'must be assigned to the main features of the religion of Mecca' ....
>
> *Diodorus Siculus, writing about half a century before our era, says of Arabia washed by the Red Sea, 'There is in this country, a temple greatly revered by the Arabs'.*
>
> *'These words must refer to the Holy House of Mecca, for we know of no other which ever commanded such universal homage ...*
>
> *Tradition represents the Kaaba, as from time immemorial, the scene of pilgrimage from all quarters of Arabia: from*

THE BUILDING OF THE KAABA

Yemen and Hadhramut, from the shores of the Persian Gulf, and the deserts of Syria, and the distant environs of Hira and Mesopotamia, men yearly flocked to Mecca. So extensive a homage must have had its beginning in an extremely remote age.'

The celebrated Greek astronomer and geographer, Ptolemy, who lived in A.D. 139, according to Musoodi, Ibn Nadim and Yaqut Humwi, gives the dimensions of Mecca as seventy-eight degrees in length, and breadth as point three degrees.

We must, however, turn to the Oriental sources to find the exact dimensions of the shrine of the Kaaba which Arzaqi provides us. Its height is given as nine yards, in length it was thirty-two yards, and in breadth twenty-two yards. This structure of stone erected or repaired was so rough and ready that it boasted neither roof nor doors; and it is not without significance to remember that not till Qossay Bin Kullab—about whom we will have much to say later—the Qureish tribe received the guardianship of the holy precincts, that the building was re-erected, and date-palms were laid on it to provide a roof.

At this time Mecca lay on the great trade routes over which the merchandise from the fertile Yemen passed to the rich lands of Syria. But the doctrines of pure faith were forgotten in the rush of events, in which the wild traits of the Arab race superseded whatever little of religion they had learned.

The whole country was in the grips of the grossest possible conceptions of idolatry.

Over and above the three hundred and sixty idols (one for each day of the year) in the holy shrine of the Kaaba, it was the great Hobal, the god of war, carved in red agate, however, who retained the principal position in the temple. Around this stood the images of gazelles in silver and gold, and also the representations of Abraham and his son.

MUHAMMED: THE PROPHET

Pilgrims annually thronged the city to kiss the Black Stone built in the shrine of the Kaaba, and made seven circuits around the temple.

To emphasise the dignity of the Qureish tribe, none was allowed to perform this ceremony with any clothes on. It was the prerogative of the ruling house of the Qureish only, everybody else had to run round the shrine in a nude state.

Chapter 5

THE GOVERNMENT OF PRE-ISLAMIC MECCA

The guardianship of the Kaaba—the shrine of the Black Stone, records Amir Ali, was originally an appenage of the children of Ishmael, had in consequence of the Babylonian attack passed into the hands of the Jurhumites. But another clan was gaining strength, that of the Bani-Khuzaa, who, issuing from their southern strongholds in the mountains of Yemen, overthrew the Jurhumites and made themselves the masters of Mecca.

Gradually the people of Ishmael, who had suffered almost total annihilation at the hands of the Babylonians, showed some signs of regeneration. It was during the first century before Christ that one Adnan, one of the important scions of the Ishmaelites, had married a daughter of a Jurhumite prince. The issue of this marriage, One Maad, finally re-established his power over Nejd and the whole of the Hijaz.

But whereas the adjoining provinces were thus reduced, the sole guardianship of the holy shrine still remained in the hands of the Kuzaites. Then Fihr, an able descendent of Maad, fell heir to the Ishmaelite clans with a rulership over slightly larger tracts of lands than his progenitor, but yet the control over the shrine of Mecca was not his up to the third century of the Christian era.

The power of the Khuzaites, however, gave way before Qossay, a descendent of Fihr, upon the death of the last Khuzaiter King. Qossay was the fifth in descent from Fihr, and

MUHAMMED: THE PROPHET

was born about A.D. 398.

The title of Qureish was given by this chieftain to his people, for henceforth the Ishmaelite sway was absolutely complete over the Hijaz, for the shrine of Mecca had now come within his pale of governance. Qossay, however, accomplished this about the middle of the fifth century of the Christian era. The Qureish had, therefore, come to stay in the land, for it was that section of the Ishmaelites which gave to Arabia the Prophet of Islam. Incidently, these researches place indisputably out of consideration that the Prophet Muhammed was humbly born.

Qossay as an organiser and legislator had no compeer in his predecessors. Until his rule, the Qureishite families were widely separated, even those who lived in Mecca lived very far apart from each other, and there were hardly any within a close proximity of the coveted shrine of the Kaaba, the protection of which he considered his one aim in life. Perceiving the dangers to which the national pantheon was exposed from its unprotected condition, remarks Amir Ali, he induced the Qureish to settle down in its vicinity, leaving a sufficient space free on the four sides of the temple for circumnambulation.

His capacity as a ruler soon brought forth those fruits of peace which come with good government, the wealth of the realm increased, and from his method of managing a state we can gather some interesting facts regarding the government of early Arabia.

He was perhaps the first chieftain to have had a house of representatives erected, but only the men of his own clan could be admitted to it. In this Dar un Nadwa or the Council Hall, not only civil functions were held, but disputed cases were heard and judgement was given under the presidency of the head chief, who had a council of elders, none of the members of which was to be under the age of forty years.

It was, too, at this hall, according to the foregoing authority,

THE GOVERNMENT OF PRE-ISLAMIC MECCA

that the Quraishites, when about to engage in a war, received the standard, Liwa, from the hands of Qossay. He used to attach the white piece of cloth to a lance which one of his sons bore to the chiefs of the Quraishites. It was during his time, too, that an annual poor-tax was levied, called the Rifada, out of which poor pilgrims were fed.

He was then the first man of his race to install the three historical institutions: those of the council hall, the giving of the standard, and charity for the poor pilgrims, respectively known as Nadwa, Liwa and Rifada; and from the upkeep of these institutions the ruling house of the Quraishites was ever distinguishable from all other tribes and clans.

These were regarded as the princely emblems, and no one other than the Quraishites was permitted to observe them. This priest, king and judge centralised the functions of the church and the state in himself till he died in A.D. 480, leaving his section of the Ishmaelites, the Quraishites or the Qureish, as undisputed guardians and protectors of the shrine of the Kaaba.

After Qossay's death his son, Abdud-Dar, assumed the title of the chief of Qureish and the pontiff. But as soon as the uneventful reign of Abdud-Dar closed, then the descendants of his brother Abdu Manaf began to contest the prerogatives of the great chief with the direct descendants of Qossay, namely the children of Abdud-Dar. This dispute arose, let it be remembered, on account of the maladministration of the realm by Abdud-Dar's progeny, and it was by no means due to jealousy on the part of the other sections of the clan.

A division of duties, however, was soon effected.

To Abdus Shams, the sons of Abdu Manaf, the right of controlling and distribution of the sacred well of Zam Zam was given, as well as the collection and distribution of the poor-tax.

Whilst the retention of the Kaaba shrine keys, the

MUHAMMED: THE PROPHET

distribution and presentation of Liwa, the standard, to the army and the presidency of the Council of state was entrusted to the house of Abdud-Dar; that is to say, a sort of dual monarchy was satisfactorily established. This control of the state, however, soon passed into the hands of Hashim, brother of Abdus Shams.

Hashim died in Syria in A.D. 510, where he had taken his merchandise, leaving a son named Shayba with his Yathribite wife Salma. It was then Muttalib, who journeyed to Syria to bring home his sister-in-law and young nephew Shayba—later named as Abdul Muttalib—and who was to assume the duties of state which passed to him on the death of his brother Hasham.

From this period onwards the part of Arabian history which has direct bearing upon the story of early Islam in general, goes apace with the life of the Prophet Muhammed in particular.

This is a juncture, too, where mistakes are easily made, to appreciate the events which continue to play upon the doings of the Qureish, and if essentials of the historical data of this period are not firmly grasped, the comprehension of the Prophets' work is rendered almost impossible. By knowing these details fully, one will be enabled to realize the extent of transformation which Muhammed's ministry brought about in the government of Arabia. Indeed, only by the study of an earlier chapter regarding the social depravity of the people at that time will the student be able to judge the influence which the Prophet's labours exercised upon the social side.

We had then, only two men of consequence in the then Arab polity: Muttalib and his nephew Abdul Muttalib, as the leaders of the house of Qureish. The former died in Yemen about the end of the year of A.D. 520 leaving Abdul Muttalib, his *'white-haired'* nephew, in virtual command of all that the chiefdom of the Qureish stood for at the time; that is to say presidency over both the state and the church. It was a presidency inasmuch as

THE GOVERNMENT OF PRE-ISLAMIC MECCA

the different offices of the government were divided between ten senators, every one of them holding the office as a hereditary favour. Amir Ali explains this facet of it most admirably, and I can very usefully reproduce his analysis here. According to his researches, the dignitaries were as follows:

1. The *HIJABA*, or the guardianship of the keys of the Kaaba, a sacerdotal office of considerable importance and rank. It was allotted to the house of Abdud Dar, and at the time when Mecca was converted to Islam, it was held by Osman, the son of Talha.

2. The *SIKAYA*, or the intendance of the sacred wells of Zam Zam, and of all the water destined for the use of the pilgrims. This dignity belonged to the house of Hashim, and was held at the time of the conquest of Mecca, by Abbas, the uncle of the Prophet.

3. The *DIYAT*, or the civil and criminal magistracy, which had for a long time belonged to the house of Taym-ibn-Murra. At the time of the Prophet's advent, it was held by Abdullah-ibn-Kuhnafa, surnamed Abu Bakr.

4. The *SIFARATH*, or legation. The person to whom this office belonged was the plenipotentiary to the state, authorised to discuss and settle any difference which arose between the Qureish and the other Arab tribes, as also with strangers. This office was held by Omar.

5. The *LIWA*, or the custody of the standard, under which the nation marched against enemies. The guardian of this standard was the Commander-in-Chief of the State troops. This military charge appertained to the house of Ommeyya, and was held by Abu Sufyan, the son of Harb, the most implacable enemy of Muhammed.

6. The *RIFADA*, or the administration of the poor-tax. Formed with the alms of the nation, it was employed to provide food for the poor pilgrims, whether travellers or residents, whom

the state regarded as the guest of the shrine. This duty, after the death of Abu Talib, upon whom it had devolved after Abdul Muttalib, was transferred to the house of Naufal, son of Abdu Manaf, and was held at the time of the Prophet by Harith, son of Amr.

7. The *NADWA*, the presidency of the national assembly. The holder of this office was the first councillor of the State, and under his advice all public acts were transacted. Aswad, of the house of Abdul Uzza, son of Qossay, held this dignity at the time of the Prophet.

8. The *KHAIMMEH*, the guardianship of the council chamber. This function, which conferred upon the incumbent the right of convoking the assembly and even of calling to arms the troops, was held by Khalid, son of Walid, of the house of Yakhzam, son of Marra.

9. *KHAZINA*, or the administration of public finances, belonged to the house of Hassan, son of Kaab, and was held by Harith, son of Qais.

10. The *AZLAM*, the guardianship of diving arrows, by which the judgement of the gods and goddesses was obtained. Safawan, brother of Abu Sufyan, held this dignity. At the same time it was an established custom that the oldest member exercised the greatest influence, and bore the title of Rais or Syed, chief or lord *par excellence*. At the time of the Prophet, Abbas was the first of these senators.

Abdul Muttalib, the son of Hashim, was the most influential member of the Qureish family: and, as is the custom with warrior clans, he was eager to have a large progeny to protect his house and continue his influence as the leader of the tribe. And, on account of the fact that five of the sons of this patriarch have received fame or notoriety in connection with Islam, a detailed mention of Abdul Muttalib's family is not without

THE GOVERNMENT OF PRE-ISLAMIC MECCA

significance here. His twelve sons were; Harith, Abdul Uzza *alias* Abu Lahab, Abdu Manaf, known as Abu Talib, Zubair, Abdullah, Dhirar, Abbas, Mukawwim, Jahl, and Hamza. The names of the other two sons are not known, and he also had six daughters. It should therefore be borne in mind that the government of the Qureish, with Mecca as the fountainhead, was officered almost entirely by the sons, nephews, sons-in-law or first cousins of this venerable patriarch, Abul Muttalib: he was thus the Father of the Qureish Government at the time.

Beyond the fact that in consequence of what is said above, Abul Muttalib had an undoubted pre-eminence both in the administration of the law and whatever of religion there was at the time, two incidents in his life single him out from the rest of his people. One is that he wanted to sacrifice his son Abdullah to the shrine, and Abdullah was the father of the Prophet Muhammed: the second is that it was during his time that the Abyssinian viceroy of Yemen brought his legions on elephants in order to destroy the Mecca shrine.

As a by-product of the former incident, however, we should not lose sight of the point that, in the upbringing of Muhammed, this old Chieftain's association is perhaps the most pertinent issue bearing upon the subject of this book: the life-story of the Islamic Prophet. The events of Abdul Muttalib's day, will, therefore, more than repay study.

It cannot be said that Abdul Muttalib was unduly priest-ridden or that he wished to emphasise his adhesion to the laws of his idolatrous ancestors in order to gain more influence in the eyes of his people, when towards the latter part of his life, as the father of eighteen children, he felt progressively drawn to the idea that time had arrived when one of his sons must be sacrificed to the holy shrines of Mecca. That one or other of the members of his household were always falling ill may be no more and no less than a mere incident in the workaday life of a large family, nevertheless Abdul Muttalib could not forget that, when young, he had taken a vow that he would bestow one of his sons, if he were blessed with a large progeny and lived to see them grow into hardy men and women.

The gods had fulfilled his wishes, and it was now incumbent upon him to make good his part of the bargain. The insistent illness in his house, which I have likened to mere incident and liable to occur in any large household, however presumed itself ever more rigorously on his mind as a persistent reminder of the gods to fulfil his vow.

It was in this frame of mind that Abdul Muttalib rose on that special day of which I speak. He sent word to Abdullah, his dearest son, to come to him beyond that rock-strewn valley which skirts Mecca on the way to the fruit-laden glens of the Taif highlands.

There he confided his purpose to Abdullah, and the latter, true to the Ishmaelite traditions, submitted as readily as did Abraham's son to his father. As the two walked back home resignation sat upon their brows, and the ladies of the house, being acute observers of human impulses, were not slow to guess the reason for the preparation of a feast which was ordered by their father to be ready at sundown.

Presently, cousins, sons and relatives of Abdul Muttalib gathered in the courtyard of Abdullah's sister. Wearing their proud robes they were still crowding round, for they knew that Abdul Muttalib had not required their presence without a good purpose.

The high priest had now entered, and hardly had he taken the salutations of the faithful to the shrine, that all eyes were turned towards the stony stairs, cut as they were on the side of the rock that formed the eastern flank of the courtyard.

Abdul Muttalib stood there holding the hand of his favourite

THE GOVERNMENT OF PRE-ISLAMIC MECCA

son Abdullah. Then the tribesmen knew the mind of their chief.

In the name of the three hundred and sixty gods of the Kaaba, in the name of the hoary traditions of the Qureish, he recalled the vow that he had taken. Now as he was growing old, and had lived to see his children at the heights of power and glory, he wished them to continue to flourish thuswise. Could he hope to perpetuate the happy condition of life without giving to the gods their due, to those that have blessed him with so much? He then spoke of bestowing Abdullah to the shrine of the pagan gods of Kaaba. He chose Abdullah because Abdullah was his dearest son, for Abdul Muttalib's gods will not be propitiated with an offering less precious than what was the most cherished life in the eyes of the old chief.

There was a tense silence as Abdul Muttalib sat down, whilst the elders touched their beards and eyed each other, not knowing what to say, then one bolder than the rest raised his arm: *'Nay, nay, Oh! Abdul Muttalib,'* he protested; *'worthy as thy intention is, Abdullah is just as dear to us as in thine old eyes'* proposing that camels be given to the shrine in exchange.

It was now the turn of the high priest to speak, who drew their attention to the fact that, in the past, all questions were to be decided by divining at the shrine; and men's voices were as worthless as salt on sandy hills when compared to the decision of the oracle.

The men had not done talking when a batch of women demanded the right to be heard.

Near the gate, hefty men were barring the way to the rush of a dozen women who wanted to force their way to the centre of the gathering.

They were the sisters of Abdullah and his women relations. Whatever the truth of the story, they were led by a woman who is said to have seen a radiance dart out from the forehead of

MUHAMMED: THE PROPHET

Abdullah, and the wise women of the desert alleged that young man was a forebearer of someone extraordinary in the annals of mankind.

In such conservative gatherings, as can well be imagined, when the affairs of one man really interested the whole clan, matters like the dedication of a son to a shrine always tended to become a controversial subject; so that passions were getting enflamed, the gathering soon divided into rival parties, one insisting that the lad should be given to the shrine, the other that he could be rescued in exchanging camels. But Abdul Muttalib was adamant in fulfilling his vow: and, therefore, to decide the issue, it was agreed to have the oracle speak about the affair.

A great concourse of humanity filled the holy precincts of the Kaaba. The elders of the tribes filed in one by one and stood around the shrine; the high priest taking the old chieftain by the right hand, and Abdullah by the left solemnly advanced to face Hobal, the Stone War-God, then he touched the statues of silver and gold gazelles, and went round the three hundred and sixty idols. This done, he ascended the steps at the foot of the shrine. The divining spears were drawn with the name of Abdullah in exchange for ten camels.

The oracle spoke about accepting Abdullah in preference to ten camels. For a second time the reading was taken and the number of camels was doubled. The result was the same as the first. A third time the lot was cast, but the gods still retained their partiality for Abdullah and refused an offering of thirty camels. This ought to have decided the question, had the general company agreed not to press the point further, but, to a man, the tribesmen were determined to persuade the gods.

Even Abdul Muttalib was stirred to the depths of his soul over this inveteracy of the idols; he bowed low to Hobal.

THE GOVERNMENT OF PRE-ISLAMIC MECCA

'I shall stake mine last camel, aye the whole flock before thee' he yelled, *'to see what is to be thy ultimate decision.'* And he read and reread the minds of his clansmen: for a dozen more voices rose after him offering their all to see whether Abdullah could be spared: for the Arabs, idolatrous though they were, nevertheless were simple children of nature, with children's single-heartedness towards love and hate with emotions that knew no bonds. So the high priest was asked to cast again and again and increase the number of camels each time that he drew the negative spear. What joy, indeed there was, when at last the gods were pleased to accept a hundred camels in exchange.

There are, however, two statements about this offering of Abdullah. Waqidi believes the report of divining to be more authentic, and Ibn Ishaq contends that the elders of the clan were chiefly responsible for arranging their exchange. But judging from the state of mind of old and young of Arabia of that period it is more approximate to truth that oracles were made to speak on the subject.

Abdullah now was again free to act as a sort of secretary to his old father, and was soon married to Amina, daughter of Wahb bin Abdul Munaf in the tribe of Zuhra. She was considered one of the most celebrated of the women of her time, regarding whose accomplishments such authorities as Ibn Hasham speaks at considerable length. The age of Abdullah at the time of his marriage, according to Razaqi, was seventeen years.

No sooner had Abdul Muttalib settled the question of Abdullah, and had married him, when another event threatened the integrity of Arabia and its shrine. This was the march upon Mecca of the Abyssinian viceroy of Yemen, named Abra al Arsham. It had been noticed by the Yemenites that Mecca continued to prosper and grow in strength on account of the trade that passed through it, but more in respect of the shrine to which thousands of pilgrims flocked, and thus diverted all their wealth and interests to the city of the desert in preference to the Church at the Yemenite capital of Sanaa. The only remedy was to destroy the shrine of the Kaaba.

With this object in view the Viceroy rode ahead of his troops on a highly caparisoned elephant. The desecrating army had reached almost within the sight of the temple when Abra called a halt, not only to discover about the fortification of the city, but also to calculate the resistance which his troops were likely to meet.

With all their martial traditions, the Qureish were no match to the well-drilled and organised army of the Yemenites; and therefore consternation prevailed in Mecca. The appearance of the elephants—animals quite unknown to the people of the desert, where the largest creatures known were camels—added to the havoc amongst the Meccans. The reports of the defeat of a Himyarite chieftain, Dhu Nafar, by the Abyssinian general had already reached the Qureish: and under the stress of the cumulative effect of these matters, the Mecca war-council decided to leave the shrine to look after itself, and the people, to abandon the city immediately. In the meantime, Abra's men had captured Abdul Muttalib's camels.

The southern troops remained encamped near Mecca. Knowing the weak position of the Qureish, the Abyssinians were in no haste to attack, till one day an ebony black rider, holding Abra's standard, rode up to the brow of the hill that looked directly onto the shrine of Mecca. He bore a message from his general to the chief of the Qureish, in which Abra indicated no desire to bloodshed, his only wish being to dismantle the Kaaba. But he made it abundantly clear to Abdul Muttalib that, should his people show the slightest sign of defending the temple, then the Abyssinians would spare neither the lives nor the wealth of the Arabs.

THE GOVERNMENT OF PRE-ISLAMIC MECCA

The Qureish had already made their decision: they would neither defend the shrine nor would they remain in the city whilst the acts of profanity were being enacted. A reply to that effect was sent to Abra.

The events that followed can be well narrated by what Tabiri—one of the foremost historians—records. This appears very fully in *The Literary History of the Arabs*, thus:

> *Then Abdul Muttalib was conducted by the envoy to the Abyssinian camp, as Abraha had ordered. There, he enquired after Dhu Nafar, (the captive chieftain of the Himyarites) who was his friend, and found him a prisoner. 'O Dhu Nafar,' said he, 'can you do aught in that which has befallen us?'*
>
> *Dhu Nafar answered, 'What can a man do who is a captive in the hands of a king, expecting day and night to be put to death? I can do nothing at all in the matter, but Unays, the elephant driver, is my friend; I will send to him and press your claims on his consideration and ask him to procure you an audience with the king. Tell Unays what you wish: he will plead with the king in your favour if he can'.*
>
> *So Dhu Nafar sent for Unays and said to him, 'O Unays, Abdul Muttalib is the lord of Qureish and master of the caravans of Mecca. He feeds the people in the plains and the wild creatures on the mountain tops. The king has seized two hundred of his camels. Now get him admitted to the King's presence and help him to the best of your power.' Unays consented, and soon Abdul Muttalib stood before the Viceroy.*
>
> *When Abraha saw him he held him in too high respect to let him sit in an inferior place, but was unwilling that the Abyssinians should see the Arab Chief, who was a large man and comely, seated on a level with himself; he*

> *therefore descended from his throne and sat on his carpet and bade Abdul Muttalib sit beside him. Then he said to his dragoman, 'Ask him what he wants of me.'*
>
> *Abdul Muttalib replied, 'I want the king to restore to me two hundred camels of mine which he has taken away.'*
>
> *Abraha said to the dragoman, 'Tell him: you pleased me when I first saw you, but now that you have spoken to me I hold you cheap. What! do you speak to me of two hundred camels which I have taken, and omit to speak of a temple venerated by you and your fathers which I have come to destroy?'*
>
> *Then said Abdul Muttalib: 'The camels are mine, but the Temple belongs to another, who will defend it,' and on the King exclaiming, 'He cannot defend it from me,' he said, 'That is your affair; only give me back my camels.'*

As it is related in a more credible version:

> 'The tribes settled round Mecca sent ambassadors, of whom Abdul Muttalib was one, offering to surrender a third part of their possessions to Abraha on condition that he should spare the Temple, but he refused.
>
> Having recovered his camels, Abdul Muttalib returned to the Qureish, told them what had happened, and bade them leave the city and take shelter in the mountains. Then he went to the Kaaba, accompanied by several of the Qureish, to pray help against Abraha and his army. Grasping the ring of the door, he said:
>
>> O God, defend Thy neighbouring folk
>> even as a man his gear defendeth!
>> Let not their Cross and guileful plans
>> defeat the plans Thyself intendeth!
>> But if Thou make it so, 'tis well:
>> according to Thy will, it endeth.'

THE GOVERNMENT OF PRE-ISLAMIC MECCA

Next morning, when Abraha prepared to enter Mecca, his elephant knelt down and would not budge, though they beat his head with an axe, and thrust sharp stakes into his flanks; but when they turned it in the direction of Yemen, it rose up and trotted with alacrity.

Then God sent from the sea a flock of birds like swallows, every one of which carried three stones as large as a pea or lentil, one in each bill and one in each claw, and all who were struck by those stones perished. The rest fled in disorder, dropping down as they ran, or wherever they halted to quench their thirst.

I hesitate to credit the whole of this prodigy of Tabiri, both on account of the fact that he gives also another reason of the destruction of the invading army, the cause being the outbreak of smallpox in Abra's camp: which, being a new disease in Arabia, frightened the Abyssinians quite as much as the appearance of giant animals like the elephants did the Qureish of Mecca.

The outbreak of that pestilence is quite definitely founded on historical grounds. The *Koran* throws more light on the subject: In the Chapter of *The Elephants* (one of the earliest revelations), it says:

> *Have you not considered how your Lord*
>   *dealt with the possessors of the Elephant;*
> *Did He not cause their war to end in confusion,*
> *And send down (to prey) upon them birds in flocks*
> *Casting against them hard stones,*
> *So He rendered them like straw eaten up?*

In all likelihood, if the version of the outbreak of smallpox is correct, the dispersing of an army in such circumstances cannot be thought to be beyond the range of possibility. For a similar example we might recollect the manifestation of disease that annihilated Sennacherib's men.

MUHAMMED: THE PROPHET

The appearance of birds, as spoken of in the *Koran*, is quite comprehensible, because after the soldiers died, the birds feasted on their corpses, tearing off flesh from the dead bodies and casting it on the stones.

Hence, as Mohammed Ali agrees, it is that in the concluding words, their torn flesh was compared to shred, (or strawlike), and eaten up.

Nor is this use of *'birds descending'* to eat up the dead bodies uncommon in Arab literature. We might even go to the ordinary Arab poem for a parallelism of the idea.

> *Both the Arab proverb and prosody bear witness,* says Mohammed Ali, *to birds having been spoken of as attending a victorious army to feed upon the corpses of the enemy left on the battlefield.*

Thus we have the well-known Arab proverb—*May the birds disperse thy flesh*—which is a kind of imprecation, meaning: 'may the man die, and his flesh be dispersed and eaten up by birds.'

The famous Nabighah says:

> 'When he goes out with the army, flocks of birds, being guided by the companies of the army, hover over his head.'

Here the birds are made the attendants of a victorious army, as if they knew that the army which they followed would slay the enemy, and that they would thus feed on dead bodies.

Out of this incident of the Yemenite invasion of the Hijaz arises another important point of Islamic religious law.

The story is centred around the three ideas of Idolatry, Trinity and Unity (which is yet to be pronounced). That is to say, the matter revolved around the idolatrous people of Mecca, the Christian invaders and the birth of Muhammed during the same period—a Muhammed who was to proclaim the Oneness of God.

THE GOVERNMENT OF PRE-ISLAMIC MECCA

When the Christian Viceroy, believing in Trinity, attacked a shrine of idolaters, the God of a people (Unitarians to be) sent a scourge and destroyed the hordes of Trinity; which seems to indicate to a superficial student that God in some way preferred the cult of the idols.

The Moslem Canonists, however, argue that this destruction of the invaders was, in the first instance, a sign of Muhammed's advent—since he was born in the same year—that such a man will oppose the conception of Trinity and emphasise the One God amongst the peoples of the world.

Beyond this portent, they aver that it was in fullment of the prayers of Abraham to bless the Ishmaelite with the Prophet, a prophet who will *'clean up'* the sacred house, which was built by Abraham.

One finds a testimony of it even amongst that pagan society of Arabia that was engaged in idol-worship, because though it was the only form of religion which they knew, nevertheless the conception that the Kaaba was built and sanctified by Abraham always lingered in their minds.

For it may be recollected that according to Tabiri, when the Abyssinian Viceroy sent his messenger to the Qureish, Abdul Muttalib replied:

> *'By God, we seek not war, for which we are unable. This is God's holy House, and the House of Abraham, His Friend; it is for Him to protect His House and Sanctuary; if He abandons it, we cannot defend it.'*

Furthermore, it is contended, that, as the incident was to pave the way for Muhammed's endeavors—to purify the House of God that Abraham built—-a deeper meaning lay in the matter.

To the Qureish it was to act as a warning, that when God could destroy such a powerful enemy of theirs as the invading

MUHAMMED: THE PROPHET

army of the Yemenites, it was well within His power to annihilate the Qureish if they disobeyed the man who professed to be the Prophet calling humanity towards the one and only One God.

Chapter 6

THE BIRTH OF THE PROPHET

The storm clouds of Yemenite invasion were hardly lifted from the Qureish when the world was called upon to witness a notable occurrence, commonplace in itself, the incident of childbirth—but this birth has a meaning to the story of nations.

When the Prophet of Allah was born, extraordinary portents are reported to have been seen in Mecca and beyond. Traditionists have it that fourteen minarets of the mighty palace of Cyrus fell from their proud places; the flame that burned in the holy Persian temple was extinguished; the river Sadah was dried up.

Even now some accept without questioning the sighting of the star which the Wise Men of the East followed in search of Jesus; even now some believe the inexplicable manifestations heralding the coming of Buddha; and more pertinent still, we hold by common consent that the hand of God shows itself in the course of things, the reason of which leaves the wisest of us dumbfounded and guessing.

Even today, when we claim to discover the causation of most doings, certain occurrences are still very frequently labelled by us as an *'Act of God'* because they surpass human comprehension.

Is it then justifiable not to accord a sympathetic consideration of such happenings, which are reported at the birth of the Prophet Muhammed; for it can be indisputably admitted that

MUHAMMED: THE PROPHET

that man was clearly an exceptional personality; one whose life and work was to act as the guiding star for nearly half of the world, so that an especial stage must have been set upon which this Master actor was to perform.

In the light of these circumstances, no astonishment is to be expressed that nearly fourteen centuries ago men beheld phenomena that may be likened to the finger of God pointing to the clearly marked destiny of Islam.

On the most authentic calculation of Mahmud Pasha Falki it is now proved that the birth of the Prophet took place on Monday, the 20th of April, A.D. 571. The infant was named Muhammed by his grandfather Abdul Muttalib. His widowed mother Amina fed the child from her breast for two or three days. Then Toyaba acted as his wet-nurse. Here we might usefully recount the genealogy of the Prophet.

It was then customary in Arabia that the names were remembered of only those ancestors who had distinguished themselves in some way in their national lore. As a general rule they began counting the names from one Adnan downwards, for the fact that Adnan was directly descended from Ishmael was recognised on all hands. The historian Tabiri is said to have stated that Adnan was the fortieth descendent from Ishmael, thus connecting the Prophet Muhammed with Abraham.

Here we may mention those from Adnan upwards. They are:

>Muhammed
>Abdullah
>Abdul Muttalib
>Hashim
>Monaf
>Qusay
>Kallab

THE BIRTH OF THE PROPHET

Morrah
Kaab
Lowaey
Ghalib
Fahar
Malik
Nadar
Kinana
Khazema
Mudrika
Ilyas
Modarr
Nazar
Mad
Adnan

Further in reference to what I have said regarding the curtailment in the number of names above Adnan and the reason thereof, in Bokhari the following names are also given to join the genealogical table of the Prophet with Ishmael as follows. It should, of course, be remembered that not all the forty names according to Tabiri appear here:

Adnan
Oad
Almaqoom
Tarah
Yashjib
Yarab
Tabit
Ismail
Ibrahim

EARLY CHILHOOD OF THE PROPHET

When Toyaba was feeding the infant Muhammed, the Prophet's mother Amina heard of the exodus of Bedouin women, who had been paying their biannual visit to Mecca, as was the wont of the desert folk. According to custom, many women on such visits offered their services as wet-nurses to the mothers of such children as belonged to the highest social strata of the town.

This custom had a mutual advantage to both parties. The Bedouins did not nurse the children of the aristocracy entirely on account of the good remuneration which they were to receive, rather they hoped that when a boy of the ruling house was reared amongst them, preferential treatment would be given to their tribe above all other people of the desert.

The parents availed themselves of it because they wished their sons to learn the purest Arabic language—only spoken by the tent-dwellers in the heart of the desert—also, the children, whilst with the Bedouins, would get used to hard living, imbibe that spirit, and appreciate that fire which should characterise a desert-born from a soft-living town Arab.

Not the least interesting point regarding it is that such children were taken away by the Bedouins to their encampments, where they were kept for some years to live and breathe the free air of that vastness which is called the Arabia of the real Arabs.

This practice of sending the children for a hard training was so universal amongst the Arab aristocracy, that even during the glorious days of Banu Omayah, when their power and

EARLY CHILDHOOD OF THE PROPHET

grandeur rivalled the might and splendour of Persia and Rome, Arab princes were brought up in the homes of tent-dwellers. We have a notable exception in this regard in , who for certain reasons, never saw the Bedouin upbringing, with the result that he did not speak Arabic with fluency and use apt phraseology. Iman Sahayli dilates on this subject at considerable length, and even quotes the words of the Prophet in which he is said to have attributed his skill in the use of ready expression to his stay with the Bedouin tribes of Bani Sad.

The Bedouin lady named Halima Saida, who belonged to the tribe of Howazin, was at first not particularly eager to take Muhammed—a fatherless boy—but as tradition did not permit going back without a charge whilst one awaited her, she at last was persuaded to nurse a child who was to become a Prophet, and took him with her to the encampments of the tribe. When Halima had other work to do, her daughter Shima, a comely and gentle girl, looked after the boy, little knowing what a remarkable personality those tiny feet that pattered on the hard sand around the tent in the desert were supporting.

For two years Muhammed lived with the Bedouin nurse in the desert. He would have been kept there a little longer, but even during those short months, curious happenings began to unnerve the tent-dwellers. Such manifestations, their eyes had never seen, such light playing about the boy, such straying of the infant Muhammed who always found his way back to the tent, such whisperings in the air as were passed beyond what has ever been experienced by man.

What could be the reason of it all if not the presence of the wondrous son of Amina, they thought?

So they decided to hasten his departure to his mother in Mecca, lest more doings of such an unaccountable nature baffle them.

MUHAMMED: THE PROPHET

As Halima sought the door of Muhammed's mother, she saw many corpses borne away. Men were crowding before the idols in the Shrine beseeching Hobal to ward off the plague that had visited them. A word from Amina was enough to emphasise upon Halima the necessity of taking the boy Muhammed back to her encampment, for Mecca was no safe place for whosoever had to stay in it at a time when pestilence raged in the city. Thus, Muhammed found himself back in his temporary home amongst the Bedouins. Ibn Ishaq gives the duration of the Prophet's stay with Halima as six years.

Muhammed had attained the age of six years when ultimately Halima brought the boy to his mother. Soon a journey to Medina was arranged, so that the boy and his mother could see the tomb of Abdullah, the father of the man who was to thrill the world with a Message.

No more than a month did they stay at Medina, when with Om Aman, the maidservant, the Prophet, his mother and their caravan started Meccaward. But Amina fell ill upon reaching a wayside village known as Abwa, and died there, where she lies buried. It was thus the duty of Om Aman to escort the orphaned Muhammed home to Mecca to his grandfather Abdul Muttalib.

This old chieftain of the Qureish received Muhammed with love and affection of which the people considered him quite incapable, but Abdul Muttalib had ever nursed the memory of the day when he had bartered his son Abdullah for a hundred camels; and, being a merchant whose carriers were none other than these ships of the desert, loved camels dearly. It was then the sign, the reminder, of his lovable son Abdullah, that he saw residing in the shining eyes of young Muhammed.

He therefore bestowed particular and unrelaxing care upon this orphan boy; which is important in the light of the fact that Abdul Muttalib was already the sire of eighteen children; and

EARLY CHILDHOOD OF THE PROPHET

in the ordinary way of thinking, others must have claimed a considerable amount of the old gentleman's attention and regard: nevertheless Muhammed remained always his best beloved.

Although the official primacy of Abdul Muttalib was still supreme during his waning years, when his years were passing beyond eighty, yet it was growing increasingly patent to him that the other branch of his tribe was gaining strength, and the lot of those upon whom his mantle was to fall might not be so free of cares as his; at any rate, so far as the leadership of the clan was concerned.

He wished to consolidate the position of the house of Hashim. This desire obsessed him greatly with the advancement of his age; yes, indeed, as Young says: *'Like our shadows, our wishes lengthen as our sun declines.'*

And it was as the old chieftain feared, for at his death in A.D. 579, shortly after his return from a journey to Sanaa, where he went to represent the Qureish at the court of Saif, the house of Hashim was definitely under a cloud. Not that Abu Talib, the old gentleman's son, an uncle of the Prophet, was an incapable man, but the rival factions were far too strong.

The Prophet was eight years old when he passed into the guardianship of his uncle Abu Talib. The two offices which Abdul Muttalib exercised directly in the Government of Mecca were divided between his sons. The administration of the water of holy Zam Zam was given to Abbas, whilst the collection of the poor-tax remained in the hands of Abu Talib: the latter retained the leadership of the house of Hashim in his hands, being the elder son of the old chief, Abdul Muttalib.

The presidency of the whole clan, however, fell to the share of the rival tribe of Omaya because Harab, the son of Omaya, was elected in place of Abdul Muttalib.

MUHAMMED: THE PROPHET

The orphan son of Amina and Abdullah assisted his uncle Abu Talib in his mercantile interests. When Muhammed had attained the age of twelve, Abu Talib proposed to take his merchandise to the markets of Syria.

When this biennial caravan was ready to start, Abu Talib was distinctly distressed as to who would look after the orphan during his absence: for the intense affection which the uncle Abu Talib bore for this nephew Muhammed has passed into legend. He would not touch his food without Muhammed sitting beside him, he would even start up at night in his sleep and call to Muhammed, to ask whether he was safe.

This being the degree of attachment between the two, Abu Talib could not dream of leaving the boy behind him in Mecca till his return from Syria. So Muhammed accompanied his uncle to the fertile regions of Lebanon.

THE CHRISTIAN MONK AND THE PROPHET

By easy stages the Meccan caravan journeyed northwards. The desert tracts of hard sand were now behind them, wending in and out of the many passes of the Syrian uplands the caravan of Abu Talib was nearing its destination. Perched on one of the spurs of Jabul Haroon was a monastery, stark and naked it rose above every peak beside it and this is where the celebrated Christian monk Bahira worshipped. Twisting and bending, the long line of Arabian camels zig-zagged its way below in the pass where Bahira looked out. He strained his eyes to see whether they were deceiving him: for lo! according to some reports, the trees and stones beside which a particular camel rider of that caravan passed inclined as in salutation and greeting; according to what others say, in that hot noonday sun, a fleecy cloud hovered over a rider to protect him against the sun's scorching rays.

Inch by inch the cloud moved over this especial rider, so add the traditionalists; yes, shifted its position as an umbrella high above the hills and cast a shadow upon one of the camel riders. The rest covered their heads with their head-sheets, knowing nothing of the protection accorded to that especial fellow-traveller of theirs.

'Is that the man, about whom I have read the prophecy?'

asked Bahira, but he continued to stay unbelievingly by.

The caravan was now resting in a pocket of the hill. He could see them pitching their camp for a night's rest. They were unloading the packs from their camels. It thrilled Bahira. An opportunity had at last arrived to test his knowledge about the advent of the Prophet.

MUHAMMED: THE PROPHET

Bahira had made up his mind. A messenger was hurrying to invite the wayfarers to a hearty dinner at his monastery. Bin Ibrahim relates that the messenger returned in company with the men of Mecca, whom the monk greeted at the gate of the monastery:

> 'By Lat and Uzza, our stone-built Gods of Mecca Shrine!' said the leader of the caravan, 'thy conduct doth puzzle me, O Bahira! many a time and oft have we passed by the convent; yet until now thou hast never heeded us; never didst thou dream of showing us the least sign of hospitality.'

Bahira, however, replied briefly by some non-committal words, and invited them to be seated at the table.

While the men feasted, Bahira walked about the room seeking one in whom he was interested. But none seem to correspond to the description given in his Book: for according to the Moslem historians he must have been looking for one regarding whom Jesus spoke in *John xvi. 12-13*:

> I have yet many things to say unto you, but ye cannot hear them now. Howbeit when he, the Spirit of truth, is come, he will guide you into all truth.

or again,

> Nevertheless I tell you the truth; it is expedient for you that I go away; for if I go not away, the Comforter will not come unto you, but if I depart, I will send him unto you.

The Moslem theologians do not refer to these statements as meaning the Holy Ghost, for they contend that John was filled with the Holy Ghost even before he was born; and then it speaks of Jesus receiving the Holy Ghost in the form of a pigeon: so that the above Bible references are, to the Moslems, clear enough Christian allusions indicating the appearance of the Prophet

THE CHRISTIAN MONK AND THE PROPHET

Muhammed.

It was therefore the fulfilment of these and similar prophecies which Bahira was searching out: indeed upon witnessing those abnormal phenomena of nature's protection the monk considered himself justified in instituting a search amongst the Meccan merchants.

To the narrative of the feast then, when Bahira could not find any of them to answer to the description that was in his mind;

> 'O men of the Qureish tribe!' he said, 'is not one of you remaining in your tents?'— 'Aye, one only;' was the reply; 'we left him alone at rest on account of his extreme youth.'

The monk insisted upon having the lad brought to share the feast. As Muhammed strode through the hall, the monk could not but be impressed by his free and easy gait; and when he had finished his dinner, Bahira approached him, and taking him on one side

> 'O young man!' said the monk, 'I have a question to ask. By Lat and Uza—thy great Gods of stone—wilt thou consent to answer?"

Bahira desired to put him to test at the outset by invoking the idols of the Mecca shrine; but Muhammed was of a different persuasion.

> 'Address me not in the name of Lat and Uza, for I owe no allegiance to them. Question me in the name of Allah—God that is one—and by Allah I shall answer thee.'

Bahira asked him many things, about his family, about his experiences in the desert, about those extraordinary manifestations that only good men can understand: and finally when the youth rose and gathered up his cloak, the collar slipped down his shoulder, and lo, there was a patch—a dark patch—the seal of Prophecy—at the exact spot where Bahira's sacred manuscripts had indicated as the sure sign of the coming Prophet. The monk had at last seen the mark, as foretold.

Sooner than it takes to relate, the learned Christian monk was before Abu Talib.

> *'What relation is this lad to thee, Abu Talib?' he asked, and he replied 'that he was as a son to him.'*
>
> *'Yes, as dear as a son the lad may be to Abu Talib, but he is not thy real son.'*
>
> *'Mark then my words,'* thus spoke the venerable monk solemnly, *'and mark them well, for this is no ordinary man, this Muhammed thy brother's son, but a Prophet he shall be; so heed my words and watch over him with constant care, thy charge is precious to humanity.'*

Day followed day more or less uneventfully in the life of young Muhammed upon his return from Syria, but he now could appreciate the panorama of Arab vice as complexioned in the licentious mode of living of his people. In a Mecca where tribal jealousy clouded and blackened men's hearts, where people reeled in the dust beside the wine-bibber's tavern, where gambling tables gathered the young and old; Muhammed's finer faculties revolted, but here he lived and did some hard thinking.

Now and then he would betake himself into the wilderness to brood over the misery that sat upon the Qureish, and in deep contemplation something seemed to say that the dawn of righteousness would break soon. It gave him hope, but no sooner did he return to the city and find his kinsmen in the entanglement of the vilest of sins, than those hopes woven by the reflective moonbeams were shadowed by what he saw in the wine-seller's booth, in the shameful scenes of the wayside dances; whilst men so earnestly rose and fell before the stone

THE CHRISTIAN MONK AND THE PROPHET

gods of the Kaaba, praying for victory in battle, or women supplicating for the blessing of a male child so that he could sing the poems of Arabian lore laden with that pleasure which bestows the highest praise to satanic majesty.

And in the midst of this wretched environment, the sensitive mind of Muhammed would fall into a bewildering sleep, till at dawn he saw one line of light as sharp as the glistening edge of a sabre, for Muhammed always had a hope, a horizon of boundless good, which must one day banish the wicked practices that, even now, before his Call, made his heart loathe so utterly.

To the arts of reading and writing Muhammed was a total stranger, but his capacity for trade soon won him fame. His truthfulness, correct attitude to all men, his steadfastness were acknowledged to the extent that he was styled as the *'Most Trustworthy '*. He was considered to be the best man amongst them on points of honour and virtue. Everyone looked upon him as a worthy scion of the proud and distinguished clan of the Qureish.

An incident which throws light upon his character and resourcefulness may be cited. It was about this time that his fame as a righteous person was in the mouths of all men, when he had acquired a considerable influence in business. The necessity for repairs of the Shrine of the Kaaba arose. The sacred Black Stone proved the bone of contention: for it was considered to be an especial honour to a clan to be able to build it at its former place. Every section contrived to have that honour, till the peace of the tribes was threatened, all seemingly having an equal claim to that honour.

It was therefore resolved that on the morning of the next day, whosoever entered the holy precincts first should have the honour of replacing the Black Stone. By an odd and very lucky coincidence, it happened to be none other than that Prince

MUHAMMED: THE PROPHET

of Peace-Makers—Muhammed. He was asked to perform the ceremony as agreed.

Another man would have applauded his good fortune, and, considering it a personal triumph, might have precipitated a tribal war by taunting his rivals; but not so Muhammed.

He spread a sheet on the ground, placed the Black Stone upon it, and asked the elders to take corners of the sheet, thus lifting the stone to its place; all thereby shared in the honour, and no one man could say that he alone did it. Even the cleverest brains cannot think out compromising schemes like this on the spur of the moment, it must have been a gift—and such gifts have deeper meanings than superficial observers are inclined to credit.

To those who consider the narration of such incidents as trifling and slight, I should ask them to picture the gathering of tribesmen before the shrine, a shrine for which they were willing to shed the last drop of their blood, a gathering of desert warriors who would slay a man and not regret it.

Such men crowded into the precincts: with determined faces they raised their eyes to the residence of their idols, the Bani Abed-Dar had joined the powerful Bani Adiyy-bin Kab tribe, they had filled bowls with their own blood and had dipped their fingers in it, swearing that they would sooner die than relinquish the privilege of resetting the Black Stone, and for four nights and days the contest lasted.

At any moment an inter-tribal war might have broken out, it would have blazed to the other end of Arabia and might have lasted for generations as a blood feud.

Different people look upon the items of their religion in different lights from the Arabs of that time, much indeed as the Moslems of today hold to these matters with a passion unrivalled by any craving of the materialist world.

THE CHRISTIAN MONK AND THE PROPHET

This early behaviour of Muhammed is possibly the first milestone of his ministry towards an endeavour at peacemaking: and, possessing a totally Oriental mentality—for whatever it is worth—I feel that this particular device of the Prophet saved his nation from a ruinous war.

Chapter 7

THE PROPHET AS A MERCHANT AND CITIZEN

As trade and commerce had become a family avocation in the life of the Qureish, and the Prophet's Sire, Hashim, the merchant prince of Mecca, had established business connections with countries as far distant as Iraq and Syria; these connections were very greatly further enlarged by Abu Talib, in the course of which Muhammed acted as his chief helper.

The many qualities of personal character which distinguished Muhammed from the rest of his countrymen were responsible for making him not only a general favourite amongst the people of Mecca, but in the business community his solidarity of contract and fair-dealing became a byword, so much so that men would come and trust their all to him, repose their secrets in him, and seek his advice, knowing that his judgement was so excellently executed that it must have welled up from some divine hidden source.

Abdullah Bin Abialhumsa, a merchant of Mecca at that period, relates that once he was transacting some business with Muhammed, when, leaving the business half-finished, the former had to go suddenly to attend something else, promising, however, to return presently to complete the work. For three days, Abdullah did not come: other matters absorbed his attention to such an extent that he forgot all about the affair in hand with Muhammed. Recollecting his promise after three days, Abdullah sought the other party with whom he was negotiating, and to his astonishment found Muhammed still waiting for him.

MUHAMMED: THE PROPHET

To us who have lost the real glow of virtue, and are unmindful of the high traditions of our engagements, such a long wait may appear a sheer waste of time. But it is the dross amongst us that speaks thuswise; for there are men even today who value their words more than the discomfort of a long wait; they are not the clod and stones of the earth, they have not divorced things of the Spirit and merely cultivated the flesh—flesh born of dust.

Think what an impression that waiting for three days left in the mind of Abdullah, an impression so deep that such an incident has passed into history, recorded in every worthwhile book for the last fourteen hundred years, a classic example of what man is and should be capable of doing. Yet today if a man waited for such a long time, he would be called mad: but it shows how much nearer madness we ourselves are as compared to the real issue of man's destiny.

Muhammed had now attained to the age of twenty-five years. A fine manly figure he had, of medium height, sallow of complexion, with colour showing in his cheeks, a wide forehead, with eyebrows meeting above his rather prominent nose, set proportionately over a large mouth in a rather thinish face, he was considered to possess the best type of Arab physiognomy. He had a fairly long neck, crowned by a large head with rather curly hair, eyes of dark grey, and he wore a thick beard. Much more minute details are given in Tirmizi, Muslim and in Bokhari; but for our purpose the above may suffice; although it may be added here that, between his shoulders there was a reddish growth, which has given rise to many legends that it was the place where Allah's Seal could be read; though there is no authority for this statement.

A rich widow lady, Khadija, was informed in Mecca of the increasing popularity of Muhammed in the town, and particularly regarding his business capacity. Distantly related

THE PROPHET AS A MERCHANT AND CITIZEN

to Muhammed—(a cousin by a relation in their fifth line of ancestry)—Khadija was more or less of a merchant princess, and carried on a large export trade on her own. As a capable and virtuous woman she was styled Tahira, or the Chaste, as Muhammed was known as Amin, or the Righteous. She engaged him to superintend her caravan and take the merchandise to the far-off markets of Syria. Muhammed was to receive a higher commission, due to his better qualifications.

Abu Talib, the uncle of the Prophet, was not quite at ease regarding this journey of his nephew, for although Muhammed had arrived at man's estate, nevertheless there was a strong attachment between the two, and the uncle feared for the safety of his nephew during long and arduous travel, for had the Christian monk Bahira not warned Abu Talib to protect his nephew against the Jews, according to Suliman Bin Ibrahim? He confided his fears to Maisarah, the servant who was to accompany Muhammed on his journey to Damascus, and bid him watch the safety of Muhammed, and record every incident that occurred by the way: and so, Khadija's caravan laden with the merchandise of Yemen and the Hijaz started northward in charge of Al Amin, the Righteous Muhammed.

A long line of lumbering camels wended their way in and out of those dry and parched sand dunes, which seemed to stretch to the other end of the earth. In that interminable waste of soft sands, the inexorable heat of the desert sun dried up the waterskins before the travellers reached their next water holes or resting-places. Flames of Hell itself danced and floated over the rocky defiles under the fierce noonday heat, but the caravan moved on. Muhammed, now riding, now walking, led this train, the price of which surpassed even the amalgamated wealth of the whole of Mecca merchants.

And Maisarah, like a faithful servant, watched over his master. During the time when the sun's rays were hottest, and their weary way lay between boulder-strewn passes where no shade was possible, and rocks lay throbbing with heat, beside which a tuft of grass sheltered, even the beast of burden had a taste of hellfire itself:

> *'But'* so says Bin Ibrahim, *'the servant of Muhammed was startled to see that his master did not even throw the end of his black turban to shade his eyes. He was quite comfortable.'*

Maisarah would look up and see a light cloud, like the giant feathers of a bird float in the blazing sky. These clouds, he avers, increased and met, then they were stretched out in long strands resembling the beam-feathers of enormous wings. They cast a shadow over the leader of the caravan. And thus they remained over him throughout their long marches; but when the sun's rays began to lose their intensity, the mass disintegrated into feathery shapes once again and disappeared into thin air; giving place to the azure and saffron sky till stars began to peep through the blue black vault of thc heavens, and calmness settled on the vastness, such as it can nowhere, save in the desert; giving rest to a weary caravan of men and beasts of burden.

Then soon night enveloped them, men lay in between their loads, the camels munched their fodder in deliberate fashion, the campfire was now glowing embers; yes, indeed night had descended upon them, a night of enormous silence, of mystic quiet, with a sky bejewelled with steady bunches of stars, the soothing gold-dusted desert air breathing on them like a soft caress.

But Muhammed was awake, wondering. His thoughts a hundred marches away, dwelling upon the work of man, trying to discover the purpose of creation, the whys and wherefores of life's bitter drama: while palm trees in yonder oasis beside the pool swayed back and forth as the gentle breeze wafted

THE PROPHET AS A MERCHANT AND CITIZEN

through them, making their lofty heads now meet, now part, like men in consultation; and thus gathering up velocity, lifting moving sands to a distant dune—but all remained silent, like the calm of heaven, whilst Muhammed brooded in the stillness of those desert nights as his fellow-travellers slept the sleep of the weary.

From his journey to Syria, Muhammed returned successfully, for he had disposed of Khadija's goods at greater profit than his predecessors had done. The father of the merchant princess had died by then, and although Khadija was senior in age to Muhammed, she sent a message of proposal of marriage to him. In this regard, the women of Arabia had complete control.

Three months after his Syrian journey, amongst great rejoicing in which all the elders of the clan participated, Khadija was duly married to the Prophet. His uncle Abu Talib read the marriage service and a dowry of five hundred gold pieces was fixed for the bride.

Although after the marriage Muhammed had to shoulder a greater responsibility of the Mecca trade, and business circles saw more of him, the reflective aspect of his mind began to show itself the more clearly. His desire to peer into the hidden mysteries of life and death became more intense, he pondered more seriously about the chaotic condition of his kinsmen. In the seclusion of Mount Hira—now called the Mount Of Light—near Mecca, he began to pay visits more frequently for meditation.

Gradually contemplation hardened into a passion, till by and by it became his practice to betake himself for days together to the cave of Hira, and plunge into solitude to think out the riddle of this panorama of existence. Deep contemplation began to bear fruit, for it was during those lonely nights that sensations which beggar description sprang up in his mind. Voices now rose from even the inanimate objects around him, and died

MUHAMMED: THE PROPHET

away in distant whisperings. His mind blended in tune with the infinite. Something was taking shape, an epoch was dawning.

As Ibn Hisham so aptly puts it,

> *'in the oft-benighted worldly pathways of material existence, the inner self of every lofty person has been awakened to influences unseen, but felt'*

Such were the moments that came to Samuel of yore, to Jesus in the vastness of Palestine, when they poured out their very souls to comprehend a way to save their people from the darkness; and in this pondering, these uplifters of humanity found a way. The process was the same with the Prophet of Mecca; the habit of the Great Influence is ever unchanging.

In the stillness of the cave of Hira sat Muhammed contemplating: it was day; the sun dipped behind the crags without interrupting the thoughts of the thinker. Then came the darkness swallowing everything, wrapping even the naked spurs of the Mecca hills, with a suddenness which is the magic of the desert, till stars were hung down from the velvety blackness like radiant bunches of grapes; but Muhammed's contemplations were deeper than those to be affected by the change of light and darkness.

This night, as a hundred or more before it, he was alone in the rock-hewn cave of Hira, alone with his thoughts, his ear attuned to a far-off symphony.

It was the faint ray of light that now shot up, pale yet a while, then adding another strand to it, like a pointing finger of light it grew; gradually the crest of the rocky mountains lit up. The dawn, breaking in its majesty, spreading like a river of liquid pearl growing lovelier and more gorgeous like a golden torrent; but yet the sun was hidden when a Voice spoke to Muhammed; yes, a voice like a whispering in the hush of some great Cathedral.

THE PROPHET AS A MERCHANT AND CITIZEN

'Thou art The man,' it said,
'Thou art the Prophet of Allah.'

To 'explain' such matters, human argument and causation strikes its limitations.

Explain how a man gathering up rose petals cannot affix the flower to its original stem and make it blossom, explain what is it that whispers into our hearts, aye, into the hearts of the most wicked of us— that we have done wrong when we have erred.

Such manifestations are not the things for the discernment of the eye, the nose, the brain: the Voice is of the House whence came the command, saying:

'The voice said, Cry.'
And he said, 'What shall I cry?'

as in the Book of Isaiah.

Chapter 8

THE FIRST VOICE OF TRUTH

With much contemplation, the reflective mind gets supersensitive to impulses, which a barren mind cannot respond to: and thus, great souls overcharged with this refulgence see visions to which the uncultivated eyes are blind. Messengers of God are of such make and build.

I should like to quote a Western scholar, who contributed to *Oriental Religions*, for he is free from that blight of bigotry which has settled down upon most of them, even of great names in their countries. That fair-minded scholar is Johnson.

> '*The natural relations of Muhammed's vast conception of the personality of God*,' he says, '*is the only explanation of that amazing soberness and self-command with which he entertained his all-absorbing visions*';

and then he continues,

> '*it could not have been accidental that the one supreme force of the epoch issued from the solitude of that vast peninsula round which the tides of empires rose and fell. Every exclusive prophetic claim in the name of a sovereign will has been a cry from the illimitable vastness of desert. The symbolic meaning given to Arabia by the withdrawal of the Christian apostle to commune with a power above flesh and blood, became more than a symbol in Muhammed. Arabia was itself the man of the hour, the Prophet of Islam its concentrated world.*

MUHAMMED: THE PROPHET

To the child of her exalted traditions, driven by secret compulsion out into the lonely places of the starry night, his mouth in the dust, the desert spoke without reserve.'

A few days later, however, in the placidity of the desert night in the Cave of Hira, the Voice whispered again.

It was a night in the month of Ramadan or fasting (609th year of the Christian era) when the vision spoke, once, twice and yet a third time the angel Gabriel insisted.

But overwhelmed with divine magnificence as Muhammed was:

'How can I read ? I do not know how to read!'

he replied. And here the first revelation occurred to Muhammed:

Read in the name of thy Lord . . .

spoke the angel, and the *Koran* has it:

Read in the name of thy Lord who created,
He created man from a clod.
Read, and thy Lord is most honourable,
Who taught (to write) with pen,
Taught man when he knew not . . .

This over, Muhammed woke from his trance.

A great trembling had seized him; for God's Messenger had had speech with a mere man: and fear stole into his heart.

Presently he was walking back home; in a paroxysm he lay on his bed all a-quiver, for he knew not what he had seen, or what its significance was.

Like a comforting wife Khadija was at his bedside, and listening to her husband's experiences.

THE FIRST VOICE OF TRUTH

'From thy lips never have I heard a lie,' she said, 'nor have I doubted thy virtue,' and she added, 'what thine eyes have seen and ears heard, of a truth, is odd.

But it is as thou sayst, that a Mission is placed in thy hands; thou art heralded as the Prophet of Allah.'

And, as Bin Ibrahim says, no man in Mecca was more conversant with the Holy Writ than Waraqa Ben Noful, an Arab convert to Christianity. Muhammed's wife took her husband immediately to the scholar's home.

No sooner had he heard his cousin Khadija's story about her Prophet-husband than he cried:

'By the most Holy God! If what thou sayest is correct, He who manifested His Voice to thy husband is the very same great Namus, that is, Allah's confidant, the Angel who appeared to Our Lord Moses. Doubt me not, O, Khadija,' he added, 'but thy husband is the Prophet risen out of the clan of Qureish. Go and be of good cheer!'

Bent by age, and blinded by long years of study, the Christian sage Waraqah henceforth could go to the shrine of Mecca to see the Prophet regarding whom he had read and for whom, like the Syrian monk, he had awaited.

Again he asked Muhammed of his experience at the cave of Hira, and again he tested it with his knowledge of the ancient lore and found it true.

'Ah! I should like to be still in the land of the living,' he would address the Prophet, 'when your kinsmen will send thee to exile.'

Muhammed would feel surprised by what Waraqa said, for exile outside Mecca was quite the most remote possibility for a respected citizen of the Holy City, and he a merchant-prince to boot.

MUHAMMED: THE PROPHET

'Of a surety, they will drive thee to exile,' insisted Waraqa, *'for never hath mortal man brought what thou bringest without falling a victim to the most dastardly persecution.'*

'Ah!' he sighed, *'if God deigned to lengthen my days until then,'* relates Ibn Hisham of Waraqa, *'I would devote all my energies to helping thee to triumph over thy enemies!'*

But Waraqa died soon after.

THE BEGINNING OF THE PREACHING—EARLY CONVERTS

In the beginning the Prophet had to tally his activity with the personal safety of his adherents. The plant was delicate, it required deliberate and slow growth, for the Qureish idolaters would not tolerate any other form of worship, and the Qureish were a powerful, and bloodthirsty, people.

The earliest conversion to Islam was, therefore, limited to the immediate group of the Prophet's friends and relatives.

His wife, Khadija, was the first person to embrace Islam; then Abdullah, surnamed Abu Bakr, an important merchant of Mecca, and Ali; other notables followed them, the chief amongst them being Osman, son of Affan of the Omayah family; Abdur Rahman, son of Auf; Saad, son of Abi Wakkas, afterward the conqueror of Persia, Zaid, and Zubair came within the fold at an early stage. Many people of humbler station in life also became his first disciples.

But although the Prophet's preaching had gripped the minds of many, and the circle of his adherents was growing, nevertheless all ostensible steps to popularise it were kept strictly within narrow bounds. The faithful met and prayed in a house, belonging to Arqum, some distance removed from the hub and bustle of the city of Mecca.

In the valley of that sun-smitten hill of Safa, the followers of Allah held their secret prayer-meetings. A while too, they would go to the far-off folds of the Mecca hills, and engage in their devotions hidden from the eyes of their idol-worshipping

MUHAMMED: THE PROPHET

kinsmen. It was during one of these Islamic retreats that Abu Talib, the Prophet's uncle, saw his nephew praying with his son Ali.

He watched the two standing with folded hands, facing towards Jerusalem, standing mute for a brief period of time, then reciting, and then bending and finally prostrating on the bare rocks: and Abu Talib looked on with amazement at this form of worship.

When they had finished praying:

'What form of devotion is this, the son of my brother?'

he asked the Prophet.

It was time for keeping no secrets, and Muhammed's duty was now clear.

'The prayer is of the religion of Ibrahim, Ibrahim our grand sire!'

he replied.

The single-heartedness with which his nephew and son had prayed, and the confident tone of Muhammed's speech so forcibly effected the old chief of the Hashim Clan that he permitted them to continue their worship;

'for none shall harm you, I aver,'

he asserted, though he would not himself embrace Islam. That was the way of Abu Talib.

For three years this preaching was carried on with utmost care and secrecy, till the duty of the Prophet was emphasised by the Command:

'Make known the Command which has been given to you.'

In another Revelation, he was ordered to warn his kinsmen.

He called the men of Qureish from the heights of Safa.

THE BEGINNING OF THE PREACHING

> *'O! men of my clan!' he raised his voice, 'if I tell you that an army is advancing towards us from behind the hill, would you believe me?'*

Men eyed each other, not knowing what Muhammed's real meaning was, but they had already great faith in all matters on which Muhammed made himself heard, for he was known to all as the righteous, Al Amin, one who spoke nothing but the truth. To the simple question put to them from Safa, however, they were now willing to reply unreservedly:

> *'Aye, Aye. Of a truth, if you said that an army advanced towards us from the folds of Safa, we shall all believe you; for thy word has never been found to be wanting!'*

In this atmosphere, when his people had testified to his veracity; Muhammed declared that if they did not believe in One God, and in him as the Messenger, then Allah's wrath will descend upon them.

But the minds of the men of Qureish were rusted through generations of idolatry: the tarnished disc never reflects back the glorious radiance of a mirror aglow with the light of spirituality.

The Prophet's hearers, who a short time previously had set seal on his merit as a truth-teller, were not inclined to listen to a matter which cut deep down into their hoary traditions.

> *They got wroth,* says Bokhari. *Shaking their heads in disapproval and disgust, they dispersed.*

Muhammed's uncle was also amongst them.

A few days after this, a huge feast was prepared to which the young and old of the Qureish were invited.

At the conclusion, the Prophet rose to speak:

> *'I have brought to you, all men of Qureish, indeed to the whole world,'* he said, *'that which is a stand-by, both in*

MUHAMMED: THE PROPHET

this world and the next.

In carrying on this onerous task, who will assist me?'

Men's tongues were tied with amazement to see how a mere man, a man whom they had seen grow amongst them, a man feeble and humble like all men, should dare stand before them; yes, before them, who would slay a man at sight if they found him speak ought against their idols, yet here was he standing before them preaching rank sacrilege about their stone gods, gods who had given them victory in battle, had blessed them with rain when drought came, and whose house they had defended for centuries together.

And here a man of their own flesh and blood was defying what a great empire could not do with impunity.

'Who will be with me,' asked Muhammed, 'in carrying on this great task?'

Who would you think now stood up ? None other than the son of Abu Talib.

'Mine eyes are sore, my legs may not be strong, and tender in age though I be,' said Ali Bin Abu Talib, 'I shall abide with thy mission, O Muhammed, the Messenger of God— that God Which is One.'

There was a roar of laughter amongst the guests.

Stalwart men who had wielded the battle axe and the spear all their lives, nursed their swords, these warriors of Qureish rocked with laughter. Forsooth, a weakling like Ali, and only Muhammed to carry out defiance against the might of their ancestral religion! It was ludicrous, a joke.

Gradually the number of Muhammed's followers increased to forty. There was nothing to be done by stealth now, for injunctions to the Prophet were unequivocal: henceforth he was to go forward fearlessly preaching the truth

THE BEGINNING OF THE PREACHING

Presently he was addressing the worshippers in the shrine of the Kaaba itself.

No greater offence against the Established Church could be committed. There were tumultuous scenes in the sacred precincts, angry voices were rising, jeering vituperations were hurled on the preacher; skirts were being torn off their long trailing abaya, the preacher was forgotten, the cause was forgotten, only pandemonium remained, arms were rising and falling on their tilted turbans.

Haaris Bin Abayhala ran to the sacred precincts thinking the Prophet in danger of his life.

He was tearing through the tumultuous crowd of angered men, calling *"Ya! Muhammed! where art thou?"*

Hardly had he gone ten paces through shouting, yelling men, when leaping swords descended upon the rescuer of Muhammed. Haaris was the first martyr of Islam.

Chapter 9

REASON FOR THE ENMITY OF THE QUREISH

It is pertinent here to examine the reasons which prompted the Qureish to an inexorable hostility against Muhammed's message.

First of all, we should know what conditions obtained in Mecca regarding the prestige of the Qureish, and other important clans at the advent of the Prophet. The city of Mecca was revered throughout Arabia primarily on account of its shrine of Kaaba, where dwelt three hundred and sixty idols. The ministrants of the precincts were the Qureish, and thus they were called the celestial family. Incidently it helped them in trade, and in the government of the realm, too, theirs was the whole say.

Let us note who were the officials whom the Prophet sought to dethrone. There was first Osman Bin Talha, the custodian of the Keys of the Kaaba; from the family of Noful, Hurs Bin Amir looked after the disbursement of the funds for the poor; from the house of Hashim, Abbas had the right to distribute water to the pilgrims; Yazid Bin Rabiatul Aswad was the Councillor; from Tameen was Abu Bakr who arranged the reparation: the standard-bearer was Abu Sufyan from the rival clan of Omayah; Walid Bin Mogheera from the Makhzoom family was in charge of the transport; Omar Bin Khattab, the scion of Aday, acted as the plenipotentary; the diviner and soothsayer was Sufyan Bin Omayah, and the treasury was in charge of Haars Bin Qays.

MUHAMMED: THE PROPHET

I have given these names with their family connection, because some of these dignitaries embraced Islam, and became staunch supporters of the Prophet, whilst others took a very conspicuous part in opposing the ministry of Muhammed, both in peace and war. The names of most of them, as we shall see later, will occur frequently as the drama develops; and therefore the above details will be very useful as a reference.

There are, however, half a dozen other names as well which ought to be mentioned in this regard, for although these men were not actively engaged in the discharge of any ministerial duties, nevertheless, they exercised enormous control over the people. Like the others, their names will also start up in the doings of early Islam, and therefore a familiarity with them is necessary; they are: Abu Sufyan Bin Hurb, whose father had led the Qureish army in the battle of Fijar; the next name is that of Abu Lahab, the Prophet's uncle, junior to Abu Talib, under whose protection Muhammed had enjoyed security; the third man was Abu Jahl, a nephew of Walid Bin Mogheera, and a leader of his clan; next in order was Walid Bin Mogheera, now the undisputed head of the Qureish, then Aas Bin Waal Sahmi, a rich merchant with a large following and many sons, and lastly, Otla Bin Rabiyah, another merchant of considerable fortune.

Around these personalities centred the influence and prestige of the Qureish which held the whole of Arabia within its grasp. This dual monarchy of State and Church was all-powerful.

Having regard to what is explained above, the first reason which can be ascribed to the hostile attitude of the Qureish against Muhammed's doctrine, is that it sought to dismantle the belief which had been handed down to them for long centuries, a belief, indeed, which had given them, like their forefathers, the excuse to rule over the bodies and souls of their countrymen from the north to south of the Arabian peninsula.

REASON FOR THE ENMITY OF THE QUREISH

If that belief was endangered, even in the slightest degree, their rulership would be seriously damaged, and the very existence of the Qureish as an entity in Arabia would be destroyed.

Side by side with this common menace, there was the question of acute rivalry which existed amongst the two clans of the Qureish, the House of Hashim and that of Bani Omayah. So far, the latter section held the most important posts in the government. Delicate matters of statecraft could not envisage the appearance of a man from the rival section of Hashim, and by gathering a large following, make the scale weigh heavily on the side of those whose competition was resented by the Bani Omayah. They argued that, even supposing the conception of One God, as preached by Muhammed, was tantamount to sacrilege in the eyes of everyone, yet if Bani Hashim saw that Muhammed had gathered so much strength as to help them to overpower Bani Omayah, then Bani Hashim would not have any scruples in aiding Muhammed, the man of their own clan, his *'excesses'* towards the idols notwithstanding.

It is therefore hard to discredit the opinion of many writers that the thought of their being pulled down from the pedestals of the state and trade always lingered in the minds of the Omayah's sons who so vehemently opposed Muhammed's mission. The contention, however, in no way throws in the shadow another cause of animosity, that of the dismantling of stone idols from the Kaaba.

The next cause appertains to the uneasiness felt by the Qureish about having restrictions placed upon their moral turpitude. In addition to the base and despicable licentiousness of the general public of Mecca at that time, we have evidence to show that even amongst the keepers of the shrine depravity and vice were common. Who but Abu Lahab himself stole and sold the golden idol of the gazelle, which was kept in the temple of the Kaaba? Other instances of the degeneracy of the moral

MUHAMMED: THE PROPHET

conduct would not bear mention.

Incidentally, the other reason for the opposition was also that the Moslems then prayed, directing their faces not towards idol-infested Mecca, but towards Jerusalem, a city revered by the Christians. The devotee of the Kaaba thought that what Muhammed sought to do was to accomplish by preaching what Abra, the Christian general of Yemen, had failed to do by force of arms, that is to say implant Christianity.

And through Abra's invasion of Mecca territory, to the Qureish had been bequeathed the greatest hatred for Christians and Christianity. The Meccan had on that score been *'bestowing their sweetness'* upon the sun-worshipping Persians and shunning the Christian Romans of Syria: so much so, that when the Persians proved victorious against the latter, the Qureish rejoiced.

The struggle between Persia and the Roman Empire, says Mohammed Ali, had existed for a long time. The great struggle, in which Persia was victorious, began in A.D. 602 when Chosroes II of Persia battled with the Romans. The Persians overran Syria, Asia Minor and had reached Chalcedon in 608. In 613 and 614 both Damascus and Jerusalem were taken by Shahabraz, and the Holy Cross was carried away in great triumph. Soon after, even Egypt was conquered.

When the news of this conquest reached Mecca, adds this Moslem scholar, the Qureish were jubilant, as in sympathies, they showed undoubted preference towards the fire-worshippers in opposition to the Christians, who, in common with the Moslems, were the *'people of the Book'* and thus enemies of pagan Arabia.

In the year A.D. 615-616, the *Koran* announced

> *'that whereas the Romans were defeated they will again rise and be triumphant':*

REASON FOR THE ENMITY OF THE QUREISH

'The Romans are vanquished,'

says the *Koran* in *Sura Ar Rum*,

'in a near land, and they after being vanquished shall be overcome within a few years. Alluh's is the command before and after; and on that day the believers shall rejoice...'

We have the testimony of known history that it was exactly as told in the *Koran*; the Persian Empire sank to earth within a very few years.

The causes and their effect enumerated above, one will presume, had enough in themselves to produce more militant opposition to the Prophet and his fellows. In a country where life was cheap, and dark crimes were not considered crimes at all, it would have been quite an easy matter to slay Muhammed and thus stifle his movement; especially in the beginning, the smothering of Islam's messenger could not be fraught with any particular dangers. Any ruffian might very easily have put Muhammed away. It is so in ordinary matters of the world.

Different laws govern the universe in regards to personalities who bear a torch in their hand, a torch before whose radiance the gloom of vice is to disappear.

These, however, may be my own feelings; but viewing the question from the angle of vision of the Qureish, superficially looking, we cannot escape the conclusion that they made some tactical mistake in not taking drastic steps right in the very first break of the Islamic dawn.

A more serious study of the conditions then prevailing shows us, however, that the Qureish had made no mistake. They knew their business.

To kill a man was an easy enough matter; but its consequences were far-reaching. It precipitated a clan war, a blood feud that would have raged for generations, for Muhammed belonged to the tribe of Hashim, and his kinsmen could never have left the matter alone till the blood was wiped out with the sword. Furthermore, men of other clans had also embraced Islam by now.

These followers of Muhammed would have shed their blood in the way of their master, and thus, practically the entire Arabian peninsula would have been embroiled in one great national upheaval of internal wars. Besides the wicked state of the Mecca society notwithstanding, there were still some men left who desired to have the differences arranged amicably.

A delegation of the important men of Qureish waited upon Muhammed's uncle:

> 'O! Abu Talib,' they said, 'thy influence is appreciated throughout Mecca, thy respect we cherish in our eyes and hearts; but this nephew of thine is incorrigible. He mocks at our idols, and flaunts the traditional worship of our grandsires. Wilt thou rid us of him, or shall we take the law into our hands and deal with him in our own way?'

Abu Talib dismissed them with a conciliatory reply: but Muhammed could not be muzzled, his orders were not orders of a human being: he obeyed no laws of the vice-ridden people of Mecca, and he continued to warn the idol worshippers, and invited them ever more zealously to tread the path of Allah.

A second time, the delegates of Mecca came to Abu Talib to give him the final warning:

> 'Range thyself along thy nephew O! Abu Talib,' they shouted, 'so that we may deal with thee as well, for Muhammed's ways are beyond toleration.'

The old chief promised to speak to his nephew: and sending for Muhammed, he said,

REASON FOR THE ENMITY OF THE QUREISH

> *'my beloved nephew, place not so much burden upon mine old back which I may not be able to bear.'*

Abu Talib's appeal moved the Prophet deeply. On one side you have the filial regard for a venerable uncle who has watched over Muhammed when he was a helpless orphan, on the other the mighty call of God's message. On one side the entire weight of the powerful Qureish, men with glistening swords and proud lances, who rule the heart of Arabia and beyond, who could exterminate a hundred times over the followers of Muhammed before the day dipped in the golden west, and on the other, the promise of Allah's words, yes, Allah, whose power was impersonal, hidden, mysterious, known and appreciated only by those who were fit enough to behold it.

But feelings did not battle long in the mind of Muhammed, with his characteristic boldness in such matters,

> *'In the name of God—who is One—I swear,'* replied the Prophet to his uncle, *'if they will place the moon on my right hand and the sun on my left, even then I cannot, will not, turn from my Mission.'*

The pronouncement had something of that directness and intensity which only truth can impart; and Abu Talib was palpably impressed.

> *'Go thy way, the son of mine brother,'* he said, as reported in Bokhari, *'none dare touch thee!'*

The Qureish thought of another stratagem. Is this son of Abdullah, really so dear to Abu Talib that he could not be persuaded to part with him? Could monetary considerations not affect the decision of Abu Talib?

A third time a few leaders came to the uncle of Muhammed.

> *'O! Abu Talib,'* they said, *'here is Ammarah Bin Walid, son of the most accomplished and handsomest man of*

MUHAMMED: THE PROPHET

Mecca. We bring him to thee. Adopt him for thy son, and let us take away Muhammed, for our souls hunger for his blood.'

Abu Talib refused the order. He did not want another man's son—even with financial backing—to clothe and feed, whilst giving up the one who shared the flesh and blood of his own kinsmen. The bargain was all one-sided.

Next they went to Muhammed. They offered him one of the offices in the Mecca state,

'a rich wife thou mayst have, a share in the business of the merchant-princes, indeed any thing that thy mind craveth for. But leave alone your ways of preaching. O! Muhammed, for the pleasure of thy clan thou shalt win thuswise: or prepare for the wrath of Qureish!'

Muhammed, in place of accepting their terms, reiterated the warning of Allah:

'Take heed O! men of Mecca,' he replied, and fear the wrath of God.

Banish your idol worshipping, and incline towards right living to which Islam invites you.'

And then they let loose their passions, murder was in their eyes, men foamed with rage, tugging at their beards, the youthful amongst them greeted Muhammed's words with derisive laughter, a few swords flashed in the noonday sun, spearheads showed above the turbans of the Elders who could with difficulty quieten down the more fiery elements amongst them.

There were other ways to bring a man round to think as they thought, chuckled the wiseacres of Mecca. To thrust a spear in the side of their culprit was not one of them: at least, not quite that, till it be in a pitched battle, they reasoned.

Chapter 10

THE PERSECUTION: AND ASCENSION

The persecution of the Prophet now commenced. His followers fared no better. Many a time when the sand was baking under the intense heat of the Arabian sun, Moslems were taken to those stretches, where they were made to lie, a large boulder having been placed upon their chests. Others were branded with hot irons, others were immersed in the water till they were just about to be drowned. Ibn Saad gives these and other details about the atrocities inflicted upon the Moslems.

Even women did not escape the wrath of the Qureish, Simeyah was killed by Abu Jahl, Zanerah, another pious woman, was beaten till her persecutor himself collapsed; and after taking a rest, began to belabour her till she became unconscious and ultimately lost the sight of her eyes.

Men like Abu Fakiyah were dragged through the streets by their feet; passers-by were asked to spit on them and then they were placed over the burning sands.

The treatment meted out to Muhammed was scarcely less severe. One day, while he was praying, a man, throwing his sheet round the neck of the Prophet, dragged him with such force that Muhammed fell on his knees.

On another occasion Abu Jahl caused some camel intestines to be thrown over him at the time of worship. Thorns were strewn in his way: men even cast their slops and rubbish upon

MUHAMMED: THE PROPHET

him from their windows as he passed by.

The persecution of the Moslem was getting unbearable, when the Prophet advised some of his followers to abandon Mecca, and seek refuge in the neighbouring Christian Kingdom of Abyssinia, where justice was done and hospitality was shown to the refugees.

In the first Hijra, or exile, four women and eleven men left their homeland during the fifth year of Muhammed's Ministry in A.D. 6 1 5 .

Later, others too left Mecca, and Ibn Hisham gives the total number to be eighty-three men and eighteen women. Osman, the fourth Khalifa, was one of the first batch which had left Mecca, but he returned later to rejoin the Prophet.

The Qureish, however, saw a further danger to their position by this voluntary exile of the Moslems. They feared that the followers of the Prophet would acquaint the powerful ruler of Abyssinia with their excesses and weaknesses and this might prepare the mind of the Negus to repeat the invasion of Mecca.

But chiefly did they resent this flight because the mission of Allah, so far circumscribed within Mecca, was now going to be spread beyond the confines of Arabia.

They forthwith resolved to send a delegation to await upon the Negus in order to have the Moslems expelled from Abyssinia.

The charges which the Meccans brought up against the helpless refugees were that they had abjured their ancestral religion and had adopted a new faith.

I cannot do better than quote from the oldest Arabic biography of Ibn Hisham regarding this, a great milestone in Islamic history:

'Then he, the Negus, sent for the followers of the Prophet,'

THE PERSECUTION: AND ASCENSION

says the biographer,

'When they came before the Emperor, he had convened his bishops with their books, and then he inquired, 'what is this religion by reason of which you have separated from your people: a religion which is neither my own, nor like any other?'

Jafar, son of Abu Talib, who was their spokesman, narrated how they were leading a barbarous life, worshipping idols, eating carrion, violating the ties of consanguinity and how the strong man's hand was always lifted against the weak: thus, they continued to live, he asserted, till the Apostle of Allah rose amongst them to summon them to God, declaring his Unity and offering prayers only to Him. The Prophet bade them be truthful, God-fearing, performing neighbourly duties towards their neighbours, respect the property of orphans, to give charity and abide by the moral laws; and, above all, associating none other with God.

In details did Jafar mention the cruelties inflicted upon them at Mecca, how they were induced to go back to the pagan life of idol-worship.

Then the Negus asked the leader of the Moslems to recite some passages of the Koran, *and he read the Sura of* Maryam *which, like others, was revealed to the Prophet.*

The Negus and his bishops were so overcome that they wept bitterly:

'Verily,' said the Negus *when the recitation was over, 'verily, this, and that which Moses brought, emanate from one lamp.'*

'Go! he addressed the Moslems, *'for by God I will not surrender you to them to let them get at you, nor even contemplate this.'*

MUHAMMED: THE PROPHET

Amru Bin Aas, the head of the Mecca delegation, refused, however, to be defeated in his purpose. During the evening he saw the Church dignitaries and told them that although the followers of Islam did not believe in the form of their ancestral worship, they did not in the like manner owe allegiance to the Christian ethics, more especially the followers of Muhammed had no faith in the Trinity and in the Divinity of Jesus. In their estimation, Bin Aas stated, Christ was no more and no less than a mere man.

The Abyssinian bishops were persuaded to use their influence in exhorting upon the Negus the necessity of banishing the people from his realm who entertained such ideas about the Saviour.

The stage was set the next morning when the Negus assembled his court. The machination of the pagan Arabs had apparently conquered. The bishops sat on the right hand side of the King's throne, the officers of the state stood on the left, an oppressing feeling was abroad, many heads were bent in whispers as the Moslems were asked to present themselves again before the mighty ruler of the Abyssinian warriors, and declare their views about Jesus.

Amru was certain that what the Moslems would say could not but favour his cause.

If Jafar gave an evasive reply then the leader of the Meccans would at once denounce him as a liar, for the *Koran* could be quoted to say that the Divinity of Christ was not to be believed by the faithful; and if the Moslems were truthful then the Emperor, with the connivance of the bishops, would be angered, and command the expulsion of men who in his eyes would be painted as heathens.

> '*Say what your belief is about Christ,*' *thundered the Negus to Jafar* as stated by Shibli, *and the leader of the*

THE PERSECUTION: AND ASCENSION

Moslems repeated what was told to them by the Prophet, that Jesus was to them a Voice of God, a slave of Allah and His Prophet.

The pagan Arabs chuckled in their beards, at last their manoeuvering had succeeded, and they watched with assurance the expected command from the Negus.

But the Emperor picked up a piece of straw from the ground: 'By God Almighty,' he said, holding the straw in his fingers, 'Jesus was no more than what you state, you have not exaggerated about Him as much as this thin piece of straw.'

The effect of this extraordinary pronouncement struck the bishops mute with wonderment, with difficulty they were able to control their wrath-born amazement. The Arab pagans felt as if the earth was swallowing them, were they hearing and seeing aright? There could be no doubt about what the Emperor of Abyssinia meant:

'Go, to thy dwellings!' the Negus swayed his hand towards Jafar, 'and live and worship in thine own way, none shall interfere with you.'

As a humble tribute to the justice of the king of Abyssinia the Moslem refugees strove to help the Negus against his enemies. Though small in number they could withal be of some service to the cause of their benefactor.

The Negus had taken the command in person against those who had invaded his territory. Zubair, a young Moslem, was deputed to go to the battlefield and inform the refugees if help was wanted, for they were ready to show their gratitude. Ibn Hisham gives an account of how the young lad swam the Nile by means of inflated goatskins, journeyed to the scene of war, and returned to inform his co-religionists of the victory of the Negus, over which the Moslems greatly rejoiced.

MUHAMMED: THE PROPHET

Upon the return of the Qureish delegation to Mecca, without the Moslem refugees from Abyssinia, the flames of revenge burnt the fiercer in the heart of the Meccans against the followers of the Prophet.

An organised system of persecution was now set on foot; and even the more important men of that persuasion were maltreated: despite the fact that such strong men as Omar and Hamza had embraced Islam, and there was almost a daily addition in the ranks of Muhammed's followers.

Concurrently with Muhammed's ever-growing molestation, other steps were taken to boycott not only the Moslems but also the entire House of Hashim which gave birth to the movement of Islam.

A large meeting of all the clans was held to devise the means of this ostracism, wherein it was agreed that

> *no one shall give his daughter in marriage to the men of Bani Hashim, and vice versa, no one shall carry on any business transaction with them, none shall provide them with water or any articles of food. This shall remain in operation till the Bani Hashim see their way in giving over Muhammed to them to be slain.*

Munsoor Bin Akramah, having inscribed these resolutions, says Mawahib Ladunyah, suspended them on the Kaaba shrine of three hundred and sixty idols.

And whilst the thraldom of this excommunication sat heavily upon the clan of the Prophet, the ill-treatment was increasing without restraint upon the Moslems. For three years the Beni Hashim had to bear the brunt of all the doings of Muhammed, and true to their tradition, bore hardships cheerfully. Towards the later part of this social boycott, limits of starvation had been reached: people ate dried-up leaves, and castoff leather was soaked in water and roasted for food. When children wept for

THE PERSECUTION: AND ASCENSION

food, the persecutors hailed their distress with glee.

During this period of trial, the Ascension of Muhammed to the Celestial Throne of Allah occurred, of which I shall speak presently; and it was at this time, too, that the Moslems were commanded to offer their prayers five times a day. Eventually the pagan Arabs of Mecca, who had many blood ties with the Bani Hashim, on their own accord lifted the ban, and the Prophet's clan was again free to occupy its former quarter in the city; but soon after, both the beloved wife of the Prophet, Khadija, and his uncle Abu Talib died.

There is still a controversy about whether Abu Talib embraced Islam on his deathbed; but of course we know that the spouse of the Prophet was the first Moslem and died as such: and now for the last ten years Muhammed had been carrying on his mission under turbulent circumstances with such fortitude.

As the storm of opposition raged the fiercer against the Moslems, Muhammed's resolve grew stronger. The Qureish were on the warpath, and they meant to extirpate the cause which had brought disgrace upon their idols.

If Muhammed was the Messenger of God, the pagans demanded, then let him bring down the heavens in pieces, shift mountains, erect a palace of gold or ascend to the skies by means of a ladder, and bring down a complete Book of his Laws. Nothing short of these miracles would satisfy the Qureish.

Nor was this demand of asking for miracles a new demand from the Prophet; for the same was asked of Jesus; as in the words of Professor Momerie,

> 'His immediate disciples were always misunderstanding Him and His work: wanting Him to call down here from heaven; wanting Him to declare Himself King of the Jews; wanting to sit on His right hand and His left hand in His

MUHAMMED: THE PROPHET

kingdom; wanting Him to show them the Father, to make God visible to their bodily eyes.... This was how they treated Him until the end. When that came, they all forsook Him, and fled.'

It is impossible to escape the comparison that the Muhammed's disciples never asked for miracles, they accepted the Prophet on his own merits as a model man, whose life story was not the life of a god but of a man.

In an age says, Amir Ali, when miracles were supposed to be ordinary occurrences at the beck and call of the most ordinary saint, when the whole atmosphere of Arabia and the countries encompassing it, was countenancing supernatural and occult practises, the Prophet of Allah unhesitatingly replied to the miracle-seeking heathens of Mecca:

'God has not sent me to work wonders. He has sent me to preach to you. My Lord be praised! Am I more than a man sent as an apostle? . .

Angels do not commonly walk the earth, or God would have dispatched an angel to preach His truth to you. I, who cannot even help or trust myself, unless God pleaseth.'

Here you cannot but observe the clear note of directness, with no embellishment of speech, no effort to shroud himself in mystery regarding his personality or mission: a plain man speaking in plain language the gospel which God put into his mouth:

'I am only a preacher of God's words, the bringer of Allah's message to mankind,'

and here I may again quote the passage, which Professor Momerie attests, that at no tie during his life the Prophet made any statement

THE PERSECUTION: AND ASCENSION

'which could be construed into a request for human worship.'

His miracle was contained in the tenets of his teaching, and his attitude towards mankind.

It was during this time too, as stated above, that the phenomenon of the nocturnal journey to Jerusalem and the Ascension of the Prophet took place. Before endeavouring to understand the nature of this occurrence, it is necessary to recapitulate what the doctors of Islamic law have reported about the actual happening.

Al-Isra, the nocturnal journey, and Al-Miraj, the Prophet's Ascension, are variously described.

Some think that this miraculous journey, says Bin Ibrahim, was physically accomplished, whilst others rely upon the most accredited traditions, among which is that of Ayesha, the wife of Muhammed—that the Prophet's soul alone undertook the journey, and that the phenomenon should only be looked upon as a veracious vision.

There is really no authoritative date of the journey, but according to Bin Ibrahim, who no doubt bases his statements upon the Arab writers, it was the night of the twenty-seventh of the Moslem month of Rabial Awwal, that the angel upon whom devolved the duty of directing the heavenly bodies, was ordered by the Almighty to increase the moon's brilliancy by adding a part of the sun's radiance, and that of the stars by a share of the moon's brightness, so that the firmament that night should be resplendent with light. The Angel was then to descend to where Muhammed was sleeping, and carry him to Allah through the seven zones of Heaven.

Quoth the Prophet: as reported by some biographers

—*'I was in a deep sleep when the angel Jibrail (Gabriel) appeared to me.'*

MUHAMMED: THE PROPHET

The angel taking the Prophet to the Sacred well of Zam Zam, it is related,

> 'opened his chest, and washed the heart of Muhammed with the holy water of that well. Then the angel brought Al Buraq, an extraordinary bird-like animal, so that the Prophet may ride on it on his celestial journey. The Buraq is described to be a quadruped larger than an ass and smaller than a mule. His coat was whiter than snow, his face was a man's face, but the animal was dumb. He had wings like a giant bird; on the mane, and upon his breast precious jewels were sparkling. As soon as the Prophet mounted on him, the creature flapped his great wings, and rose above the clouds, careering on and onwards.
>
> From the sacred temple of Mecca, the Prophet's mount took him to the Masjid Al Aqsa in Jeruslem with great rapidity. Alighting from the Buraq, Muhammed fastened the bridle to the ring used by the prophets of yore in Jerusalem, and now one appeared before him holding two cups. One contained milk and the other had wine. The Prophet took and drank the milk and refused the wine; and the angel, who had accompanied him to Jerusalem and had thus offered him the two cups, spoke approvingly: 'If thou hadst preferred wine to milk,' said the Angel, 'thy people would have preferred Error to Truth.'
>
> After visiting the mosque, the Prophet climbed up to where the great rock of Sukhra lies near Al Aqsa, in the sacred Harem of Jerusalem. He remounted the Buraq, and being led by the angel, proceeded towards the skies.'

During his ascent he is reported to have met many prophets of old, Adam, Abraham, Jesus, Moses, Idris;

> there he saw the paradise in which the believers will be lodged, and in it rose a edifice of pearls, the earth of the paradise being of musk and the Prophet's grandsire

THE PERSECUTION: AND ASCENSION

Abraham was reclining against the wall of the Noble House, in which seventy thousand angels entered every day.

Proceeding further a 'station' was reached, where he could hear the Pen scribbling the account of world's destinies and work of nature; beyond it he spied the Tree of Eternity, and beyond, which nothing can penetrate. The refulgence of God's radiance played upon the Tree; and this Light of Heaven enveloped the Prophet as well. The Great Angel here disclosed himself in his true lambent light; for Allah's nearness was now in sight. It was here that the Command to perform fifty prayers every day was conveyed to Muhammed from the Celestial Throne.

On his way back the Prophet was asked by Moses regarding the orders which had been given to Muhammed 'Thy flock is too weak to bear the burden of fifty prayers,' said Moses to Muhammed, 'go back and seek a reduction in their number.'

To the Throne of Allah did Muhammed return and begged for the reduction in the number of prayers. They were reduced by five; but Moses again reminded the Prophet of the frailty of his people, and again did Muhammed go before the Throne seeking further reduction. The request was granted; and yet a third time Muhammed found himself before Allah's Celestial Light till the number of prayers were reduced from fifty to five; but whereas, it is stated—the number of prayers is thus reduced, the virtue of fifty is vouchsafed into five.

This concluded, Muhammed returned to Jerusalem from the skies and found all the previous prophets awaiting him. Moses and Abraham were already bending low in prayer.

He described Jesus as:

'*a man of medium height, fair complexioned with long*

MUHAMMED: THE PROPHET

flowing hair. He looked as clean as one that emerges from the bath: the physiognomy of Moses was mentioned as of a tall man, with sallow complexion and curly hair. The prophet Abraham or Ibrahim resembled Muhammed himself.'

As the dawn was breaking, all filed up to offer the morning prayer, the Prophet leading the congregation; and ultimately Muhammed found himself in the great Temple of Mecca.

'What eyes can pierce the veil of God's decrees?
Or read the riddle of earth's destinies?
Pondered have I for years threescore and twelve,
And can but say these things are mysteries.'

So far the reports of the many biographers have been set down. Much of it, if taken literally, may sound as a legend; but it can admit of an explanation.

In the history of the philosophy of Islam we have ample evidence to show that this *'transportation'* is possible, as such flights have been of the nature of a trance, which are not unusual manifestations with men gifted with the powers of the occult.

Muhammed, as we know, was an extraordinary man, his message had already singled him out from his fellows; and there can be no shadow of doubt that during a time when hebetation settled on the body and he was just about to sleep, a feeling of other-worldliness crept upon him, which, in essence, was of the nature of the Divine.

Whilst Muhammed was in this state of mental and spiritual exaltation, his mind's eye became opened; he had gained possession of knowledge beyond human comprehension; his soul was soaring high above the clouds of sinful humanity as he lay beside the Kaaba in the temple of Mecca.

Step by step he proceeded, unveiling mysteries of ages, into

THE PERSECUTION: AND ASCENSION

the unknown region of thought, on and onward towards the grail of true searches, to the Throne of Allah.

Meditation, constant prayer to the One God, had exalted him in purity and holiness to see and experience things which are inaccessible to men of the common herd.

Long flights of spiritual thought transported him to the highest realms which only a mystic can reach; those wings of spiritual ecstasy bore him into that rare atmosphere where he could perceive the Light of the Divine Cause and the Origin of All: and so what is described about his journey with such a glory of colour is nothing but the illusions of a wondrous soul endeavouring to interpret, to the profane, that impulse which prophets can only comprehend.

Those facets of this stupendous journey where the travel of the Prophet to Jerusalem is spoken of, and during which the injunction of five prayers during the day was made absolute, are of especial interest to us; because, whereas they lay the cornerstone of the Islamic form of devolution in one case, in the other, they explain the reason as to why the Moslems turned their faces towards Jerusalem when in prayer.

Finally, they mark the turning point in the career of Islamic preaching, for during this period, the *Koran* warned the people of Mecca for the last time before the wrath of Allah might descend upon them: and in it, the ground was paved for the Hijrah, or the Flight of the Moslems, from idol-ridden Mecca to Medina.

Chapter 11

HIJRA, OR THE FLIGHT

The struggle between the Moslems and the Qureish was now open and often violent. Incidents of molestation of the Prophet's followers were growing in number, but the Torch of Truth was fully alight, and Muhammed remained steadfast towards his duty. In spite of the growing strength of the Moslems, they were not allowed to recite the *Koran* aloud nor pray in the Mecca temple freely; till the Prophet went to the uplands of Taif, near Mecca, to preach his gospel of One God.

The agents of the Man of Sin had forestalled Muhammed, and his words, therefore, fell upon deaf ears; indeed it was not without difficulty that the Prophet was able to return from idol-infested Taif with a whole skin. He was spat upon, stones were thrown at him, he was jeered at, in short his peracute reception at Taif was on par with that of the Mecca disorder which took place when the Prophet described his journey to Jerusalem to the pagans.

Nothing daunted, this apostle of Allah returned to his home town even more resolute in his mind to proceed with the Mission. The pilgrim season was drawing near, and the Qureish feared that at those gatherings Muhammed could not but preach to all and sundry, which would be positively harmful to the cult of the idol-worshippers. At a public meeting of the clans it was decided to depute men from the Qureish who should warn the pilgrims of the desert regarding the *'sacrilegious'* beliefs of one of them—Muhammed—and his

MUHAMMED: THE PROPHET

followers. They were to style him as a wizard, his mission as a farce; and if they found him to be capturing the attention of the men of the desert by reciting the passages of the *Koran*, then one of the Qureish should immediately pronounce the Holy Work as a man-made poem with no religious motive but calculated for the self-aggrandisement of the Prophet.

Muhammed, however, was prepared, for he reposed his trust in the duty before him. Preach, he would, he thought; and let the world judge of his words on their own merits. On the healthy soil the seeds which he would cast should grow, and thuswise his mind was made up.

The pilgrims came to Mecca from the far off corners of Arabia. They trekked from the green uplands of Yemen, from the burnng sands of the Arabian no-man's-land, from the Red Sea littoral and from the heart of the desert they came to rejoice and to pray before the three hundred and sixty idols of the Kaaba; and to seek from their stone gods the gift of children, or rain where drought dried up their crops, or victory over their wandering enemies.

During the ceremonies, they sold and bought in the markets of Mecca, made merry at the taverns, drank wine till their legs could not support them; and in the midst of it all a call startled them. It was Muhammed who was speaking.

A man was reeling in the dust in an inebriated condition. Clinging to the curtain of the shrine of the stone gods, he uttered incoherent prayers that he might win at the gambling table; another kicked him saying how dare he beseech in that manner when the gods had already promised him success; a woman wailed under the swaying curtain supplicating to the god Hobal to give her back her dead child; the haughty Qureish pranced about collecting offerings from the poor pilgrims: and here Muhammed rose to speak in a thronged courtyard of the Temple.

HIJRA, OR THE FLIGHT

He invited the pagans to come to the way of One God, he warned them of the evil day which they will see if they did not mend their ways; he gave them the glad tidings that the Light of Truth has been ushered in, and that no man had any excuse to grope in the dark any further:

'Come to Allah, the Compassionate, the merciful,'

he called out again and again.

Men stared at him with eyes of astonishment: what have they heard? What force more potent than their ancestral idols that presided at the shrine had made him so bold as to utter such profanity? The noise subsided as birds quieten down before a thunderstorm: and then the Qureish realised what had happened. Muhammed could have been torn limb from limb, but something stayed their hands, that very thing before which unrighteousness withers and dies. But whereas the time was not yet for these words of Muhammed to sink into the minds of the desert-born; the seed was cast; for shortly afterwards he spoke to some men of Yasrib or Medina about his mission. They were the people of the Khazraj tribe.

These six men of Medina, with whom Muhammed now conversed at the hill of Aqabah, were not entirely ignorant regarding the advent of a Prophet, because a number of Jews living in their town had often related to them the prophesy about the coming of the Prophet. When, however, they heard the *Koran* recited, with such glow and warmth which Muhammed only could give, they felt convinced that the verses were none other than those from a Holy Book, and the reciter the man spoken of before. They embraced Islam, and undertook to carry the message of peace to their people.

The new converts to Islam, upon reaching Medina, worked for their new faith with such zest that during the next twelve months their original number was doubled. At Aqabah, again,

MUHAMMED: THE PROPHET

they met the Prophet and took an oath of fidelity; but although not wanting in energy themselves, it was felt by these men of Medina that if the Prophet could depute a religious teacher of Islam with them, it will undoubtedly provide a greater vigour to the preaching of Allah's religion; consequently Musab Ibn Umr was sent to Yasrib with them.

In the beautiful city of Medina the air was free from those sordid influences which hovered over the Qureish at Mecca; the teaching was favourably received, people were more amiable to reason, and Islam began to thrive in its new environment with great rapidity; till there was hardly a single family in the town of Medina, where dwelt the two clans of Khazraj and Aus, in which some of the members did not adopt Islam, for now the number of the converts had reached to seventy-five.

In the full blaze of their zeal, the Moslems of Medina trekked to their usual meeting-place of Aqaba to meet the Prophet. They had not only heard of, but seen, the atrocities inflicted upon Muhammed's flock in Mecca. They had witnessed the gleam of truth in the mind of their religious teacher Musab, and Musab was but a particle of the Sun that Reflected the Master Mind. The life of that Fountain Head of Islam was in jeopardy, and it stirred up feelings of racial and religious pride which showed themselves in the desire to have the Prophet amongst them, where in Medina they could guard him, and what he stood for, with their very life-sap.

This request of having Muhammed in Medina was placed before the Prophet during the night preceding the second day of Tashriq. Bin Ibrahim repeats the narrative of one of the Moslem pilgrims.

> 'We made up our minds,' Kab Ibn Malik related, 'to keep our movements secret from our idolatrous fellow-citizens, amongst whom we slept till one-third of the night was

HIJRA, OR THE FLIGHT

passed. We then went out, one after another, stealthily, making our way slowly and silently towards a pass on the slopes of the Aqaba, where we all met together to await the Prophet. He soon arrived, accompanied by his uncle Abbas Ibn Abdul Muttalib.

He had not yet abjured the religion of his ancestors, but he had great affection for his nephew from whom he wished to ward off all misfortune, following the example of his brother Abu Talib. Having been informed of the plans of the people of Yasrib, Abbas wanted to see for himself what amount of confidence Muhammed could have in their proposals. Abbas was the first to address the meeting and spoke as follows:

'O, Assembly of the Khazraj and the Aus! my brother's son, as you know, holds high rank amongst us, and although we do not share his convictions, we have hitherto protected him against his fellow-citizens. In our 'qawm' he finds honour and safety. Nevertheless, at the present hour, he turns towards you, and desires to settle in your midst.

'Reflect! if ye decide to remain faithful to your promises and shield him from all dangers whatsoever, it will be well. But should ye fear to be forced one day to throw him over, and give him into the hands of his enemies, it would be better, now at once, to confess that your purpose is not steadfast by withdrawing your proposals and leaving him with his own party.'

"Without the slightest hesitation,' says Kab, 'we answered Abbas: "Thou hast heard what we proposed. Thou canst rely on us absolutely!" '

Then we turned to Muhammed: 'Speak, O Prophet! What dost thou want of us, for thy Lord and for thyself?'

MUHAMMED: THE PROPHET

After having recited a few passages from the Koran, and recapitulating the fundamental principles of Islam, the Prophet added: 'Swear that ye will fight to defend me and my disciples, as ye would fight to defend your wives and children.'

'We took the required oath with unanimous enthusiasm: By Allah! we are war children, and our fathers have taught us how to manufacture all weapons—"O! Prophet" broke in Abul Hasham, "there exists a compact between the Jews of Yasrib and us, which we shall have to break, perhaps, in order to uphold thy cause. What would be our position, in our land, if, after being victorious thanks to us, thou didst go back to thy 'qawm'?"

Let the observer pause and think here, whether in this private and secret parley, only material gain prompted these simple lovable children of Arabia to speak in the manner in which they were speaking. Was it bargaining? Were the people who were willing to shed their blood to protect the Prophet hungry for the spoils of war? Abul Hasham had made it abundantly clear. They would be slain before any harm could reach the Prophet, and as the reward for their services, all they wanted was to retain his presence amongst them; no more and no less. Can human affection attain nobler heights?

And let us note as to what the Prophet replies!

'The Prophet smiled,' writes Kab, 'and protested: "Rest easy on that score. Your blood hath become my blood, and your honour, my honour. He who wrongeth you, wrongeth me. I will fight the enemies you fight, and support whom ye support. Ye are mine and I am yours! Choose then twelve Najibs amongst you as leaders."

Nine Khazraj and three Aus having been selected; 'when we brought the twelve men to him, 'adds Kab, 'he said,

HIJRA, OR THE FLIGHT

"ye shall be my delegates in your Qawm, as were the apostles of Jesus, son of Mary, among their people."

'The Najibs pledged their words, but just as the solemn oath was about to be sworn, Bin Zarara rose and said, 'O, Assembly of the Khazraj and Aus! have ye reflected seriously about the consequences of the compact ye intend to make with this man? In his sake you swear to go on war with white, brown and black men. But if, in days to come, seeing your property pillaged and your nobles massacred, ye were to forsake him, shame would be brought upon you in this world and the next!'—'We are resigned in anticipation to the loss of our property, and to the death of our best men, if such a sacrifice is useful for the cause of Islam,' we replied unhesitatingly, 'but may we ask the Prophet what shall we receive in exchange?'

He replied: "Paradise!"

The oath of fidelity was then taken. First of all the leader of the Medinites, Abwal Hasheem, placing his hand in the Prophet's hands, swore allegiance. Then followed Al Bara and the others. They promised to protect the Prophet, undertook not to acknowledge any partnership in God's prerogatives, desist for ever from theft, adultery, killing of their children and speaking untruths: and henceforth were entitled 'Ansar', or 'the helpers'.

The whole pact was so well carried out that the pagan Arabs who travelled with the Moslems from Medina had no knowledge of it; so that when the Qureish complained about the secret negotiations, the non-Moslems refused to believe that such an understanding was sealed whilst they slept in that camp.

As to what potent instrument this negotiation at Aqaba was, the succeeding chapters of Islamic history will amply reveal.

MUHAMMED: THE PROPHET

The embracing of Islam, and the appointment of twelve nobles of Medina as the Prophet's delegates, created a situation wholly unthought of by the Qureish of Mecca. Clans after clans in Yasrib flocked to the preachers of Allah; the Ansar, or the converted Medinites, were working with passion, so that the Prophet may find it convenient to be with them and rid himself of the dangers which played on him at Mecca. The enemies of Muhammed were not unaware of the preparation which the people of Medina were making to receive their master; and when the reports of the rapid spread of Islam in Yasrib became frequent in Mecca, a large meeting of the pagans was called to discover ways and means to deal with the new menace which they now felt.

Elder after elder rose to speak in the infuriated gathering beside the yawning mouths of their stone gods in the temple of the Kaaba: each had a new and more gruesome device for destroying the creed of Muhammed. They suggested his being burnt alive, others thought of torture, for anger had seized them as a tempest seizes a slender tree; yet the meeting broke up, the only agreement arrived at being that the people of Medina are to be warned not to assist their arch-enemy and his faith.

The Ansar knew their mind and took no heed of what the Qureish demanded, and the Mecca threat dropped at their feet like a spent arrow.

From under the gathering of this storm at Mecca, the Prophet and his followers were watching the clearing sky at Medina. The day, however, came when it was evident upon the Leader of the Faithful to advise his disciples to leave Mecca for Medina: with care and deliberation a slow trek of the Moslems began from the land of the persecuting Qureish to the friendly town of the Ansar; till a very large number of the followers had left Mecca without exciting any undue suspicion of the Qureish. Amongst his immediate friends, however, only Abu Bakr and Ali remained.

HIJRA, OR THE FLIGHT

Repeatedly did his staunch supporter, Abu Bakr, request the Prophet to betake himself also to Medina, but Muhammed waited, waited for the Command. The time passed on, Abu Bakr would remind him how the Ansar awaited him, the Prophet would, however, sit in the temple like a graven figure, lost in silence and meditation, with his face in his hand, and waited and let the time roll on, for his Orders had not yet come: and he could only obey the God of Islam.

Then the Voice came, Abu Bakr was to accompany his master to Yasrib, and a joy like the morning sun entered his heart, for were they not going to a city where Islam's standard was fluttering, where the slim and tender creed of Allah was to find a root, from which would arise the tree of One Supreme Being, casting its shade upon the weary and sore-hearted, and from whence the light would dart out to the four corners of the world to let people sift right from wrong?

And Muhammed was happy too, for, in Medina, he would enthuse men and women with greater vigour, so that he could share the blessings of the *Koran* with all mankind, because, as the sun shines not only for a few trees and flowers but for the wide world's joy, so God sits effulgent in heaven, not for a favoured few, but for the universe of life: so action was forthwith taken, for the future of Islam was contained in that resolve during the thirteenth year of the Ministry of Muhammed.

Call it coincidence or what you will according to worldly imagining, but it just so happened that at the time when the Prophet was preparing to leave Mecca, the Qureish were engaged in a secret conclave to put a stop once and for all to the activities of Muhammed. Once again they were suggesting, and had ultimately agreed, to kill the father of the Islamic movement, so when someone pointed out the danger of starting a tribal war on account of the assassination of Muhammed, Abu Jahl jumped to his feet with a ready reply. He had been thinking over the matter for a long time, and had now hit upon

MUHAMMED: THE PROPHET

a plan whereby the dark deed could be done without implicating any one person. The scheme was that one man from each clan should be selected; and, composed of all the tribes, the assassins should waylay the Prophet, and let all their swords descend upon him at one and the same time. In this manner the blood of Muhammed could be shared, and no one man could be held responsible.

This decided, they hied forth to Muhammed's house. The night had now gathered and spread itself over the crags of Mecca, plunging the city in the gloom of darkness like a threatening shadow of a storm.

Just round the bend of the house of the Prophet the swordsmen waited, but passion burnt in the heart of one bolder than the rest upon seeing the doorway of the man they were seeking. His scimitar leaped out of the folds of his robe as he ran towards Muhammed's door. He would slay the man himself and alone: *"Tarry a moment, you fool!"* spoke Abu Jahl, clutching the man by the sleeves, *"tarry a while, he will come out, Muhammed, I aver, will not see the dawn of another day."* But other plans were made for Muhammed.

And whilst the Qureish waited and foamed like tethered cubs beside the house, Ali had occupied the Prophet's bed and Muhammed, together with his friend and compatriot Abu Bakr, was away out of the town. After winding up the Prophet's affairs, Ali was to come to Medina.

Beyond the hills of Mecca the two men of God wended their way through parched valleys of the desert: for their friends in the northern city of Medina were eagerly awaiting them.

In the stillness of the night these two gentle wayfarers trod the earth with lightsome heart, hearts full of hope and joy of what was before them—the growth of Islam—and then the moon rose, touching the distant rocky heads with pale cold silver, and the stars smiled with that languorous smile of

HIJRA, OR THE FLIGHT

aloofness which only the stars possess, and the coolness of the desert increased till it was chilly; and now the night air was distinctly cold as the sun-smitten particles of sand always lose their warmth at night: and the two lone Moslems were wrapped in the magnificence of thought born of solitude; for

> . . . *All form a scene*
> *Where musing solitude might love to lift*
> *Her soul above this sphere of earthliness;*
> *Where silence undisturbed might watch alone—*
> *So cold, so bright, so still.*

The two distinguished refugees hid themselves in a cave, about three miles right of Mecca, in the folds of Jabel Soor.

When the morning dawned, and the Qureish found Ali in place of Muhammed in bed there was general consternation.

> '*And what are you here for?*' *thundered the leader of the Qureish to Ali,* '*thy master has fled, and thou?*'

The youthful companion of the Prophet stated that he was there according to his instructions. They dragged Ali before the shrine of the idols.

> '*Slit his tongue,*' *shouted one, who bound Ali to a log, and, when the Elders had gathered, their wrath knew no bounds. The victim had slipped from their very hands:* '*and leaving a weakling like thee, he fled, Bah!*' *they jeered.*

It was then that Ali spoke. He reminded them that although their thirst for Muhammed's blood was insatiable, every man of Qureish considered the Prophet the most honest man in Mecca, or else why did they deposit every thing of value to them with Muhammed? Even at that hour, said Ali, there were such deposits of the Meccans in Muhammed's house; and it was to return those that Muhammed had instructed him to remain behind; for the Prophet was scrupulous to a fault regarding other's property.

With gnashing teeth in evidence, a man ripped his sword from his girdle: the noonday rays making its silver alive, he advanced to slay Ali. But they held him back, for Ali was to return their goods and, after all, Ali was not the man whom they sought to kill. At last he was freed.

Presently search parties were out in the ravines, over the sun-baked face of the desert looking for Muhammed. Camel riders dipped and rose amongst the sand dunes to discover the trail of those who had escaped. Savage-looking men of Qureish, maddened by the defeat, sang war songs as they rode up and down the hill where the Prophet hid. Then there was a patter of feet, a camel grunted, its rider was leading his party, in hot chase: the voices of men could be heard, their remarks very audible.

Just round the shoulder of the rock, *'Ahey,'* shouted a pagan soldier, *'I see some traces of feet,'* he thrust his face forward, two cruel eyes scanned the pathway, he was now within earshot of where the two sat in the cave.

A few yards ahead of him lay the cave, a cave where Abu Bakr felt a little anxious for the life of Muhammed: *'Allah is with us!'* whispered the Prophet to his companion: and there in a few moments a man with a bared sword in hand was drawing nearer and nearer to their hiding-place.

Had he got the scent? He was sure of it, they are here; but anon! he stopped, rubbed his eyes, was he seeing aright? The trace of human feet on rocks was a phenomenon which he had never seen; and suddenly that trace was gone: the man was frankly puzzled.

The ugly marks of his face burnt in the midday sun, in wonderment he looked around, he was following no trail, again it baffled him, his features stood out as if they had been chiselled

HIJRA, OR THE FLIGHT

with a very blunt instrument, and he retraced his steps: for God's ways are very mysterious.

How men passed to and fro, near and round about that cave, how one almost hit the trail, how an open and unprotected cave, with no trees, shrubs, or stones sheltering it, kept its secret hidden from the eyes of even such as had believed to have seen human footprints; all are matters over which no further emphasis is necessary.

Whose hand worked from behind the Veil, who threw a curtain before the eyes of the assassins are points which demand reflection, such occurrences are not normal: the meaning of all these manifestations can be comprehended by the mind's eye rather than described.

And so the futile search ended.

For four days did the Prophet and his companion remain in hiding. Every day the young son of Abu Bakr went to the city to find out as to what further plans were being made by the Qureish. According to Bokhari, the slave boy of Abu Bakr brought his herd to the cave to provide milk for the refugees, and the Prophet's sister-in-law sent food regularly to the cave.

On the fifth day the two started Medina-ward, knowing that sixteen marches lay between them and their friends, the Ansar. But the Qureish were not yet beaten. Every tribe in the neighbourhood was informed that whosoever could capture Muhammed alive or even bring him dead to Mecca, shall be given the reward of a hundred camels.

Distressed with thirst and munching dried bread and corn, the Prophet and his companion continued their journey. Their trust was in Allah, and indeed how different this journey as compared to his former leadership of the camel train bearing rich merchandise to the fertile regions of Syria!

But now both the value and purpose of Muhammed had

grown. During his youth he was only an agent, however respected as a mere man engaged in commerce, a man of little better significance than a merchant-prince; but now he held the standard of a movement destined to change the face of the world. His name was now in the mouths of men in the four corners of Arabia. When swaying in the saddle with the lumbering tread of his camel, Allah's name and prayers on his lips, the blaze of the desert sun was naught to him. On the way he would see signs and portends, his mind in communion with God eternal, hundreds of miles of sand stretched right and left of him, but the wilderness was peopled with that which his prophetic eyes could only discern:

> *'and thus our lives, exempt from public haunt,*
> *Find tongues in trees, books in the running brooks,*
> *Sermons in stones, and good in everything.'*

till all of a sudden a cloud of dust rose in the far horizon. It was rolling on towards Muhammed: it became enlarged by the fact that, now towards the evening, a slight haze arose from the surrounding hills; and when, within the distance of two or three arrow-shots, the dust was seen to envelop a horse rider, gauntly did he sit in his saddle urging his mount forward.

He had no doubt that the men who journeyed towards Medina were none other than the Prophet, his companion and Abdullah the guide; and Siraqa, as was the name of this wild warrior, was bent on possessing the price of a hundred camels by slaying Muhammed, but just at that instant his horse stumbled and fell. It was a bad omen for the price-seeker, and he drew his arrows to divine whether he was to attack the defenceless refugees. The oracle spoke in the negative. But the allurement of a hundred camels was great: leaping into the saddle, he spurred his mount towards the Prophet, this time the horse's legs sunk into the soft sand. Siraqa alighted to divine anew, and again the reply was against attacking the wayfarers.

HIJRA, OR THE FLIGHT

It had a marvellous effect on the man, for humbly he approached Muhammed and begged forgiveness, which was ungrudgingly given.

The people of Medina had already been informed of the coming of the Prophet. Both the Ansar and those Moslems who had arrived from Mecca were anxiously awaiting the arrival. From early dawn till late at night people sat on the parapets of the city walls, staring into the vastness of the desert, their eyes straining to behold the one whom they loved.

Day passed day in this anxious uncertainty. Some went further to the plains of Hira on the south-west of Medina, shading their eyes from the glaring sun, hoping to catch a glimpse of the Apostle of Allah, but only the blackish grey boulders deflected the rays and the bouncing waves of heat rising from them, melting into the shimmering sands beyond with no sign of the approaching Man of Allah. On the other side of the town they now cast their glances, but here also, nothing but vacant and glimmering sand and shale glowed in the distance, without a trace of the noble caravan from Mecca.

And thus did men come and wait and go back home without having welcomed the man of their longing.

It was thuswise, when the Moslems had waited one day the whole morning and at last returned to their homes; that a Jewish scholar looked out of his window into the desert. Two men, clad in white flowing garb, were but a speck in the far distance, their progress was slow, and the Jew watched them awhile: then he cried,

> 'O ye the Men of Islam,' he ran through the town, 'the one that you seek is coming, in yonder direction he and his companion are now approaching the city.'

There was a joyous roar of compliments throughout Medina, men buckled up their armour, and, putting on their best clothes, were now running in the direction from which Muhammed was approaching. A more sincere welcome is hard to conceive.

About three miles from Medina, that part of the town which lies on a higher plain, is Quba, where many Ansar had their houses. In that quarter of the city the Prophet, according to Bokhari, stayed in the house of Amru Bin Uof. Many other important Moslems, who had arrived in Medina from Mecca, were also staying in the same house. In all for fourteen days Muhammed is reported to have resided there.

The very first thing which engaged the Prophet's attention was the erection of a place of worship. In an adjoining plot where dates were dried, Muhammed laid the foundation of a mosque with his own hands. Like the ordinary labourer he worked to have the building erected, he carried stones, mixed the mortar, dug and levelled as one of his flock. This day of the Prophet's entry into the suburbs of Quba is authoritatively indicated to be on the eight of Rabial Awal in the 13th year of his mission, and as the fact of Emigration definitely turned a new leaf in Islamic history, the Moslem Calendar is counted from that date of Hijra, which according to the European method of calculation corresponds to A.D. 622.

Lest the significance of the romance of this first mosque at Quba be lost in the study of that plethora of events which now followed; it should be emphasised that the Leader of the Faithful was not above rolling up his sleeves to work in the building of the first real Temple to Allah's Truth, and in striking at the very root of social or official superiority in the discharge of a common duty.

In the eyes of Allah all Moslems are brothers, the master and the servant, with no distinction of colour or nationality, all standing on one plane, before one Supreme God, and dwarfed by no material status of social rank: for as labourers go, it would have been quite possible to engage local labour if not for all the

HIJRA, OR THE FLIGHT

Moslems, certainly to substitute the Master Teacher of Islam; but it was not resorted to, the Prophet desired to have it deeply stamped in the minds of his followers that Islam has no distinction of that kind.

The merit, too, of the prayer and building of this mosque was particularly great, for regarding this *'Mosque of Fear'*—*Taqwa*—as it is called, the *Koran* says:

> '. . . *certainly a mosque founded on piety from the very first day is more deserving that you should stand in it; in it are men who love that they should be purified, and Allah loves those who purify themselves.*'

Chapter 12

ENTRY INTO MEDINA

After two weeks' stay at the house of Banu Amru, the Prophet was now ready to make his formal entry into the city of his refuge. The streets were lined by men before Muhammed mounted his camel. The youth of the town, holding banners and slashing the empty air with their glistening blades, pranced about leading the procession, warriors resplendent in their shining armour strode proudly forward, but when the populace saw the Prophet's camel, a roar of *'Allahu-Akbar'* (*'God is great'*) rose from the throats of hundreds of men and women.

They were holding on to the gear of the camel as a mark of honour to themselves, and women shouted greetings from the tops of the houses; young girls were chanting the praises of the Man of Allah: the Ansar, sometimes together, sometimes singly, welcomed the Prophet. Again and again the shouts of *'Allahu-Akbar'* rose and fell like notes loosened by the different stops of a giant organ, as Muhammed, sitting meekly on his camel, responded to their felicitations as he passed from street to street—but where was he going?

There was not a single man amongst the Ansar who did not wish to have the honour of being a host of the Prophet. To every man who begged to lodge him he replied:

'Let my camel go where he wishes. I shall stay where the camel may sit.'

And the camel, his reins loosened, wended his way through

many street twists and turnings before stopping in an open space. There he knelt down, but as the Prophet did not alight he grunted and rose; but again sat down, where Muhammed decided to stay. It was a barn of one Abu Ayub Ansari: and henceforth he was the proud host of the Prophet.

Abu Ayub's double-storied house was then the residence of the Leader of the Faithful for seven months; and shortly after that period when the Mosque of Nabi was erected, living accommodation was built near it, and the Prophet moved to those quarters.

During that period too, Zaid was sent to Mecca to bring back with him various female members of the family to Medina. But the very first item which engaged the attention of the Prophet, now as he was in Medina proper, was the building of a mosque. The space in which it was to be built belonged to two orphans, who wished to offer the piece of ground free of charge, but Muhammed had more than ordinary regard for the property of orphans, so the ground was bought from them, even though it was to be used to erect a house of worship.

The building itself was unpretentious enough. Its walls were of mud, the pillars of ordinary date palm tree trunks, and for the roof nothing better than mere thatch, and it faced towards Jerusalem. On one side of the quadrangle of the mosque, a room was provided for such Moslems as had no home, and around the mosque existed the living quarters of the Prophet's family.

This is really the birthplace of early Islam.

Scornful of worldly trappings, an utter disregard, even an abhorrence of the things of luxury, in which the simple and direct mind of Muhammed felt that true and pure living can only be maintained by doing without the tarnished dross of the earth, which wealth has ever proved itself to be since the beginning of time.

SETTLING DOWN IN MEDINA

When a state of tranquillity was thus secured in Medina, the organised form of worship was ordered. Various devices of sounding the horn or ringing of bells in order to summon the faithful to prayer, which were suggested, did not appeal to the Prophet. The calling of the worshippers to prayers five times a day in a loud voice was the form fixed, as well as the form of prayer when standing in a row behind a leader, as adhered to up to this day, were then prescribed.

The question of worship having thus been commanded, the Prophet next turned his attention towards the organisation of the Society of the Moslems; that is, the relations that were to exist between the Moslems of Medina and those who, having left their all at Mecca, had left their native town with, after or before, Muhammed.

As the financial capacity of the Meccan Moslems was practically nil, the Prophet gathered together all of them, and asked the Ansar as to what they proposed doing. The people of Medina were willing to give the half share in all their property, land or business to the immigrants from Mecca. Every one of the forty-five immigrants was *'connected into a brotherly accord'* with forty-five men of Medina: if an Ansari was a businessman, he took an immigrant as equal partner in his trade, in case of his being a farmer, half of the lands he gave to his co-religionist from Mecca: till the system grew so common that when a man from Medina died, his whole property fell in

MUHAMMED: THE PROPHET

the share of the Meccan immigrant, for the verse in the *Koran* commanded:

> 'Surely those who believed and fled (their homes) and struggled hard in Allah's way with their property and soul, and those who gave shelter and helped— these are guardians (brothers) of each other ...'

And thus the relationship was determined between the men of Medina and those of Mecca. The world's record shows no parallel to this.

But noble-minded as the support of the Ansar was, the Meccans were loath to take undue advantage of their hosts, the example of one Abdur Rahman Bin Auf is a case in point, when offered half of the property of his Brother Ansari or Helper, he declined the offer with thanks, and only asked the way to the market-place, where he soon opened a small shop, and before his career was over, the Refugee had a flourishing business.

No one, of course, wished to burden himself upon the Moslem friends in Medina if he could rationally help it, not even excepting the Prophet, for one day when Muhammed could not find it within his means to entertain a guest he reluctantly asked Abu Talha to see whether he could do anything. It so happened that Abu Talha had not a greater store of food; so he put out the light in the house and placed his own and his wife's food before the guest, and, sitting away in the dark alley, made gestures such as in eating so that the guest should consider that they were also partaking of the food.

This welding of Islamic federation naturally produced significant influence in the civic activities of the people of Medina: so it was thought important to establish a more thorough working arrangement between the Moslems and the non-Moslems. To this task the Prophet addressed himself next:

SETTLING DOWN IN MEDINA

for what a few months ago was only a scattered and loose batch of poor and helpless refugees had taken a shape of a well-disciplined civic unit of Moslems, showing every sign, both on account of its growing numbers and its efforts in trade and husbandry, of wielding a mighty power.

It behoved the leader of this organisation, living and spreading as it now was, to proceed in the direction of forming an alliance with its neighbours. The Jews of Medina had a decided voice in many matters. They used to enter into alliance with the tribes of Aus and Khazraj, says Mohammed Ali, and to take part in their internecine wars. Though Arab by descent, they formed a distinct unit by reason of their adoption of Judaism, and were therefore divided into three clans of Banu Qainuqa, Banu Nazir, and Banu Quraiza. Unfortunately, the two Arab clans of Aus and Khazraj —those who were not Moslems—were always at war with each other: and two tribes of the Jews, namely Banu Quraiza and Banu Nazir, sided with the Arab clans of Aus and Khazraj respectively.

A very large number of the above-mentioned Arab clans had now embraced Islam, so that the voice of the Aus and Khazraj became the voice of the Prophet. In the light of new events, since the arrival of Muhammed in Medina, it was necessary to have a treaty with the two Jewish clans: therefore the Prophet contracted a pact with the men of Banu Nazir and Banu Quraiza. As this was the first political understanding between the Moslems and the non-Moslems the mention of its terms here is not without interest.

The first clause of the Instrument provided that:

the Moslems and the Jews are to live in peace henceforth.

Secondly,

the contracting parties may keep to their own faiths and be unmolested in consequence.

MUHAMMED: THE PROPHET

The third laid down that:

in the event of war with a third party, each was to come to the help of the other, provided always that the latter were the aggrieved and not the aggressor.

The forth clause had it that,

in the event of an attack on Medina, the city was to be defended by both parties.

Fifthly:

that in giving the peace terms to the enemy the other party shall be consulted.

Sixthly,

that Medina was to be considered holy and sacred by both, and all bloodshed within its bounds was strictly prohibited;

and finally, that:

the Prophet was the final court of appeal and arbitrator in all matters in case of a dispute.

The Jews set their seals gladly to the document: and the foundation stone of an Islamic State was thus formally laid.

INTERNAL TROUBLE IN MEDINA

Soon after taking up residence in his new environment, it was now beginning to be borne upon the Prophet that although the Moslem position had apparently assumed a more peaceful and organised form, yet deep currents of intrigue, distrust and possible menace for his followers were to be discerned by the seeing eye: indeed, the situation, if anything was even worse than at Mecca.

In the city of his birth a unified system of laws existed amongst the people that lived in and around Mecca. Their traditions were the same, the evolution of their history had marched on parallel lines, in national outlook and aspirations they were not different, in short, a unity of purpose and mind existed amongst the people of Mecca.

That that unity was used against the Prophet is beside the point, what is important to note is that Muhammed knew his people well; and, therefore, he could in a measure safeguard their interests by employing means, which he, in virtue of his familiar knowledge of his own folk, could devise the more effectively. But here in Medina, the most generous hospitality of the newly-converted Moslems notwithstanding, he and his flock of seventy-five Meccan Moslems were strangers, and may perhaps be sympathetically regarded if they did not find things in Medina exactly in the shape and form to which they were used in their own town. I do not refer to the method of ordinary living, or avocations of life, food or clothing or the like; but to

MUHAMMED: THE PROPHET

matters of a more profound nature with which the new Moslem community had to reconcile itself at Medina.

Amongst others, we must first of all note that in Medina there were several peoples who had a say in the affairs of men's lives. There were three different clans of the Jews; two Arab tribes: the body of the citizens was therefore now composed of six elements, namely, the Jews, the non-Moslem Arabs and the Moslems both of Mecca and Medina. In such a mixed society, presided over though it was by Muhammed, as the Leader of the largest party, working at cross purposes could not be wondered at.

But it was more: some men of Medina, mostly Jews, had embraced Islam not for the sake of the religion, but to act in their own interests, to get whatever they could secure out of it, and perchance to help the enemies of Islam if it suited their purpose. This element within the gates of Medina was a greater danger to the people of the town than an attacking army of the Qureish of Mecca. The Monafiqeen, as these subreptive sections of Medina population were called, were helped in their duplicity by the fact that the Moslems, like them, turned their faces towards Jerusalem, hence by dissembling thuswise they stood to lose nothing towards their real faith. A rival Arab chief like Abdullah, feeling that his importance in the town was dwarfed by the advent of Islam in Medina, was not slow to grasp the opportunity of inciting his kinsmen, the Jews, and others, against the Prophet.

In the meantime, of course, a tremendous change occurred when a verse of the *Koran* was revealed, in which the faithful were commanded to turn their faces towards Mecca—the Qibla—instead of towards Jerusalem. This, being a Test Case, showed the hypocrites in their true colours, and the Jews and others were now frankly inimical towards the Moslems.

A point of considerable importance springs up in the minds

INTERNAL TROUBLE IN MEDINA

of serious students, regarding the appointment of Mecca, towards which the Moslems were to pray. Mecca at the time was pagan, its shrine was idol infested; and Muhammed, who proclaimed the Unity of God, preached the abhorrence of all idols, and sought to dismantle the cult of heathenism, was now not only commanded to have his flock pray towards Mecca, but had himself prayed in the quadrangle of the shrine there, even before the above-mentioned verse of the *Koran*.

Moreover, many of his followers used to go to perform pilgrimages at Mecca, such as Saad Bin Maaz. How can it be consistent with the preaching and tenets of Islam?

Here we must examine what exactly is the object which the Moslems were to worship in Mecca. Was it the courtyard of the Great Temple, its bricks, stones or mortar, the structure called the Kaaba, its idols or walls, or the Black Stone, which is built in the wall of the shrine?

From all available authority of Moslem writers it can be deduced that the Moslems prayed to none of the abovementioned structures of earth, stone and mortar, and least of all to the idols. The only thing of importance was that House of God which Abraham and Ishmael had built, as a memory of what sacrifice man is capable of making, that is, the highest sacrifice, the blood of his own son—and rendered the occasion and the House holy by that Association.

It is now, as it was then, the sacredness of that offering which invests Mecca's shrine, with the holiness to which the descendants of Abraham (Ibrahim in Arabic)—the Moslems—bow their heads.

The fact of all the faithful turning their faces towards that Emblem emphasises the idea of Unity of God and His Purpose. Hence it was so that Muhammed prayed in the courtyard of that shrine.

MUHAMMED: THE PROPHET

It was, too, on this account that his followers went on a pilgrimage to Mecca; and precisely for that reason the Qibla, or the temple where a Memory Lingered, was made the place to which all Moslems must turn when in worship.

In addition to the fact that Allah intended to make all Moslems as one people by having them turn their faces to one direction, so as to set one goal before them, and establish a unity of purpose with Mecca as the centre, it is justifiable to deduce other reasons for the Command:

> '... then turn your face towards the sacred mosque (Qibla at Mecca).'

The reason is that God wanted to fulfil His promise of accepting the prayers of Ibrahim when the Father of the Faithful prayed:

> 'Our Lord! make us both submissive to Thee, and raise from our offspring a nation submitting to Thee ... And raise up in them an Apostle from among them who shall recite to them Thy Communications ....'

This prayer was accepted, according to the Moslem belief, an Apostle was sent, he was Muhammed (as argued elsewhere in this book), the Book which he brought was the *Koran*; and the place which Abraham or Ibrahim built as preferred was therefore justly accepted as worthy of reposing a memory of the Sacrifice and the acceptance of Abraham's supplications. The House was then the Qibla on that score.

If, during the progress of time, that very same association was darkened by the heathenish ways of the myriads of pre-Islamic generations, it should not necessarily disturb the continuity of the Purpose, especially when regarding the advent of the Prophet, it was clearly pointed out that he was to purge the House of God of its loathsome idols and bring the people back to the original Call of Abraham.

INTERNAL TROUBLE IN MEDINA

Secondly, as pointed out above, this re-establishment of the Qibla distinguished the real Moslems from the Pretenders; who stood out clear before the faithful as people not to be trusted, as so remarkably told in the *Koran*:

'And even if you bring to those who have been given the Book every sign

(both the Christians and the Jews are called the People of the Book by the Moslems because the original Bible and the Torah are considered as the Holy Work of Allah)

they would not follow your Qibla, nor can you be the followers of their Qibla . .'

(their Qibla obviously was Jerusalem):

so that after sixteen months of constant facing towards Jerusalem in prayer, the Moslems turned their worship Meccaward.

The above discussion was necessary to explode the fanatical theory that the Moslem adoration of Mecca was a remnant of pre-Islamic polytheism, because the idea of Moslem worship avowedly begins from the time of Abraham/Ibrahim: and the Father of the Faithful was anything but idolatrous.

Chapter 13

ESTABLISHMENT OF OTHER ISLAMIC INJUNCTIONS

The turning of one's face towards Mecca when in prayer having thus been settled, instructions were given as to the actual method of the prayer.

The faithful shall first wash themselves, then will attend the mosque where the Muezzin or the Caller of the Prayer Call shall be chanting in a loud voice certain formulae. The faithful shall thus range themselves in a row behind an Imam, or the leader of prayer, folding their arms over their abdomens they shall stand, then bend, and finally touch the ground in front of them in unison following their Imam, and then sit, folding their legs under them, to the end of the prayer. The various movements in the prayer, together with what is recited at each move, and their philosophy and meaning, will be described in a later section of this book.

The next Command was the observing of fast during the month of Ramadan. Prior to this period, says Bin Ibrahim, for three days did the Prophet fast every month: till the verse was revealed:

> '*As to the month of Ramadan, in which the Koran was sent for men's guidance . . . as soon as any one observeth the moon, let him set about to fast . . .*'

Total abstinence from food, drink, smoking, or using anything '*to feed the body*' was enjoined upon between sunrise and sunset during the entire month of Ramadan, or the Month

MUHAMMED: THE PROPHET

of Fasting. As to its reasons and usefulness I shall speak later. Wine was also prohibited in all shapes and form: the Revelation Commanded:

> 'They will ask thee concerning liquors . . . say: In them is great sin. . . .'

The third Commandment lays down the rule of Charity: or Zakat; which was to be given on the assessment of a man's property and earning; it was intended only for the poor.

Gambling too was banned:

> 'O, Believers!' says the Koran, "wine and game of chance, and statues and divining arrows, are only an abomination of Satan's work! Avoid them, that ye may prosper.'

But whilst these orders were being enforced, and men's morals were being brought in line with the way of Islam, storm clouds were gathering fast and furiously in and around Medina against the Prophet and his followers.

The local dignitaries, led by Abdullah Bin Ubay and helped by the Jews, were intriguing with the Qureish of Mecca, and the Bedouins of the desert who lived on the Mecca-Medina route. They were being made to instigate trouble in order to nip in the bud a movement that threatened to dismantle the power of the idol-worshippers of the Kaaba, and which was incidentally a thorn in the side of those non-Moslem Medinites who had suffered in their overlordship since the Prophet and his men had come to Medina.

The trade was passing from the hands of Abdullah, the Arab chief of Medina: the Jews found that they could lend money only on justifiable interest, the magisterial power of the non-Moslem Arabs was not permitted to deal out justice in its own way; and in the midst of it all lived Muhammed, trusting, hoping, and confident in his prayer for the cause he had at heart and the men who clung to him.

ESTABLISHMENT OF OTHER ISLAMIC INJUNCTIONS

His prayer had a force and life and wisdom: for,

> *'More things are wrought by prayer*
> *Than this world dreams of. Wherefore let thy voice*
> *Rise like a fountain for Me night and day.*
> *For what are men better than sheep or goats*
> *That nourish a blind life within the brain,*
> *If, knowing God, they lift no hands of prayer*
> *Both for themselves and those who call them friends?'*

Presently matters progressed much beyond the limits of endurance, the security of the Moslems was now definitely threatened, wild sons of the desert had already been seen brandishing their swords near the walls of Medina;— that they were in league with the non-Moslems in the town was also patent.

The Qureish had invited the Bedouins to attack Medina first. On the wake of those marauding parties, the Meccans planned their own organised attack; and, of course, concurrently, the anti-Moslem population of Medina would fall upon its Moslem townsmen. With utmost secrecy and deliberation the whole scheme was thought out. Advance parties of the enemy were already sighted in the neighbourhood.

The anxiety of the Prophet could be imagined. With such a small and unequipped following, a handful of refugees to battle against the mighty forces of the Qureish with men and resources ten times as much as those of the Moslems was at first nothing but courting disaster: and then the thought of bringing their peaceloving hosts into a fight—a fight which could not be called, racially or nationally, that of the people of Medina— appeared to Muhammed an unnecessary burden to impose upon the Ansar.

Finally, what can be said about the Jewish population, who were ready to fall upon the men of Islam as soon as the enemy thundered at the gates of Medina?

MUHAMMED: THE PROPHET

Moreover the very name by which the faith of Allah is known, being Islam, meaning Peace and Resignation, connotes humbleness, and not the ferocity of war or the clashing of sabres in the heat of battle. Muhammed was clearly puzzled, but not for long, as the Revelation came to him:

> *'. . . And fight in the cause of Allah against those who fought against you: but commit not the injustice of attacking them first....'*

The Command was clear, and war preparations were begun to defend Medina, yes, the Defence of Medina was the point of view, but let it be well remembered, so far as the Moslems were concerned: they did not invite battle first.

Chapter 14

THE BATTLE OF BADR

Relations between the Moslems and the Qureish were already strained, and now actual skirmishes began to take place between the reconnoitring parties of the Medinites and the enemies of Islam. The Meccans were exerting strong pressure upon the headman of the non-Moslem Arabs of Medina, vowing that unless Muhammed was expelled from the town, the Qureish would attack the city. The most notorious warlord of the Qureish had actually threatened a Moslem pilgrim with death at Mecca if his people did not get rid of the Prophet, and as clear evidence of the state of war, which the non-Moslems precipitated, was the action of one Kurzur Bin Jabar, who had raided the Medina grazing grounds and had decamped with the Prophet's camels.

The Moslems, however, still hoped that if the Mecca caravans could be harassed as they passed in the vicinity of their town, the pressure thus exerted might bring the Meccans about to a more amicable frame of mind, and that they might make peace with the Moslems; for the Prophet above all wanted to avert war; but as these excesses had already taken place, his followers were taking all precautions.

When such tension prevailed, rumours of an oncoming war were in the air: all sorts of reports added to the nervousness of the opposing parties: news, however, reached Mecca that the merchant prince Abu Sufyan, who was bringing his merchandise from Syria, was maltreated near Medina and his caravan looted. The report of course was not true: but before it could be counteracted, mischief had been done and it incited the Qureish to speed up their war preparations.

In the meantime, about the end of the month of Jamadul Tani in the second year of Hijra, the Prophet ordered a party to go into the desert, look round, and report the results of their reconnaissance. Sealed orders of this mission were given to the leader, one Abdullah Bin Jahsh.

When the Moslem party reached Nakhla, and the instructions were read—instruction for only reconnaissance—these were unfortunately not fully acted upon, for the blood of the leader of the Medina troopers boiled to see three Mecca merchants on their way back to the city of the idol-worshippers. Hot words were exchanged, then swords leaping into their hands worked their way into the body of one of the Meccans, he was slain, and his two companions brought in chains before the Prophet. And then did the Prophet get wroth, for the over-zealous officer had exceeded his orders.

This incident was very gravely looked upon by the Qureish. In the ordinary way, the matter could have been settled quite easily by paying blood-money, but the Qureish were in no mood to make peace. War was declared on Muhammed and his followers, and the Qureish vowed that Medina would be razed to the ground and its people butchered in cold blood before their swords seek their scabbards: a pretext for revenge had been found and it should be war to the finish, thus resolved the warlord of the Qureish.

This is the story of Badr.

A thousand warriors gathered in the shrine of the idols, and a hundred horsemen lined outside, when they placed their arms near the foot of the temple. Lifting their arms in supplication, the Qureish looked at their god of War which resided in the idol of Hobal. To him they sang hymns, and sought a sign for

THE BATTLE OF BADR

victory against the Prophet of Allah: but no sign came.

That the idol did not lift an arm to bless them is readily comprehended; but could that discourage the men of Mecca, and they eleven hundred strong? Holding their spears and swords aloft, they burst into one mighty song of war as the foot-soldiers marched out of the town behind the cavalcade of their cavalry.

Their shining armours, set and determined faces, and gleaming swords were a pageant of colour, for now the groups of dancing girls with sparkling eyes, radiant faces, and bedecked in their gala dress, thumping on their tambours, came dancing along the line of the soldiers.

The poets recited heroic poems of old, the bards were there too, to sing the war tales of long ago, and so the army of Qureish marched on to meet the foe; a foe small in number, weak in defence, ill-fed and ill-equipped and loving no idols. Thus, day by day, they marched in proud array to win victory.

Here in Medina the Prophet was not unmindful of what was in the air. As a leader of men in peace, so a leader in battle, Muhammed had now the situation well in hand.

On the twelfth day of the month of Fasting, with his three hundred and thirteen followers he emerged from Medina. They were journeying towards the village of Badr, some eighty miles from Medina, where the Syrian caravan route is sandwiched by high and rocky mountains.

On the way the Prophet held a war council to make sure whether the men of Medina were prepared to fight. Need he have asked them? The Ansar were prepared to shed the last drop of their blood in the cause of Muhammed. By five easy stages the Moslems were in the neighbourhood of Badr, and the Leader of the Faithful was informed that the Qureish had already taken their position on the other side of the ravine; so

MUHAMMED: THE PROPHET

the Moslem warriors encamped on the near side of it.

With the dawn, the opposing armies faced each other: the Qureish resplendent in their shining armour, with sparkling battle-axes, sabres and scimitars ablaze with the rays of the sun. Pinions flirted from the tall lances of the horsemen, their leader rode in between the lines a hundred strong.

On the other side only three hundred and thirteen men of Islam stood erect, gaunt, their hearts aglow with the warmth of the faith.

Muhammed, their general, arranged them in rows. There was to be no war cry raised by the Moslems, no savage yells of pre-Islamic time were to be employed. War was a serious matter, a life and death struggle at any time, between any two rivals; but this was no ordinary battle; here the question of a mighty faith was involved, glory in being victorious at Badr meant the dispelling of gloom.

Death meant dying in the cause of Islam, a worthy reminder of the sacrifice which Abraham/Ibrahim made at Mecca, and which gave Islam its name.

That tradition, the Prophet was called upon to uphold. A feeling had pervaded the soul of Muhammed on that fateful day, he was praying, earnestly beseeching for the termination of strife, so that as few lives as possible should be destroyed; for bloodshed was the one thing the Prophet abhorred.

Presently the Qureish were within striking distance, phalanx after phalanx of their men strode forward, confident of victory. The swordsman Utba, the renowned soldier of Mecca, stepped forward into the arena with his son and brother. Three Moslems went to meet them. The proud Qureish inquired the names of his adversaries.

> 'Oh! Muhammed,' he shouted to the Prophet, 'what three men to battle with us, three soft men of Medina.

THE BATTLE OF BADR

Nay, send those amongst thy ranks that belong to the warrior blood of Mecca, and be worthy adversaries of mine blade!'

The three best fighters, namely Hamza, Ali and Obayda, were now facing the pagan Arabs. They whirled round, they jumped about, avoiding each other, blade beat against blade, the women of the Qureish yelled, shouted, singing war songs, urged their warriors till the sword of Hamza made a clean slit in the side of the leader of the Meccans. Ali despatched the other, but the third Moslem was wounded, till Ali, turning round, was able to slay the remaining swordsman, and bore his wounded compatriot back to the rank of the Moslems: and the two opposing armies watched the duel, with yells on one side and prayers on the other.

Another round was now fought, in which the victory of the Moslems was repeated. Then the attack became general. Maddened with the adverse results of combat, the Qureish fell pell-mell upon the Moslems, a force of eleven hundred rushed towards a mere handful numbering three hundred and thirteen men, a proportion of less than three to one.

Sabres and scimitars rose and fell; lances and spears and arrows were doing their evil work, the shouting and yelling of warriors blending with the thud-thudding of women's drums, their cymbals crashed, war chants rent the air, moans and battle cries mingled, again and again the Qureish charged to dislodge the Moslems, each time they were repulsed, then the din of battle began to grow less, it lessened further for the mighty legions of Qureish were now retreating, fleeing as quickly as their legs could carry them.

The enemy were routed. Leaving their dead on the field, they fled.

The victory was won against eleven hundred men by three hundred and thirteen men. Call it a miracle, or chance, or fortune of war, the fact is clear that the victory was with those who feared Allah, and who fought to defend themselves and were not the aggressors, who had acted upon what the *Koran* had commanded:

> *'and fight in the cause of Allah against those who fought against you: but commit not the injustice of attacking them first....'*

There were fourteen casualties amongst the Moslems. Seventy of the enemy were slain, and as many taken prisoner. The Prophet had even the non-Moslems buried.

After the battle, express orders were given by the Prophet regarding the treatment to be meted out to prisoners. They were provided with new clothes, the people of Medina were to give them the best available food, not even the advice of such an important personage of Islam as Omar would the Prophet take, when it was suggested that two of the teeth of a war prisoner were to be extracted so that he should not harangue the people so successfully against Islam in future.

These men, in the eyes of the Leader of the Faithful, were the guests—uninvited withal, but guests all the same—and where ransom could not be provided for some of them, such men were required to act as teachers for a time 'to pay for their release' so to speak.

Many of those nobles of the Qureish who had offered a sturdy opposition to Muhammed were slain in the battle of Badr; Abu Jahl was one of them.

Chapter 15

THE BATTLE OF OHUD

The complete victory of the Moslems at Badr had now consolidated the position of the Messenger of Islam; but the people of Mecca could not afford to let the news of their defeat percolate into the far corners of the desert: otherwise their prestige as the keepers of the Shrine, and above all, their leadership in trade, would be irrevocably lost.

Also, the idea of revenge in the hearts of the Arabs is keen to a degree; therefore arrangements for another attack on Medina were immediately started.

It was the year 625 of the Christian Era, and only three years after the date when the Prophet had left his native city to work his way for Islam amongst his friends in Medina.

Benefiting from the experience of the battle of Badr, the Qureish at Mecca wished to take no chances but those needed to ensure victory, and so in addition to their own resources they considered it advisable to contract an alliance with the tribes of Tihama and Kinena.

The veteran soldier-merchant, Abu Sufyan, was now placed at the command of the combined forces of the Qureish and the desert folk.

At Ohud, where walls of hills interspersed with red sandstone and granite, roll into deep valleys, about three miles from Medina, the two armies met.

Like the battle of Badr, a small body of Moslems, only seven

MUHAMMED: THE PROPHET

hundred, faced three thousand of their enemy hosts.

One of the interesting features of this battle being that women took an active part on both sides.

With his usual care, the Prophet had planned the position of his men so as to leave no point of vantage through which the enemy could launch a surprise attack. At a cleft in the hills, he specially posted a strong body of archers to guard the opening and remain at their places, even when the battle was finished.

The battle raged furiously, the clashing of arms was deafening, women were urging their Qureish warriors.

> 'Courage! Ye sons of Abu Dar; courage' they shouted, 'Courage! Ye defenders of women! strike home with the edges of your swords!'

The Qureish rushed at the Moslems with flashing swords, the Moslems, defending, hacked their way into the thick of the battle. They slaved, they cursed, they yelled, Hades itself was let loose upon the Moslems. Hamza, the renowned warrior of Islam, cut his way to the heart of the Qureish legions, men fell before Ali like chaff, Omar's sword was showing no mercy.

Again and again the Qureish attacked and were repulsed.

Then Talha, the pagan standard bearer, stepped before Ali, and brandishing his sword defied him crying:

> 'You Moslems say that our dead will go to hell, and yours to heaven; let me send you to Paradise.'

The young warrior of Islam accepting the challenge replied: 'Be it so!' and as they fought, Talha was struck down.

> 'Mercy, O Son of my uncle,' cried the standard-bearer.

> 'Mercy be it,' replied Ali, 'for thou dost not deserve the fire.'

The battle had already showed gain to the Moslems; step by

THE BATTLE OF OHUD

step the enemy were retreating. *'Glory be to Hobal!'* shouted Abu Sufyan, *'Glory be to God!'* shouted back Omar by his stand.

The Qureish were now definitely weakening, and the Moslems made one great dash to dislodge them.

The main body of the troopers were now seen to be in a demoralised condition, and a roar of victory rose from the throats of the Moslems. But it rose too soon. The archers who were commanded by the Prophet to guard the opening of the key position, deserting their posts joined the main body of their compatriots. The cleft was left undefended. And Khalid Ibn Walid, the cavalry commander of the Qureish, seeing the opportunity, rushed into the opening and attacked the Moslems from the rear: and then a battle royal raged.

Men were falling right and left, clouds of arrows swam into the midst of mingled fighters; everybody was so jammed that often the Moslems fought against Moslems; the Prophet was attacked, the weapon of his enemy fell on the head-piece of his armour, making it cut his face, arrows rained on all from all sides.

Moslem women were attending to the wounded, the women of Mecca were fighting like their warriors. Hamza fell, then others, there was confusion amongst the Moslems; more confusion occurred because someone shouted that *even the Prophet is slain.*

But before the vicious report was corrected, the Moslems, losing hearts, threw themselves upon the enemy with such recklessness that many were slain: the carnage was appalling.

A grey pall began to float over the battle-field, both parties were exhausted, the Moslems still held the heights of Ohud, and the Qureish could not even then force the issue and take advantage of their superior position.

MUHAMMED: THE PROPHET

After mutilating the slain enemies, the Qureish retreated.

'On returning to Medina' says Amir Ali, *'the Prophet directed a small body of the disciples to pursue the retreating enemy, and to impress on them that though worsted in battle, they were yet unbroken in spirit, and too strong to be attacked again with impunity.*

Abu Sufyan, hearing of the pursuit, hastened back to Mecca with his tattered army, having first murdered two Medinites whom he met on the way. He, however, sent a message to the Prophet, saying that he would soon return to exterminate him and his people. The reply, as before, was full of trust and faith:

"God is enough for us, a good guardian is He."

Although the battle of Ohud did not decide any issue for the contending parties—as battles go—yet it was certain that the serious loss of life which had been sustained by the Moslems had not added to their prestige in the eyes of the wild Bedouins, who were anxiously watching the trend of events.

The men of Qureish, moreover, hastened to announce that the power of the Moslems was no match to their warlike clans, which incited the sons of the desert to try conclusions with Muhammed's followers on their own; and, of course, enrich themselves with such depredation as are the means of livelihood of the desert born.

These resolves were, for obvious reasons, applauded by the Qureish, and even active support was promised to the tribes against the Moslems of Medina.

Emboldened and encouraged in this manner, on the first of Moharram in the 4th year of Islamic era, Talha and Khowalid, the two chieftains of the tribe that dwelt in the uplands of Faid Qutan threw their men into the field against the Medinites.

THE BATTLE OF OHUD

The matter did not even reach the extent of a skirmish, for the attackers, seeing a hundred and fifty men of Islam under Abu Sulma marching out of Medina to face the marauders, took to their heels.

Shortly afterwards, from another one of the uplands of Ghurta, Sufyan Bin Khalid led his men against Medina: his followers were also dispersed by the Moslems under Abdullah Bin Anees. The leader of the recalcitrant tribesmen fell in the battle. But perhaps the worse treachery of these lawless clans was manifested during the month of Safor, 4th Hijrah, when Abu Bara Kalabi, chief of the Kalab clan, presenting himself before the Prophet, averred that the time was ripe for his clan to adopt Islam.

The ground was already paved, all that was needed was some religious teachers who could speak to the people about the tenets of Islam and to invite them to partake of the blessing of Allah.

The Prophet felt reluctant to send any of his missionaries to a hostile people, specially when no one could protect them, should the tribesmen themselves prove unfriendly, but Abu Bara guaranteed their safety.

Seventy picked men, well versed in the law of Islam, were consequently ordered by the Prophet to go.

When they reached the territory near the Kalab tribe, a messenger was despatched to the head chief of that clan to announce the arrival of the Moslem Missionaries. The messenger was forthwith put to death, and before these Moslems could realise the peril of their position, they found themselves surrounded by hostile clansmen.

Sixty-nine of the Moslem missionaries out of seventy were butchered in cold blood. Amru Omayah was the only man who escaped out of the whole group that had been invited to preach in Nejd by the Najdi clans themselves.

MUHAMMED: THE PROPHET

Similar treachery is shown by the two other clans, namely Adal and Qarah, to whom ten missionaries were deputed at the request of the tribes.

Eight of these Moslem teachers were killed in an ambush by the very same people who had invited them, and the two, Khabeeb and Zaid, were captured and taken to Mecca as slaves.

The sons of Harrés bought the former at the slave market in order to slay him in blood revenge, and Zaid was executed by the order of Sufyan.

The tragedy of these executions is no greater than other cruelties of the Qureish upon the Moslems, but in the scene which proceeded the slaying of Khabeeb, a thinker feels a thrill of religious spirit.

Before the executioner severed the Moslem's head, the culprit requested to offer a short prayer, which, being granted, Khabeeb stood in prayer for the last time. A crowd had gathered to see the gruesome spectacle, there was a man with bared sabre in hand, the Moslems stood reciting

'O Allah thanks to Thee, the Lord of Mercy and Compassion,'

he paused,

'To Thee we pray and from Thee only do we seek help,'

he continued,

'lead us to Thine own way....'

Then he bent low, and touched the ground with his forehead, calm and resigned and even cheerful, death staring into his face; and he thanked Allah, sent blessings to Muhammed; yes, to a God who even then did not lift His Mighty Hand to save His slave, and a Muhammed who could do nothing for a man whose life-sap was to be spilt.

THE BATTLE OF OHUD

A materialistic mind might turn away in despair. Had he said that he no longer loved Allah and His Prophet, the pagans would have spared him: but that was not and shall never be the spirit of Islam.

The man rose from his prayer, walked to the block of wood, placed his head on it quietly, the executioner's sword trembled for an instant in the sun, and Khabeeb was no more. There is a lesson in steadfastness for one's conviction in such prayer-of-death, so to speak; there is music in their words as they pray; yes, music which still resounded in the ears of those who care to listen, who have an entrée into the Temple of Spirituality:

> *Where music dwells*
> *Lingering, and wandering on as loth to die;*
> *Like thoughts whose very sweetness yieldeth proof*
> *That they were born for immortality.*

And though small engagements in themselves, these skirmishes were indicative, as shadow ripples show the sinister movement of darker waters below.

The entire desert area was now bestirred against the Prophet.

That these stirrings were engineered by the Qureish requires no proving: it was necessary, as a war measure, to weaken the resistance of the Moslems by these smaller conflicts, so that when a Qureish attack of greater magnitude would be launched, the Meccan troops might find it all the more easy to conquer Medina and extirpate the Prophet and his preaching from their midst.

Chapter 16

THE JEWISH REACTION

The dealing of the Moslems with the Jewish population in Medina, and those who lived in the neighbouring villages, has a very pertinent bearing upon the early government of Islam.

In order to understand fully their relationship with the Prophet, we shall have to recapitulate some early Moslem-Hebrew negotiations.

We have seen that as soon as Muhammed had consolidated his position in Medina, he was made alive to the necessity of bestowing the friendship of his followers on the Jews.

These people, divided in three clans of Qinqah, Nadheer and Qariteh, lived in and around Medina, and they controlled practically the entire financial dealings of the Medinites.

A large number of the inhabitants owed money to them, virtually the whole trade of Medina was in their hands; also the Jews, being the *'People of the Book,'* were more educated than the Arab population of the city.

The Law of Moses, of course, was not obeyed by these Jews with any rigidity.

The passing of an Arab debtor's wife into such a Jewish money-lender's harem, and the buying of the defaulter's children, were not unusual practices in Medina, when the Prophet had set himself to reform society.

There were, of course, no moral restraints of any kind.

MUHAMMED: THE PROPHET

> *'Do you not stone the sinner for adultery according to the Law of Moses?'*

once asked the Prophet of a Jew.

> *'Oh! yes,' replied the Jew, 'we apply the strap on the back of a wealthy evil-doer, but the poor must receive the full penalty.'*

According to Isbabul Nuzool, it was resolved to equalise the punishment by only flogging the person who may have committed that misconduct.

The Prophet's amazement can be imagined when he noticed such a flagrant breach of the Heavenly Law: but, perhaps, at the time, it was the affair of the Jews.

The only reason of my quoting this incident is to show the condition of moral degeneracy that existed amongst the Jews of those clans at that period of early Medinite history.

The checking of many of these questionable practices, which the preaching of Islam now placed in Medina, infuriated the Jews. They disregarded the Pact which had been signed between them and the Moslems.

They were now in league with the enemies of Islam. they plotted with the non-Moslem section of Medina, and were in free communication with the Qureish at Mecca.

One of their renowned poets went to Mecca, in order to incite the Qureish to take revenge for the lives of those who fell to the Moslem swords at the battle of Badr.

Nor were his efforts concerned with Mecca alone, for he journeyed far and wide in the hidden folds of desert valleys, amongst the nomads and tent-dwellers, swaying people with the witchery of his poetry and spitting venom against Islam and its preacher.

THE JEWISH REACTION

Another example of the breach of Agreement between the Jews and the Moslems is provided by Nadhir, who was active in anti-Moslem propaganda in his desert area around Khaiber, a region which is some four or five days' journey to the north-west of Medina.

The behaviour of the Prophet was, however, faithful to the Pact. As the Jews observed fast on Ashorah, Muhammed, out of respect for their fellow-citizens, had ordered all Moslems to keep fast on that day. He paid tribute to the dead by standing up whenever a Jewish funeral passed him.

It was the Prophet too, who smoothed matters for the Jews on an occasion when they were to be roughly handled by the Arabs of Medina.

But the intrigue and animosity of the Jews increased daily, till, as is related in the collection of hadith known as the Sunun Abu Daud, the Jewish clans of Qinqah, breaking the Pact, declared war on the Moslems. But they were besieged in their forts, and when these forts surrendered after fifteen days, seven hundred of them left the town.

The next clan of the Jews, Nadheer, followed in the wake of their co-religionists, according to Ibn Hisham, in the month of Rabial Awal in the fourth year of Islam: but a section of this tribe had already grafted itself at Khaiber.

The position of Islam and its enemies should now be borne in mind. There were the hypocrites amongst the Arabs of Medina, the hostile clans of the pagan population within the gates of the city, there were the unfriendly nomads in the desert, and then the arch-enemies of Muhammed at Mecca.

In the midst of all this opposition, the only refuge for the Faithful was Medina, and a handful of the Ansar, believing that their master-mind was there to defend the truth of Allah:

MUHAMMED: THE PROPHET

Get but the truth once uttered, and 'tis like
A star new-born that drops into its place
And which, once circling on its placid round,
Not all the tumult of the earth can shake.

In this great family of the enemies of Islam, it was therefore not difficult to raise an army formidable enough to crush the Believers with one united blow.

This was the suggestion that was made from the Jewish clans of Khaiber; the Qureish heartily welcomed it, and the nomads were not slow to avail themselves of an opportunity which might bring welcome spoils of war to their tents in the desert.

So a coalition army of ten thousand strong under Abu Sufyan, the veteran Qureish general, was on its way to put a stop to Muhammed's activities once and for all.

It must, however, be to the abiding glory of the Moslems, that in practically every military engagement, they had thrown an infinitely smaller number of men into the field than had their adversaries: and in every one of the engagements, the victory had been on their side.

In material resources, and even in war training, they were in every way inferior to their enemy, and yet they had triumphed without an exception. In facing the legions of the combined forces of Arabia—a force of ten thousand well-equipped tough soldiers, hardened to the craft of war—the Moslems, as usual, again put in the field a number of less than one-third, namely three thousand fighters.

When the host of the Qureish arrived near the city, there was not a single Moslem to oppose them.

'Have they fled, are they all dead?'

they asked: but it was soon discovered that a new system of warfare had been resorted to—new to the Arabia of that day—

THE JEWISH REACTION

deep trenches were dug round the city, and soldiers thus sought to defend Medina.

A siege was, therefore, laid. The remaining clans of the Jews would not come to the aid of the citizens of their native town. Not only had they broken the Pact with the Moslems, but in this hour of trial they were not prepared to defend the city against the common foe: instead they openly sided with the attackers of Medina.

When the gravity of the situation grew unbearable, the Prophet sent two of his messengers to persuade the Jews to come to their help. This was not merely a question of Islam, but of common citizenship, of keeping to the most solemn Agreement, which must be kept at a time when the annihilation of the whole people could so easily take place.

In the name of truth and honesty, the Saad Brothers appealed to the Jewish chieftain. In the name of the Apostle of Allah they reminded him of the Pact. Was he going back on his promise, asked Saad, on his pledge, on the terms of an instrument which was contracted?

> '. . . the Moslems and the Jews shall enjoy the same security and freedom; the guilty shall be pursued and punished; the Jews shall join the Moslems in defending Medina against all enemies, the interior of Medina shall be a sacred place for all who accept this Charter....'

The reply of the Jews was defiant:

> 'Who is Muhammed, and who is the Apostle of God that we should obey him? There is no bond or compact between us and him.'

A refusal to help in an hour of trial was possible only because the Jews, like the Qureish, were confident of victory: and on the eve of a triumph all previous Pacts, however solemn, were treated as mere useless scraps of paper. But history took its course.

This was clearly not the time for the measuring of swords in an open field, according to the war tactics, the smaller party was well-advised to avoid facing those who were more than three times their number: so the Moslems bided their time in the trenches and kept a careful watch over the walled area against an attack by the Qureish, with whom now the Jews of Medina had joined issue.

So the siege lingered on.

In a desert town where inhabitants depend upon imported food and the trade of the passing caravans, it is never possible to lay in a store of provisions. That was the predicament at Medina. Food was exhausted, and there was no hope of getting milk for the children. Men ate berries, dried husks, or went about for days without even one fourth of their ordinary rations.

Thus, utter and devastating starvation ensued. Women sat holding their children in their laps and saw them expire for want of nutriment.

Dried skins were boiled; in that soup chopped-up hay was soaked to give it 'body'—this for days was used as the only article of diet; but even these sources have their limits.

Warriors, not even excepting the Prophet, tied up flat stones over their bellies, a familiar device to bear starvation till men fall down dead with absolute hunger.

One day, one of the watchmen jumping down from the parapet, ran to Muhammed; tearing away his shirt, he showed the stone that he had tied to his stomach—he could hold out no longer.

The Leader of the Faithful tried to revive him by saying that a man can go much further than he thinks even when he gives

THE JEWISH REACTION

up hope, especially in the cause which is worth defending, and quite definitely put the man on his feet, when the Prophet bared his abdomen displaying not one but two stones, which he had tied on to ward off his own hunger.

The siege had now lasted twenty days.

The restless tribes of the desert were growing restive of this method of warfare.

Repeatedly they rushed the trenches, and as often, were repulsed.

But although there was privation inside Medina, the armies of the Qureish, their Jewish allies and the Bedouins outside the gates of the city had all feasted too lavishly; soon their stores began to show depletion.

An army of ten thousand men, with followers, grooms, camels and beasts of burden needs an elaborate system of transport in order to be supplied with rations.

With such necessary arrangements of this kind, the early fighters of Arabia were not fully competent; and besides, there were no fertile valleys or villages, or even a constant stream of caravans, which could keep the Meccans provided with the barest of war rations.

Both the animals and the men were in the throes of famine before they had even realised the situation.

The morale of the men now showed distinct deterioration. To this should be added the rivalry of the various chieftains and their disagreement over the booty of Medina, should they succeed in ravaging it.

Horses and camels began to perish, and the men had no moral obligation to bear starvation, such as was the case for the besieged Moslems of Medina.

MUHAMMED: THE PROPHET

It was one of those nights in the city when the Prophet's followers were changing guard a little after midnight.

The man in the foremost corner of the part of the wall which he was watching rose from his place with a start.

He had heard the voice of a woman. Looking round, his eyes met those of his wife.

'And what do you want here?'

he asked the Moslem woman,

'do you not know that women are not in this game of war? and this infant in your arms!'

The woman had come to keep watch with her husband, to do duty like a soldier of Islam, because, she asked, if in the eyes of Allah *all Moslems are equal,* why is she denied the privilege of doing her bit?

As to the infant, that was dead. A starved-out mother's breast could provide no food for the new-born.

'And Allah hath given, and Allah has taken back!'

they said, as the child was lowered under the sod.

Then the man shaded his eyes, he blinked, did he see aright?

And the woman agreed that her husband's vision was not deceiving him, stars which hung down like radiant bunches of grapes were not so bright, as a haze was floating on the face of the moon, there was a rustling of wind, rather an unusual phenomenon, thought the Moslem watchman, as he gathered up his cloak around him. The woman took his place whilst he stood in prayer.

Then what they doubted became a reality: gust after gust of wind was now rising, the clouds had gathered, the moon and the stars were gone, rain-laden thunderclouds were now rolling

THE JEWISH REACTION

overhead like leaping giants, lashed by the crack of vivid lightning.

For a fraction of time the wind abated, the clouds thickened, forming and reforming like gargantuan slabs of black marble, till the watchman could see, away and beyond, the tiny campfires of the besiegers going out one by one. He could no longer see the link of the huge bonfires before which the Qureish danced and sang their warsongs of Arabian revenge.

The wind rose again, it moaned, and sighed and howled, driving its herd of clouds before it like an infuriated shepherd. Then the storm gathered force such as chills the heart of the children of the desert, the tents of the mighty Mecca legions were uprooted, ponies broke loose, men were shouting and yelling, cursing their leaders for having brought them to that stormridden country; till a crash of thunder drowned their voices, sending torrents of rain, sweeping everything with the fierce velocity of angry wind—such a storm as the Moslem soldier and his wife, sitting at the watchtower, like many others in the trenches and all along the walls of Medina bore that night —had not been experienced for generations in Arabian history.

In the half light of the dawn, when the Muezzin, or he who calls the faithful to the morning prayer, climbed up the steps to do Allah's bidding, it was quiet and serene and fresh.

The storm of the previous five or six hours had left the world as pure and fresh as a bride in her wedding raiments. Little pools of water catching the light reflected it; and as for the host of Qureish!—they had fled with the storm.

Starvation, quarrels amongst them, the risk of life, were bad enough, they thought, but the very elements were now against them: the wrath of the skies drives the fear of death into the hearts of men who are not used to such furious exhibitions of nature's moods; and so they had gone, dispersed in confusion,

MUHAMMED: THE PROPHET

obeying no order, owning to no chief, leaving their uprooted tents, the dead camels—even some of their weapons were littered about where, barely ten hours ago sat men bent on murder and plunder and rape —gone and melted like a waxen image against a fire, their dismantled camps bearing no impression of the things they were!

Medina was again free to live and preach in Allah's name.

This anxious time for Islam during the fifth year of Hijra, February A.D. 627, is to be considered as another milestone passed in the atrocities inflicted upon the Faithful.

But although the Qureish had been dispersed, the position of danger persisted at Medina for the fact was that the Jews, who had so callously turned their faces at the time of life and death struggle, were still intriguing against the Moslems. They had proved themselves traitors, and had gone back on their own sworn alliance at so critical a juncture when the whole of Medina might have suffered from the invaders: and yet they continued to plot.

The Moslems could not be blamed for seeking some kind of satisfaction from such unreliable neighbours.

Any such attempt was impudently disregarded by the Jews: so if a siege was laid on their quarters, this was immediately raised, for they proposed their surrender on the stipulation that in the manner of punishment they could only accept their own laws.

As they were guilty of treason against the realm, the Law of Moses, as in *Deuteronomy xx. 13*, was pronounced by the Ausite chief, Assad Bin Muaz. The Law decreed:

> *'And when the Lord thy God hath delivered it into thine hands, thou shalt smite every male thereof with the edge of the sword....'*

THE JEWISH REACTION

Nearly four hundred traitors were put to the sword, and, as is quite natural, a great deal of capital was made out of this occurrence.

> *'It was a harsh, bloody sentence,'* wrote Lane Poole, *'worthy of the episcopal generals of the army against the Albigenses, or of the deeds of the Augustan age of Puritanism; but it must be remembered that the crime of these men was high treason against the State during a time of siege; and those who have read how Wellington's march could be traced by the bodies of deserters and pillagers hanging from the trees, need not be surprised at the summary execution of a traitorous clan.'*

Before forming an opinion upon this execution, we must examine anew the nature of the crime for which the punishment was inflicted.

They had first of all contracted a friendly alliance—not only did they break it, but they helped the pagan Arabs to reduce Medina.

Even after the disappearance of the hostile forces from Mecca, they still plotted against the State when besieged and defeated: they chose their own judge—a non-Moslem, by the way—and desired to be treated in accordance with their own Holy Book.

It was the *Torah,* and the *Old Testament,* which decreed what was meted out to them.

We cannot but agree with Grote—the greatest of all European historians of his time—that it was

> *'a strict application of admitted customs of war in those days.'*

And do the people even now judge of the massacres of King David according to the lights of his time when . . .

MUHAMMED: THE PROPHET

'the conquered Ammonites he treated with even greater ferocity, tearing and hewing some of them in pieces with harrows, axes, and saws; and roasting others in brick-kilns.'

Compare this with the Moslem attitude.

They inflicted none of these barbarities; the vanquished called for their own laws, their own judge, and the punishment was given strictly according to the Jewish Book, not the *Koran*: and yet a cry is raised to say that pardon ought to have been given, about as much, perhaps, as Cromwell could show at the promiscuous massacre of the Irishmen of Drogheda!

A war is a serious business; in it you do not enter with love of the enemy welling from your bosom.

If you fall in a battle, your adversary rejoices: if he is killed, there is one enemy less.

And whether the war is a good or a bad thing is a totally different discussion, regarding which the sober part of humanity has always found itself in agreement, and is as often over-ridden by the herd instinct of the beast in man.

Reverting, however, to the original point under review, no blame of the punishment given to the Jews after their treachery at Medina attaches to the Prophet: thenceforth the Moslems were immune from the machinations of the enemy in their midst. But the Jews were to try conclusions with the Moslems later, as we shall presently see.

Chapter 17

THE ARMISTICE OF HUDAIBIYYA

The Moslem State at Medina had, by the 6th year of Hijra, taken a definite shape.

Many battles had been fought and won.

Medina had been defended, the establishment of the Moslem law was now recognised as the only guide for the people.

But the hearts of the Moslem refugees ached for the sight of their native town of Mecca, for once one makes oneself at one with its mystic atmosphere, whosoever is the person who cannot but yearn for it?

Even I, who have seen the height of wealth and experienced the depths of poverty, and whose heart flies to the uplands of his native glens, was captured by the enchantment of the sunbaked crags of Mecca.

It is the one place on God's earth which has no replica, it must be made of a different clay, different air must waft in Mecca, for why does its atmosphere so grip the soul; why its draw?

When men of nationalities living on the other side of the world from it feel so keenly about the sacred city, how much more the men whose cradle it was?

I can almost hear Bilal, the negro who called the Faithful to prayer, sing with passion for the swaying heads of the Mecca palms, its rocks ablaze in sunshine; its rich, leaping burns of

MUHAMMED: THE PROPHET

Majanh! And Bilal was not the only man who pined to go to Mecca.

For six long years the Meccan Moslems were in exile—six long years of anxiety and battle and distress.

They had borne with fortitude for the glory of Islam, but these Moslems were after all humans; their hearts were in Mecca—Mecca their homeland. Besides, the father of the Faithful, Abraham, had built the House of God at Mecca, where they ought to perform pilgrimages.

This latter fact induced the Prophet to make up his mind to take his followers to the city rendered holy with the memory of the Sire of Ishmael.

With fourteen hundred pilgrims, the Prophet journeyed towards the House of God, the Shrine of the Kaaba. As behoves the peaceful pilgrims, no one was armed except with their swords, and even these were in their scabbards.

The taking of the swords was as perfunctory during those days as the carrying of our walking sticks is to-day. The animals for sacrifice were also with them.

The Qureish, however, began to prepare for war. But the Prophet communicated to them at Mecca that he was coming with his followers in peace, only to perform the pilgrimage and had no warlike intentions. But the people of Mecca forbade the entry of the Moslems to the Holy City.

Messengers from both sides were sent to each other's camps, a few skirmishes ensued, then negotiations were opened again at which a ten years' Armistice was signed between the Moslems and the Qureish.

There were six clauses:

1) That year, the Moslems were not to perform their pilgrimage.

THE ARMISTICE OF HUDAIBIYYA

2) Next year they could do so, provided they did not stay longer than three days in Mecca.

3) The Moslems should bear no arms; their swords must be encased in bags.

4) No Moslem resident shall be taken back from Mecca to Medina; nor any such Moslems, who from among the pilgrims that wished to remain behind at Mecca, shall be forced to return to Medina.

5) All such Moslems who leave Mecca shall be made to regress by the Moslems.

6) The tribes of the desert shall be free to choose as to whom they may ally in battle. There shall be no coercion in this regard on the part of the Moslems.

Practically everyone took the terms of the agreement to mean an unqualified triumph of the pagans of Mecca.

Muhammed was humbled after all, they rejoiced, little thinking that the Prophet was commanded to consider it as victory, for the *Koran* says:

'I have made thee victorious.'

The significance of the Revelation was not understood until events that followed justified it.

When the Treaty was being written, and Suhail, the Qureish delegate, waited; some men ran to remove the chains from the feet of a refugee.

The unfortunate man was staggering with privation and fatigue of the journey. The Moslems brought some water and washed his wounds where the chains had eaten into his flesh. Then before he could relate his story, he fainted. Every effort was made to resuscitate him, and when he revived, he was taken before the Prophet.

MUHAMMED: THE PROPHET

One horrified look he gave to Suhail, the Qureish, who sat beside Muhammed.

The treaty was being signed. It was the turn of Suhail to speak.

> *'To signify that you are faithful to your contract,'* he addressed the Prophet, *'an opportunity has just arrived.*
>
> *This man is my own son, Abu Jundal: because he has embraced Islam, befitting punishment is being given to him. That he is in chains is the proof of what I say.'*

He looked at his son, and then with that cruel voice with which the men of the desert knew Suhail from afar, he insisted that the man who stood before them should be returned to Mecca in chains, in virtue of the treaty just signed: this sad commentary on the love of a father for his son, in the pagan heart, is difficult to realise.

Fourteen hundred warriors stood around the Prophet, warriors who had won battles. Even now, they could throw themselves upon the heathen father who would tolerate, nay even require, the torturing of his son, his own blood and bone, because he so hated Islam.

The men of the desert were not a whit behind in military skill to this vile Qureish, and he was alone in their midst—so what if his blood flowed, he richly deserved it—and above all a Moslem's life was in danger, a Moslem who was so utterly helpless that even his father desired his persecution.

What seas of passion must not be heaving in their hearts, what fire must not have been burning in their eyes! And would the Prophet now command; why did he wait?

> *'But the treaty was not signed,'* said the Prophet to the delegate of the Qureish, *'when your son entered the camp'*:

THE ARMISTICE OF HUDAIBIYYA

but Suhail looked at the man in chains like a viper that devours its own serpent-born,

'Aye, aye,' he said, *'but the terms of the treaty were agreed upon.'*

You require to have a heart of stone not to be moved by this human drama, but the faithful engagement was considered above all other consideration, a word of a Prophet was something holy, something which admitted no ambiguity, a contract which could not be broken.

In silent resignation Abu Jundal was borne away with his chains;

'. . . and Allah shall open a way for thee,'

said the Prophet to that true son of Islam.

After this Armistice, the Qureish did not stay their hands from persecuting the Moslems at Mecca, for they knew that even if such men left for Medina, the terms of the agreement could be pressed and the refugees extradited.

Soon after the sad case of Abu Jundal, another Moslem, Atba Bin Aseed, escaped from Mecca. No sooner had he arrived at Medina than two men from the Qureish were despatched to exhort upon the Prophet the necessity of enforcing the terms of the engagement, and to demand the return of the Moslem Meccan.

Atba too, much against the inclination of the Prophet, was made to leave Medina with the two pagan guards.

But Atba was resourceful, for on the way, pouncing upon one of his guards, he killed him. Chasing the other out of his sight, he hid himself near the village of Aais on the coast, where he thenceforth lived in peace.

Gradually other Moslems of Mecca joined Atba till a fair

MUHAMMED: THE PROPHET

sized colony was formed, and soon sought revenge upon the passing Qureish caravans. The pagans of Mecca, finding themselves unable to control these exiled colonists, begged the Prophet to do away with the clause which governed the extradition: and thus Allah found a way as was promised; for Rumi says:

> 'Union exists beyond all thought and speech
> Between great Allah and the soul of each.'

Chapter 18

THE FALL OF KHAIBER

The 6th year of the Prophet's Flight from Mecca was now coming to a close, when the Moslems believed that their worst difficulties were over.

But the Jews, in their mountain fastnesses in Khaiber, were perhaps even as active now as when they lived within the Medina region.

Khaiber, some two hundred miles north-east of Medina, is a barren enough place today; but you can still see the inaccessible heights on which the Jews had built their forts.

The word Khaiber itself means fortified place.

Here the exiled Jews settled amongst their kinsmen, and soon sought revenge from the Moslems by sending their emissaries far and wide to the Bedouins of Arabia, inciting them to war against the followers of Islam.

In their new environment, they were not handicapped from proceeding with such plots as might strike deeply into the system of the Medina government: with their marvellous power of recuperation, the trade soon came back to their hands, chiefly because in the moneylending business none could rival them in Arabia at that period.

The sons of the desert always found the need of extra cash, which they could only secure from the people of Khaiber, often on exorbitant interest of course, but the money was readily loaned, and that was all that mattered to the impecunious Arabs.

MUHAMMED: THE PROPHET

Be that as it may, the march to Khaiber was not the choice of the Moslems. When the heights of the enemy's strongholds appeared before the Faithful, the passion of religion could not be controlled, and the warriors shouted the name of Allah loud and long, till the cry echoed and re-echoed in the parched gulleys beyond.

The Prophet, resenting it, commanded that no such behaviour was to be shown.

> *'You do not shout,' he said to his troopers, 'as if to a deaf one who is hidden.'*

for, as it is related in Bokhari, Muhammed meant that Allah hears all and sees all, which makes it unnecessary to invoke his support in so unseemly a manner.

The army had not moved very near the Jewish forts when a few women of Medina were brought before the Prophet. This was a serious offence, for in a dangerous game of war, women have no place: till they explained that they wished to attend to the wounded and care for the sick.

Nor was this the first occasion when Arab women thus offered their service, for, as in the battle of Ohud, even the wife of Muhammed dressed the wounds of the soldiers, and in the thick of the battle distributed water in the full blaze of the midday sun.

The women also gathered the spent arrows of the enemies and brought them to their own warriors at a time when one did not know one's own soldiers from those of the other side.

It was in the late afternoon when the Moslem legions almost approached the outer fortifications of the forts of Khaiber.

The Jews awaited the attack, but the Faithful stood to prayer, after which rations, consisting only of roasted oatmeal flour, were distributed amongst the ranks.

THE FALL OF KHAIBER

The Prophet had no better fare than this, a halt was called for the night there, as, according to the Islamic practice, no attack was to be made at night on any villages.

At dawn the fort of Naam was attacked. The Jews showed unprecedented courage, but it was soon reduced, and the adjoining ones followed suit in rapid succession, but the defence of Qamoos proved too formidable even to the repeated rushes of the veteran soldiers of Islam.

The night had gathered, but the fort retained its defiance. Further action against it was postponed till the next day.

On the morrow, the Prophet gave the command to Ali.

Younger in age, and in experience, withal a fighter amongst fighters, Ali led his men up the battlements: again and again he charged, a thousand arrows rained from behind the parapets, boiling oil was thrown upon the attackers, stones were hurled, severed limbs of the Faithful fell on the ground as they climbed up the walls of the Jewish fortress.

It was now midday, party after party of the Moslems, with prayers on their lips, approached, and were as quickly dispersed by the Jewish archers.

And then did Ali swear not to dishonour the standard of Islam; holding the flag in one hand and surrounded by men who fought for the defence of the faith, he made a frenzied rush for the gate.

Now they were madly hurling stones, throwing oil and showering arrows as the Moslems battled and hammered at the gate. It crashed: and then there was such a heaving of bodies, the play of sword-blades, hacking and slaying as never before.

For fully two hours the battle surged; battle-axes rose and fell, arms shot up and fell limp and cold, till another rush was made.

MUHAMMED: THE PROPHET

Then all was over, the fort was reduced, the banner of Islam was on the brow of the hill, the last stronghold of those who would be satisfied with nothing less than the total annihilation of the Faithful fell at the feet of the Prophet.

Twenty days more and this was accomplished.

The enemy had been defeated, and the enemy was non-Moslem who believed, not in the *Koran*, but in *Torah*, the Law of Moses.

Should the punishment be given to the vanquished according to the Jewish law: to strike all male members with the sword, or according to the wisdom of the Prophet?

The decision now rested not on a judge who would decree, as before, according to the Hebrew law, but upon Muhammed.

He would not put every man to the sword.

Not even their entire farm yields were taken from them, but henceforth they were to give only the half of what they grew.

Not even were they forced to embrace Islam, but were left free to the practices of their own religion.

No regular taxes were levied upon them, as on others within the realm of Islam.

An undertaking was given to the defeated foes that they should even be protected by the Moslem arms; and thus, with the reduction of the Khaiber forts closes a chapter of the friction between the Jews and the Moslems.

Chapter 19

THE EXPANSION OF ISLAM

The time that followed the reduction of the Jewish insurrection was one of peaceful penetration of Islam into various corners of the world. The terms of the Hudaibiyya truce, which stipulated that no Moslems shall be allowed to leave Mecca, had to be struck off at the request of the Meccans themselves.

A general interchange of visits between the Qureish and the Moslems of Medina now ensued. People began to come and go freely between Mecca and Medina. The Qureish caravans passed through Medina on their northward journey; and beyond the fact that Islam, as a religion, was still frowned upon by the pagans, the intermixing of the population of the two assumed its normal aspect.

During this period, Khalid, the great cavalry commander of the Qureish who had so materially changed the aspect of battle at Ohud, and was rightly considered the greatest warrior of his time, now embraced Islam of his own accord: with him came Amru Bin Aas, equally renowned in battle, and who, placing his hand between those of the Prophet, attested to his belief in the faith of Allah.

As we shall see, the former led the Moslem legions to victory against the Greeks, and the latter brought Egypt within the Islamic fold.

Many other notables bowed allegiance to the Prophet during

MUHAMMED: THE PROPHET

the time when the Moslems were not implicated in any war, which goes a long way to prove that the expansion of the faith was elected, not by dint of sword, but in virtue of what people had seen and experienced of it in times of peace and goodwill at Medina: else it would have been quite easy for the Moslems to impose their religion on the defeated Jews at Khaiber; but the *Koran* had commanded:

'there is no compulsion in religion—'

an order which was scrupulously obeyed throughout the time of the men who proclaimed the law of Islam to the world.

With the consolidation of the Commonwealth at Medina, various sections of the Moslems, who were scattered by the atrocities of the Qureish, arrived at the recognised seat of Islam: and the government of the Prophet had now taken a definite shape.

It was during this 'recess', too, that frequent attempts were made on Muhammed's life: the most notable amongst them being the case of a Jewish woman who served up poisoned meat to him.

One of his followers, upon eating the food, never rose alive from the table; and the Prophet, although he had spat out the morsel, is said never to have recovered from the ill effects of the poison he had swallowed.

Another feature of this period was the Moslem invitation to various kings and state dignitaries of neighbouring kingdoms.

Envoys were therefore sent to the courts of Heraclius, the Emperor of Greece, to Negus of Abyssinia, to Khusra Parviz, the King of Persia, to the ruler of Egypt, and the chieftains of many Arab principalities. When the Moslem envoy, Wahiyah Kulbi, reached Palestine, he was informed that the Emperor was celebrating his victory over the Persians by paying a visit

THE EXPANSION OF ISLAM

to Jerusalem—the cradle of his faith, and thus it was here that the Prophet's Letter was given to him. With great pomp and show, the durbar of Heraclius was prepared to receive the Moslem envoy.

Surrounded by the high officials of the Church, the Emperor, his crown sitting awry on his brow, strode to the dais, where he first summoned Abu Sufyan, the pagan anti-Moslem Merchant prince of Mecca. The testimony which even this avowed enemy of the Prophet gave regarding the personal excellence of Muhammed, and the good which Islam was doing to Arabia, amazed Heraclius. Abu Sufyan stated that the ancestry of Muhammed was very high placed, that in the family of the Qureish to which the Prophet belonged no one had ever before proclaimed himself as the Messenger of God, that the people who first were fascinated by his religion were poor, that according to his religious principles Muhammed did not enjoin upon his followers to rebel against the law and order of a state, that he is very faithful to his engagements, that in battle as in peace, his attitude is found to be strictly correct; and—added Abu Sufyan, the enemy of Islam himself—that Muhammed required all to obey God, Only One God, to be truthful, to pray, and to lead an honourable and chaste life.

The Emperor observed that prophets are, as a rule, men of high birth, that according to what Abu Sufyan had said, if Muhammed's clan had been the bearer of Kings, one might presume that Muhammed wished to revive the old traditions of rulership, but that clearly did not seem to be the craving in the Prophet's heart.

In all other attributes of good conduct; that is of worship, prayer, honesty, truthfulness; these and many others which characterised Muhammed, remarked the Emperor, were just the sort of qualities which distinguish a Messenger of God from the dross of humanity to whom he is sent as a beacon light of virtue.

MUHAMMED: THE PROPHET

'If that is so,' predicted Heraclius, *'then his domain will stretch far beyond my Kingdoms. I have known that such a Prophet shall rise,'* he added, *'But naught did I think of such an advent in Arabia. O! I wish that I could wash his feet if I could only go there!'*

The report of this declaration of the mighty Emperor cannot be believed by those who have taken undue pains to call Muhammed an impostor; because their *'Knowledge'* surpasses the wisdom of the greatest philosophers and scholars and kings: for the rest it will suffice to draw the attention to the facts of history to show how the vaticination of Heraclius was fulfilled by the march of events, because the Moslem legions had reached provinces even further than entered the mind of that Great Greek Conqueror.

Then the Prophet's letter was read aloud, which, rendered into English, is as follows:

> *With the name of Allah, the Compassionate, the Merciful. This letter is being sent by Muhammed, the slave of Allah and His Messenger, to Harqoul, the Emperor of Roum. I invite you to embrace Islam. If you will become one of the faithful then God shall give you a double reward, but if you do not adopt Islam then the sins of your people will be upon your shoulders.*
>
> *You that are a believer in A Sacred Book,* (that is the Bible, therefore, believing in one of Sacred books of Islam) *and between us there is common ground of worship:*
>
> *Come to that form of devotion we both may worship, a unity—a One God—and that neither of us should recognise any other deity than One God. But if you do not agree to this then we make you a witness that we worship One God.*

THE EXPANSION OF ISLAM

Abu Sufyan's statement, then the observations of the Emperor, and finally, the definite and clear-cut exposition of the Islamic invitation could not but create a tense atmosphere amongst the Clergy present at the Durbar.

The King did not embrace Islam—it was differently ordained—but the Moslem Envoy was returned to Medina bearing the felicitations of the Emperor.

In direct contrast to this reception was the wrath inflicted upon Abdullah Bin Hazafa who was sent from Medina to the court of the Persian King.

Gallant soldiers of Chosroes held their swords aloft when their monarch, enraged by the language of the Prophet's letter, paced the hall of audience. Holding it in his hands,

'this letter, this mere application of an uncouth Arab,' he shouted, *'begins not with my name—I the King of Kings,'*

he tore the epistle into shreds.

'Who is this Muhammed, of what account is he?'

he roared: forthwith he dictated a command to his viceroy at Yemen to send a couple of troopers to Medina to arrest Muhammed, and bring him in chains to the city of the Persian King of Kings.

The incident is not without its humorous situation: for two soldiers, obedient to the order of the Persians, did actually ride into Medina; they did approach the Prophet; yes, they had the audacity of conveying their orders to that man, to whose preaching nearly one seventh of the human race was to bow allegiance.

'Like unto the shreds of mine letter,' calmly replied the Prophet, *'the Kingdom of thy king be.'*

And within a short time pagan Persia had crumbled to dust:

for hardly had the Yemenite soldiers reached home, than proud Chosroes had been assassinated by his own son.

Regarding the message to the King of Abyssinia, Tabiri records that the Negus had embraced Islam at the hands of Jafar, and had sent a reply to say that he attested to the Prophet being the Messenger of God, and the same authority mentions that the Abyssinian Emperor had sent his son with delegates to the Prophet, but the boat in which the delegation sailed was sunk in the Red Sea.

Presents accompanied a very courteous reply from Egypt; but varied in tone and results were the replies received by the Arab chieftains: one of them from Hozah Bin Ali was of interest, because he showed his approval of Islam provided he was given a share in the government, which naturally could not be given as a price for the support of anybody.

The acceptance of Islam on its own merit, was the Summum Bonum of life.

As the origin of the battle of Mutah is linked up with the despatching of these Islamic invitations, its details are pertinent here. Mutah is situated in Syria, where Hauris Bin Amir was sent as the Prophet's Envoy to Busra.

The ruler of the province, Sharjeel Bin Umru, was a Christian Arab, who, being a vassal of the Romans, dared not envisage a cause so decidedly different from the faith of his Christian Emperor. But he went a step further by having the Moslem envoy slain, and returning a *'reply of war to a peaceful approach.'*

This gross breach of peace necessitated an expedition. The Medina Commonwealth could not possibly brook an affront of this description, and so an army composed of only three thousand Moslem warriors marched northwards to avenge the death of their peaceful negotiator.

THE EXPANSION OF ISLAM

A hundred thousand strong were mustered against these men of Medina, who trusted only in Allah; for reposing trust in God is the expression, because this insignificant force of the Moslems was ill-equipped, insufficiently armed, and naturally enough, had no great reassurance of reinforcements or imperial resources such as the Syrians could command.

An undecided battle was fought, the Moslems lost many lives, amongst them Jafar, the uncle of the Prophet; and beyond the fact that the Emperor of the Romans realised that his vassal could not commit atrocities with impunity, little else was gained: but to a student of history, a most remarkable evidence of the equality and impartiality of Islam is shown by the fact that the Command of the Moslem expedition was placed in the hands of one Zaid, the liberated slave of the Prophet.

Let me examine the point here, for without it, we are apt to lose sight of the real significance of Muhammed's preaching.

At that early period of Arabian history, as indeed, even today in many regions of Asia, blue-blood counted above every other distinction in men's lives.

People counted their ancestry to forty generations and more, the exclusiveness of blood-stock was something over which people prided themselves. The *'purity'* of their blood was the one criterion to judge between the *'salt of the earth'* and the common masses.

The Qureish of Mecca were the men who were the *'best of men,'* the purest of Arabs. They held the trade, the guardianship of the Temple and the prestige of race. The oligarchy of these factors, none dare dispute.

Now, amongst the Moslems at Medina, there were all sorts and descriptions of people, the Qureish of Mecca, the desert tent-dwellers, the tradesmen of the town, and those who did nothing better than to mind the camels or graze sheep.

MUHAMMED: THE PROPHET

Whosoever embraced Islam had to forfeit his haughty attitude of race, colour and tradition. He was merely one of the Moslems: *'All Moslems are brothers,'* is the injunction.

The *'blackest'* negro Bilal called the faithful to prayer, the sallow-complexioned Persian philosopher Sulman, an ordinary work-a-day helper towards the cause, the rich and proud Qureish and the humble tradesman of Medina were on equal footing; brothers all, with no distinction of colour, race or social distinction.

So in this battle of Mutah, whom did you find leading the men proud of race and traditions, the men of Qureish, but Zaid, the liberated slave of Muhammed—a slave as the standardbearer of free-men with such mighty warriors as Khalid, the Cavalry Commander of Qureish, and even Jafar, the uncle of the Prophet, under him.

If we value this incident as an index of what equality meant to early Islam, it is because prior to that time, equality did not exist; and certainly equality between the slave and the free-men was inconceivable.

The above example stands as a monument of worthy endeavour in the annals of man, to show how one has *'to lose one's caste'* upon entering within the pale of Islam; for rank, ancestry, wealth were nullified before the searching test of the law of the *Koran*: thenceforth they ceased to be Persians, Arabs, Syrians, wealthy or poor, tradesmen or warriors of haughty grace, but simply Moslem workers in the cause of Allah, whichever way it may lead them.

For this alone, if for nothing else, I, as a Moslem, shall always consider Muhammed the first and the foremost man of all times.

History has shown its value, nor can it ever show a nobler disciple of Allah to humanity than Muhammed.

Chapter 20

THE MOSLEMS VISIT MECCA

According to the terms of the truce of Hudaibiyya, towards the close of his 7th year of the Flight of Hijra, the Prophet started for Mecca in order to perform the pilgrimage, from which he had been turned away on the previous year.

Before we go any further into the details of this journey, the discerning eye sees a contrast.

Muhammed, it will be remembered, had reached the confines of Mecca during the last pilgrimage season.

A large armed following he had, and in view of the fact that he was being denied the offering of prayers at the cradle of his religion, a right which was not withheld even from the pagan Arabs of the desert, would he have not been justified in having entered Mecca and fighting his way to the shrine—

'War in the name of Allah . . .'

is a clear injunction, and is this command not pertinent in a situation when the faithful are not allowed to perform one of the five principle religious duties?

But Muhammed abhorred war, hated to shed blood, so he turned back to Medina, turned back even when his entire following thirsted for the sight of the holy shrine; no, the Prophet cared not to fight unless goaded into it: first, he tried all other means, even to the extent of signing a treaty which some of his disciples considered humiliating.

MUHAMMED: THE PROPHET

He did this to secure peace and to avoid war. And yet men blinded with prejudice will stigmatise him as a man of the sword, deliberately suppressing facts of the life with a parallel: but, in this entry of the Prophet into Mecca for the purpose of a pilgrimage, there is more than the mere recording of the fact that with a large number of the Moslems accompanying him, and after a three days' stay in the city, they left it as peacefully as they had entered it.

We must look closely into this visit. This pilgrimage was being performed according to the treaty of Hudaibiyya, in which it was stipulated that no armed man should enter Mecca; consequently, the Moslems left all their arms at a place some eight miles from Mecca with a party of two hundred men to guard them.

The city was deserted: the Qureish had left the place and retired in their tents on the adjoining hills. But a few real admirers and sympathisers of the Prophet had gathered in Nadwa, the Council Hall overlooking the Temple of the Kaaba.

Some lighthearted youths sauntered along the streets, mockingly remarking that the soft air of Medina had rendered the Moslems less able to retain the vigour of the desert-born; that those of the Meccans, who, having adopted Islam, had joined issues with the Prophet, would rather be in the sheltered life of leafy Medina than face the heat and the fatigue of pilgrimage ceremonies, especially after a long journey.

A point small in itself, and yet of deep significance, for in those days, as indeed ever in the history of man, a tired-out foe, physically weak, who drags his feet, as it were, has a decidedly encouraging value to an adversary.

So the Prophet ordered his men to show to these men of Mecca that the Moslems did not suffer from any such weaknesses. For days they would march, thirsty and on short rations, and yet

THE MOSLEMS VISIT MECCA

retain a strength equal to the greatest warrior of the day.

The faithful were commanded, therefore, to run or to encircle the temple with quick paces, holding their heads erect, showing no fatigue or exhaustion, calling the name of Allah; and then, during the last circumnambulations, slow down to their normal gait.

This practice is still carried out by the pilgrims at Mecca.

Ibn Abi Shayba, following Isa Ibn Talha, describes the various scenes of the time very graphically:

> '*addressing the Black Stone,*' he says, '*the Prophet declared: verily, I know that thou art nothing more than a stone, powerless to do harm, or be of any use. Then he kissed it . . . Abu Bakr followed, then Omar, and the rest came and kissed the stone, saying: By Allah, I know thou art nothing more than a stone, powerless to do harm or be of any use, and if I had not seen the Prophet kiss thee, I should not have kissed thee!*'

Then, they did honour in the usual manner to the memory of Hagar, who

> '*being too weak to carry Ishmael any further, her child that was succumbing to thirst, Hagar placed him on the ground in the shade of a shrub and ascended a hill, hoping to see from afar a well or spring; but all in vain. Then, fearing that her son must be dying, she ran up another hill for the same purpose, but with no better results, till in anguish she climbed down to where her child lay smitten with heat and thirst.*'

> '*Seven times did she run in despair between the two hills, when, worn out, she was now near her child, who, as she thought, may be dead by that time; but lo! a stream lay nearby, and it was the Zam Zam, a well by the mercy of Allah, the Compassionate, the Merciful.*'

MUHAMMED: THE PROPHET

In order to keep the memory of that incident of Hagar running seven times between the two hills of Safa and Marva, a practice called the Saey was performed by the faithful with the Prophet—as it has continued to be performed year by year by thousands of pilgrims at Mecca to this day throughout the last two two centuries of Islamic history.

Following this, the sacrifice was made, the pilgrim costume of Ahram consisting of only one sheet with no stitches or attachments was discarded, and the Moslems were again before the shrine of the holy Kaaba with the Prophet.

The *Koran* had enjoined upon its believers to keep their contracts, to be faithful to their treaties, and Muhammed was showing by his actions at Mecca that he was a model of what he preached.

During that stay of three days, it would have been quite possible to occupy that *'vacant city,'* arms were easily accessible: but the Prophet was incapable of such treachery. The Moslem pilgrims went about the streets of Mecca honouring the memories of early days, behaving peacefully like pilgrims in Allah's way, true to the truce which their leader had signed.

> *'It was surely a strange sight,'* says even Muir, whose love for Muhammed was never deep, *'which at this time presented itself in the vale of Mecca—a sight unique in the history of the world. The ancient city is for three days vacated by all its inhabitants, high and low, every house deserted; and they retire, the exiled converts, many years banished from their birthplace, approach in a great body, accompanied by their allies, revisit the empty houses of their childhood, and within the short allotted space, fulfil the rites of pilgrimage. The inhabitants, climbing the heights around, take refuge under tents or other shelter among the hills and glens; and, clustering on the overhanging peak of Abu Qubay, thence watch the*

THE MOSLEMS VISIT MECCA

movements of the visitors beneath, as, with the Prophet at their head, they make the circuit of the Kaaba, and the rapid procession between Safa and Marwah; and anxiously scan every figure if perchance they may recognise among the worshippers some long-lost friend or relative. It was a scene rendered possible only by the throes which gave birth to Islam.'

On the eve of the third day, the Qureish approached Ali to say that the stipulated time was over, so just as peacefully as they had come, the two thousand Moslem pilgrims left Mecca after the pilgrimage.

There is, no doubt, of course, that this visit of the Prophet was of great value to the cause of Islam in Mecca and around. People had the opportunity of witnessing, perhaps for the first time, how devoted the followers were to their leader of Islam. They also saw, with their own eyes, that the religion of Muhammed had very considerably reformed the personal behaviour and outlook of many whom they had seen before in Mecca.

The safe return of the pilgrims to Medina was an occasion of great rejoicing in the city; and the Prophet set about knitting his system more closely to the requirements of the new commonwealth.

What situation, however, obtained now in Medina? The greatest European scholar of his time, A. von Kremer, attests that the Prophet founded a political system of an entirely new and peculiar character—peculiar, of course, in the sense that no such law was given to the world before—it was a system in which the Church and the State worked hand in hand, the one being an integral part of the other.

In the beginning, as we have seen, he invited his people to believe in the One God—Allah—but, as Von Kremer thinks:

along with this, he brought about the overthrow of the old system of government: that is, in place of the tribal aristocracy under which the conduct of public affairs was shared in common by the ruling families, he substituted an absolute theocratic monarchy.

We shall have an opportunity a little later of again examining this point.

Chapter 21

THE CONQUEST OF MECCA

According to the terms of the treaty of Hudaibiyya, the Arab tribesmen of Khizaah had been allied to the Moslems of Medina, and thus were more or less immune from the raids of their old enemies the people of Banu Bukr, but soon the latter attacked these Moslem allies, during which the Qureish of Mecca openly helped the aggressors.

Pressed by their enemies the tribesmen of Khizaah sought the sanctuary of the Temple, but here too, their lives were not respected, and contrary to all accepted traditions, Noful, the chief of Banu Bukr, chasing them into the sanctified area—where no blood should be shed—massacred his adversaries.

When the aggrieved party sought justice from their Moslem allies, the Prophet, as the leader, demanded an immediate redress, not only for violating the treaty but also for slaying people in the sanctified area.

Three demands were made; the acceptance of any one of them was claimed: firstly, that blood-money should be paid, secondly, that the Qureish should terminate their alliance with the Banu Bukr who had so ruthlessly disavowed the truce, and/or, finally, that the truce should be considered as null and void.

The Qureish, proud of their strength, agreed to the third condition; that is, that no truce of Hudaibiyya was binding upon them. Neither in spirit nor in deed could the Qureish give a clearer ultimatum to the Moslems and their Allies.

MUHAMMED: THE PROPHET

Providentially, in such tragic circumstances, the promise of Allah was now to be fulfilled; and the Prophet was destined to claim the House which his greatsire Abraham dedicated to the sacred name of Allah at Mecca. But Abu Sufyan, the leader of the Qureish, was sent later to Medina in order to reopen the negotiations. He, however, met with no success.

On the tenth day of Ramadan, the Moslem month of Fasting, the Prophet led his ten thousand warriors Meccaward. Many more tribesmen, throwing in their lot, joined the expedition on the way. A large army thus encamped outside Mecca.

Again Abu Sufyan was sent to stave off the attack, but the time had come when mediation of this description only showed how the Qureish wished to launch fresh treachery.

This great enemy of Islam, Abu Sufyan, who had been instrumental in inciting the tribesmen against the Moslems, who had plotted the assassination of the Prophet more than once, who had led his men again and again against the believers, was arrested: but having regard to the merciful behaviour of the Prophet, he was not beheaded.

In the morning, the Moslems surged over the hills and vales of Mecca, but the Prophet had ordered that no one must attack first, there should be neither looting nor plunder, no one who took refuge with Abu Sufyan was to be molested, nor any one harmed who might shut himself in his own house.

Company after company of the Moslem warriors entered Mecca unopposed, not a stone was thrown, not a single battle cry raised, not an arrow discharged; the might of Islam had chilled the courage of the men of Qureish: but, anon, a party of the Meccans rose from behind the boulders on the height occupied by the cavalry under Khalid, and before the Moslem commander could realise his position, two of his men lay dead, arrows piercing their vitals.

THE CONQUEST OF MECCA

That was the solitary occasion when resistance was offered, when Khalid pursued his assailants, inflicting thirteen casualties upon the Qureish. The rest was quiet, and Mecca was occupied practically without any opposition.

And now notice the situation: the government of Medina was in the hands of one man, all tribal recalcitrancy was reduced to submission. An army of ten thousand strong and more enters into a town where men can offer no resistance, where the treasury of the Temple is overflowing with the accumulated wealth of generations, where merchandise is at the mercy of the conquering army, where, in the temple, men who had persecuted him stand before Muhammed, who exiled him, where Moslems were tortured—what would be the first impulse of a conqueror?

Should he not have all his enemies slaughtered now, as they were in his grasp; should he not appropriate the treasury; should he not give up the city to plunder? Has it not ever been done in the annals of man, and has the world not condoned such actions, for the defeated must suffer for their sins?

What did Muhammed do in his hour of triumph? He ascended the steps of the idol-infested Kaaba and knocked down the idols, saying,

> *'the truth has arrived, sin is removed, for infidelity is a thing which perishes!'*

One by one, the stone-gods were dismantled, the pictures and effigies deleted, and the black liberated slave Bilal was commanded to ascend to the roof of the Kaaba and call the men to prayer, to the prayer of One God, the One God Who has no partner in His realm, Who was not begotten by any one, and begets none as human beings do.

To the men and women of Mecca he gave a general amnesty. Only four, and strictly speaking, only two men were to be executed for murder, the rest was peace and goodwill, nor were the vanquished compelled to adopt Islam if they did not want to, and the promise was then completed that a descendant of Abraham shall one day clean up the sacred House of Allah.

The truth of Islam was made absolute: for, indeed it has been justly remarked that in the story of men there has been no triumphant entry like unto this one of Muhammed's entry into Mecca. To Muhammed the conquest of Mecca meant only one thing, the preaching of Islam, and not in any way a desire of megalomania. So, true to his mission, he started his work without delay.

On the height of Safa, near the shrine of Kaaba, sat the Prophet. Batches after batches of men came up to him, placing their hands in his, they embraced Islam, the women dipped their hands in a bowl of water after him to take the oath of fidelity, and thus he sat long, carrying on with the work for which his heart had hungered so long.

They came from far and near, in pairs, singly, in hordes, to pledge the oath of Islam by saying:

> 'We shall not adore any but the One God, we shall not commit larceny, adultery, or infanticide, nor utter falsehood, nor speak evil of women.'

Once again he emphasised the equality amongst the Moslems:

> 'O! You men of Qureish,' he addressed them, 'the pride with which you carried yourselves before during the period when you were in darkness, is gone; gone never to return: for God willed it so. All men are the sons of Adam, and Adam was built of clay.... In the sight of God those only are nobles whose actions are pious and free from evil ...'

Leaving Maghaz in Mecca to continue the preaching of Islam, the Prophet left the city for Medina, after fifteen days.

Chapter 22

THE BATTLE OF HUNAIN AND AFTER

Hunain is the valley which lies between Mecca and the uplands of Taif.

In its neighbourhood, also, is the region of Zulmajaz, the famous market, and a meeting-place of caravans.

This valley was chosen by the combined forces of the tribes of Howazin and their allies to attack Mecca before the Moslem power grew too strong for any effective opposition.

In self-defence an army of ten thousand Moslem soldiers proceeded to check the advancing desert warriors: and this was scarcely after one month of the reduction of Mecca by the Moslem arms, when the faithful thought that the time for a rest had arrived.

In the beginning, when the two armies met, Moslems charged, with the fury of battle surpassing any hitherto undertaken by them.

The enemy fell back, but it was only a passing phase, the archers of the desert played havoc amongst the Moslem ranks, men fell like leaves in autumn, the warriors of Islam were in confusion: a section retreated, then another, and a third, till at one time it appeared that a general rout had taken place.

The knoll on which the Prophet stood was now isolated: the archers concentrated their attack upon it, the enemy was making straight for that spot.

MUHAMMED: THE PROPHET

'I am the Prophet,'

shouted Muhammed,

'I am the true Messenger of Allah,'

he called to his followers.

Abbas, his companion, shouted too: gradually the fleeing soldiers tarried, and forming and reforming, closed their ranks. Throwing themselves upon the enemy with the frenzy of religious devotion, they stemmed the tide and fought to kill or be killed.

The defeat was changed in a trice into victory, the pagan Arabs were completely defeated. Six thousand prisoners were taken, whilst a section took refuge in the walled fortress of Taif.

The booty which fell into the hands of the Moslems was colossal judging from the standard of those times, for the defeated foe left behind forty thousand sheep, four thousand ounces of silver and twenty-four thousand camels. These were divided amongst the soldiers, the fifth portion going to the State Treasury and for the poor.

Returning to Jarana, where the captured Howazin were kept, the Prophet found a deputation awaiting him, says Amir Ali, which solicited the release of their relatives who had been taken as prisoners at the battle of Hunain.

Aware of the sensitiveness of the Arab nature regarding their rights, he adds, the Prophet replied to the Bedouin deputies that he could not force his people to abandon all the fruits of their victory, and that they must at least forfeit their effects if they would regain their relatives.

To this they consented: and, according to Tabiri, the next day, after the prayer of the dawn, Muhammed had the deputation repeat their requests before the gathering of the faithful.

THE BATTLE OF HUNAIN AND AFTER

The Prophet then replied:

> 'My own share of the captives, and that of the descendants of Abdul Muttalib, I give you back at once.'

His disciples, catching his spirit, immediately followed the example, and six thousand prisoners of war, attests Ibn Hisham, were set free without any further difficulty.

I do not need to draw any conclusions here, an impartial judge will readily see what hold the Prophet had upon his people, and also what real magnitude of mercy he could show.

Mention might now be made of the Moslem expedition to Tabuk in Syria, where the Christian vassals of Imperial Rome, notably the Arab chieftains of Ghassan, Lagham and Jazam had persuaded their overlord to help them in attacking the Moslems at Medina.

A force of forty thousand men was being gathered, but the Moslems marched to defend themselves with their usual deficiency in numbers and resources under the leadership of the Prophet.

Many Moslems perished with thirst and lack of provisions before they reached Tabuk, between Medina and Damascus, where a halt was called.

But what was the surprise of the Medinites upon hearing that the muster of Roman troops could not take place, and that the Emperor had his hands full at home.

For twenty days the Moslems waited at Tabuk for a foe that never came, and that in the heat of the desert during the month of Fasting too. The Moslems returned to Medina.

Soon after the return of the Prophet to his headquarters, a deputation of the refractory tribesmen of Taif waited on him.

The leader of the delegates, one Otwa, embracing Islam, hurried back to his people carrying with him the glad tidings of his conversion, but his people were of a different mind, and they literally stoned him to death.

The martyr's blood, says Amir Ali, soon blossomed into faith in the hearts of his murderers.

Seized with sudden compunction, the men of Taif sent another deputation asking for Muhammed's forgiveness, and requesting to be allowed to embrace Islam.

They begged, however, a brief respite for their idols: for two years they could not destroy their stone gods till their people could be persuaded to detach their attention gradually from their objects of worship.

The Prophet could not allow it.

Then, a very short period of three months was asked for, but it was refused, for Islam and stone gods could not exist together: and lastly the people of Taif requested that in the beginning they may be exempted from the five daily prayers; and Ibnul Athir records that the Prophet was emphatic on this point, for he replied that without devotion, religion was of little account.

The Taifites then had to accept all the principles of Islam, prayer and worship, destruction of idols, and the practice of the Moslem code of morals.

But as the worship of idols was born in their bones, they sought the good offices of the Prophet to excuse them from destroying the idols with their own hands.

And whom do you think was deputed to perform the duty of breaking these false gods of stone and clay but Abu Sufyan himself—the selfsame Abu Sufyan, archdeacon of the great shrine of Kaaba, who had led his men in the name of idol-infested Kaaba against the Moslems on many occasions, and who now was a faithful follower of Allah's Messenger.

Many more deputations of Arab clans now came to Medina

THE BATTLE OF HUNAIN AND AFTER

and embraced Islam: the chiefs of Yemen, Mahra, Oman, Bahrein and other regions swelled the ranks of the faithful, till, to all intents and purposes, the entire Arabian peninsula from the Persian Gulf to the Red Sea, from the southern uplands of Yemen to the northern confines of Medina, was Moslem.

And be it known that the expansion, the real expansion of Islam, took place after the period of warfare.

Practically, the nine years which followed Muhammed's flight to Medina was a time of constant defensive wars and expedition; none of the battles proved the fact that Islam made any but incidental and almost insignificant progress as the results thereof.

The Qureish were beaten, the Jews reduced: to the Romans it was made known that their northern legions would find hard adversaries in the Moslems, and a few tribal forays were repulsed.

But when one examines the net results of these campaigns, it is surprising to note that during the eight or nine years of incessant fighting, Islam, as a religion, progressed but slowly.

Nevertheless, as soon as a centralised system of the Moslem commonwealth was definitely established at Medina, the zenith of which may be said to have been reached only after the Moslem expedition to Syria, the various tribes, and clans came to Medina on their own accord and embraced Islam.

This is perhaps one of the most peculiar facets of Islam's progress, and explodes the myth that the preaching of Islam was effected by the sword.

To all intents and purposes, the sword was sheathed at Medina at the close of the 8th year of Hijra, so that there was no military compulsion upon those who sent their deputations to the Prophet.

MUHAMMED: THE PROPHET

Nor, indeed, can it be due to the fact that these warlike sons of Arabia, still strong and proud of their racial traditions, were suddenly seized by the fear that the Moslems will throw themselves upon them for the propagation of the faith.

In the first place, these tribes were always able to hold their own against the Moslems in battle, or again, might very easily form a federation against the growing power of Medina.

Furthermore, in case of war, they could always contract treaties of good neighbourliness with the Moslems and retain the right of worship in their own way, such as was the case for the terms that were accorded to the Jews: indeed, even to those Jews who were defeated at Khaiber.

What possible excuse is there then for not believing that these Arabs did come within the Islamic fold of their own accord; and what facts defend the theory that Muhammed spread his doctrines by a flaming sword?

And finally, if you are at war, does it necessarily mean that you have been an aggressor?

But you must pass judgement only when in possession of the full facts—facts without prejudice—and not those that are based on inferences, such as in Muir's writings, though truth sometimes escapes even through his lips, for instance, when he wrote:

> *'Never, since the days when primitive Christianity startled the world from its sleep, and waged a mortal conflict with heathenism, had men seen the like arousing of spiritual life,—the like that suffered sacrifices, and took joyfully the spoiling of goods for conscience's sake.'*

THE ISLAMIC PILGRIMAGE

Although Mecca had fallen during the 8th year of the Hijra, yet the full injunctions of Islamic pilgrimage were postponed till a later date: so after the expedition of Tabuk, when the time of the pilgrimage drew near, in the 9th year of Hijra, the Prophet commanded that it should be performed in complete obedience of Islamic canons.

Consequently three hundred pilgrims under the leadership of Abu Bakr, with Ali as standard bearer, and preachers were sent to Mecca from Medina.

This being the first pilgrimage on the lines of the original pattern of Abraham, Abu Bakr read the sermon proclaiming that various ceremonies were to be performed strictly according to Islamic practices on that occasion and ever after, detailing the method of performing the several rites and prayers.

This concluded, Ali rose and recited some verses of the *Sura Barat* from the *Koran*, and announced on behalf of the Prophet of Allah that, thenceforth,

> *no non-Moslem shall enter the Holy Precincts of the Kaaba, and no one shall encircle the shrine unless properly clothed; and that all engagements and treaties with the heathens after a lapse of four months should be considered null and void.*

The last item of the announcement is significant to show that at a time when truth had been acknowledged on all hands, and the government of One God was an established fact, there was no room for idol-worship.

Even in this instance, the Moslems were advised to carry through their engagements up to the date of their termination, which was then only four months.

It quite definitely meant that the belief in One God was the only idea on which the Established Church of the Prophet could have dealings with other people: otherwise, how could the heathens be bound to their commitments in a treaty with those who were not heathens?

The underlying fact here being that paganism is, in fact, devoid of all religious conception, and therefore of the basis of honour on which the foundation of solemn pledges between two peoples are founded: hence with such people, peaceful negotiations would ultimately dwindle down to war, and wars above all, the Moslems did not want.

Chapter 23

THE HOME LIFE OF THE PROPHET

After giving a detailed narrative of what Muhammed did as a public man, it is pertinent to examine his attitude towards his friends and relatives, his wives and children: and this facet of his character is of the utmost value, because in essence it is not detached from his public virtues, for he had no dual personality.

He married Khadija, a widow of forty years of age, when he himself was fifteen years her junior.

During the lifetime of Khadija he had no other wife, but upon her death he married a virgin, Ayesha, the daughter of Abu Bakr, his age then being fifty-two.

Others he took in marriage were the relative of Omar and other ladies. Towards his daughter Fatima, the wife of Ali, and his grand-children Zainub, Hasan and Husain, his love was great, for he had seen no grand-children from the male side of her descendants.

On closer examination we find that he practised polygamy. He acted in circumstances which best suited the condition of life obtaining then; practically all of his wives were women of an advanced age, and also widows that had been rendered destitute by the afterwar results in which their husbands had given up their lives for Islam.

There can be no question of sensuality here, no question of any considerable wealth which might have come to the Prophet by contracting such marriages.

MUHAMMED: THE PROPHET

In not a few cases, as historical instances show, it was a political necessity, and a gracious act for protecting the honour and liberty of Moslem womanhood, and also due to giving support to those who needed support, and deserved it.

The life of such women in the harem of the Prophet was not enviable from the point of view of worldly goods: for without exception, all of them lived from hand to mouth.

Indeed, when some of them hoped for a measure of comfort, they were told frankly that Muhammed had no power and right over the state treasury beyond that of an ordinary member of the faith.

A distinct example of this is furnished by the report of Omar, who visited the private apartment of the Prophet and found him sitting on a bare cot, the various other items in the room being a mat, a bowl, a skin for keeping the drinking water: and the name of this man was in the mouths of monarchs and kings and chiefs of Arabia from north to south.

But what is this law about the plurality of wives according to which Muhammed acted; the *Koran* says:

> '... then marry such women as seem good to you, two or three or four; but if you fear that you will not do justice (between them) then (marry) only one....'

By this injunction no obligation to marry four women is made, only permission is granted and a limit imposed.

It is, strictly speaking, both a negative and an affirmative command, for it is conditional upon one bestowing the equal love and to doing justice between one's several wives.

This condition is the crux of the situation: if that equal justice cannot be done, then polygamy is strictly banned.

Now for a man to be equal in his devotion and just treatment towards his several wives at one and the same time is a task

THE HOME LIFE OF THE PROPHET

much beyond any average man: whosoever succeeds in this is decidedly not an ordinary man.

The review comes to the point when one may ask, was Muhammed such a husband who could treat his wives with equal justice: and facts prove it to be so.

He treated them with kindness and courtesy, their maintenance allowances, though meagre, were the same: they all behaved towards him with equal kindness.

Judging from the state of common society, one will be inclined to think that if these ladies were not perfectly satisfied, they would have showed it only too readily, because, even at the time when the power of Muhammed was at its zenith, the society of the desert was not free from evil tongues, and how great would have been the delight of the enemies of Islam to give wings to the reports of a discord in the Prophet's family.

We have no record of such evil reports; indeed, so great was the love between the wives of the Prophet towards each other that when evil was spoken of Ayesha, her rival bore testimony to her virtue.

This is probably the most extraordinary proof, clear and undisputed, of how the wives of Muhammed agreed amongst themselves, which in turn indirectly supports the belief that the Prophet's treatment was that of justice towards his womenfolk. And so, if there be a man like unto him who could dispense equal justice amongst his wives; ordinary laws which frail man has made for himself are not valid, he is a man apart, a model to strive after.

In this regard we should not, of course, forget that monogamy was only made a matter of legislation in Europe by the Emperor Justinian, a Roman and a Pagan jurist.

In his manner of speech, Muhammed spoke very slowly and deliberately with a firm and clear voice, and never hurried over his words. When speaking, his gaze was often lifted towards the sky. He never spoke without reason, when he gesticulated his arm rose from his side; he scarcely ever laughed aloud, but always had a smile on his lips. He walked very quickly, and his eyes did not roam as he paced in the market.

His dress was always simple, often patched, and of coarse cloth. A long shirt covered the upper part of his body, the lower by a sheet, and he never used trousers. On his feet one never saw anything but sandals: and, of course, he tied a turban upon his long flowing hair.

On account of poverty—for even in the days of his greatest glory he continued to be poor on account of giving away everything in charity—he neither cared about nor generally found good food, but he liked honey, olive oil and vegetables, whenever procured. He was neither very fond of, nor was often able to buy, meat.

When on his death-bed, he asked Ayesha, his wife, to give away the last remaining gold coins in the house to the poor: so that when he died his personal belongings consisted only of an armour—which was also in mortgage with a Jew—a mattress of dried palm leaves, and a water skin.

His daily routine, when in Medina, was a curious blending of work of the Church and the State. After the prayer of the dawn he held an open court: rich and poor alike assembled to tell him of their public and private matters. Cases were heard and justice given, envoys received and despatches dictated, and then after a brief sermon, he used to rise to pray.

The public function now over, he used to go to one of his wives, make his bed, fill the water receptacles, sweep the floors, mend his sandals, or saddle, or do any other odd job which his good wife wanted him to do, even go to the market for her shopping.

THE HOME LIFE OF THE PROPHET

Then another short prayer was performed, after which he visited the sick, and the poor, calling at the houses of his friends, seeking news of their welfare. Muhammed was an ideal citizen.

In the afternoons, before a large gathering of men and women, the various religious items were explained by him. Any man could come and have his doubts removed or his wrong redressed: the prayer of the late afternoon terminated this sitting, when Muhammed made a round of his harem, a few minutes with each wife, for an hour or so, till children claimed his time, with whom he played, and now the black liberated slave Bilal was calling the Faithful to the prayer of the sunset, when the Prophet was again leading the Faithful in prayer.

This done, a short sermon was then given, a brief court held, and Muhammed went to any one of the houses of his harem where all womenfolk were assembled, and talked to them till the last prayer of the night, when he retired to solitary prayer and rest.

He slept for only a few hours, then rose and prayed and meditated, and used to go to bed again for a brief time, rising again to pray and to bed till dawn when the day's work began.

The energy of the man was extraordinary, he never complained of fatigue, never asked for food till it was brought, never lost his temper: *'for anger is thy greatest enemy,'* he used to say.

Reverting to his durbars and meetings, it is significant that he destroyed the emphasis on dignity and rank, and instilled equality amongst the Moslems; to the extent that when strangers used to come to the durbar they had to ask as to which was Muhammed. But despite this, there was a distinct etiquette of the meeting. No one could ask anything while he was standing: no interruptions were permitted.

MUHAMMED: THE PROPHET

On one occasion an uncouth Badu of the desert barged in, and in a loud voice asked the Prophet as to when will be the Last Day of the world.

As the Prophet was engaged in answering the question of someone else, he did not reply. The son of the desert insisted, and called out more loudly than before for an answer. Again the Prophet ignored him for he had not completed his reply to the other man: eventually he turned to the Badu:

> *'The Last day of the world shall be,'* said the Prophet, *'when the custodians will not respect their trust!'*

The man of the tent-dwellers did not understand as to what that meant:

> *'it means,'* enlightened the Prophet, *'a time when the government of the people will go into incompetent hands, and justice has left the world.'*

It was on a particularly hot day when the government of the Moslems gathered in the quadrangle of the Mosque at Medina, awaiting the Prophet.

In the meantime the gathering of the Faithful was split up into two sections: one section deliberated on the pure ethical questions of the creed, and the other, sitting under another tree, were grappling with some practical points.

> *'I am a practical man,'*

said the Prophet upon entering, as he joined the latter section:

> *'for I have been sent to show to the people how to live as God wishes them to live.'*

The courtesy of Muhammed, of course, has become a proverb; or *Ikhlaqay Muhammedi,* the courtliness of the Prophet, is still an expression common amongst the races of the East.

He is never reported to have said Nay to anyone. He never

THE HOME LIFE OF THE PROPHET

contradicted anybody unless it was opposed to the Koranic laws, never did he get wroth with any man because of a personal affront.

He paid equal regard to the humblest and the richest, he would turn away his face when anyone spoke ought but good of a person.

And above all, his pertinacity was *par excellence*, and this has been proved over and again in every walk of his life both in peace and war, in matters of state or in his family life.

He was slow to arrive at a decision, but once whatever was resolved, he meant to carry through in the face of all opposition and even persecution, as we have noted in his career.

He had a charming way in giving practical lessons to people; as for instance, when someone came to him complaining of extreme poverty and sought alms.

The Prophet asked him whether he had any belongings at all:

> '*Belongings, forsooth,*' replied the man, '*I have only a bowl and a cot, and that is all I possess.*'

He was commanded to bring the cot and the bowl, which Muhammed auctioned for a small sum.

> '*Take half of this money to thy children, and with the other half buy a rope and an axe, go into the country and gather wood and sell it.*'

After a time, the man presented himself before the Prophet, and showed his good earning.

> '*Verily,*' said Muhammed, '*thou art blessed, for thou hast worked and earned by the sweat of thy brow: for Allah does not love begging.*'

Here is a practical lesson for you, if you want any.

MUHAMMED: THE PROPHET

Regarding his strong sense of justice, we have instances to show that once, when laying the law against theft, a woman of Arab aristocracy was charged, he said that even if his own daughter committed the crime she would be punished like a common criminal: in the eyes of Allah all are equal, and none so pleasing as he who abides by the law.

Another point about Muhammed which is apt to be forgotten is that he left an indelible mark upon the history of mankind for one particular reason, that alone distinguishes him from others.

Quite apart from the fact that he is acknowledged as a Prophet, even as a personality, as a general, as a statesman, a mercheant, a father and a husband, he has created a pattern infinitely superior to anything known in the story of man.

And that is in terms of his personal influence, his personality.

In this particular, Muhammed has no rival, for within his own lifetime people so far apart as Basra and Mecca, Medina and the cities of Yemen were behaving, acting, even thinking in the way Muhammed did.

It is shown by the fact that he transformed a pagan people, and such inveterate warriors as the Qureish, into a humble peace-loving people—and to act according to the injunction of God to the Prophet is possible only for a man whose claim for the mastery of the world is indisputable.

His birth was shrouded in no mystery: from a human father he was born, he lived an ordinary life, and yet lived to deliver his people from the slough and degradation, all within ten years.

This is a task which staggers the imagination.

If all of that does not mean a personality without a compeer, what else is it?

If this did not mean that his message had a more than

THE HOME LIFE OF THE PROPHET

ordinary potency, how would one account for the progress, such rapid and firm progress, of the law of Allah?—proclaimed in as wondrous language as the *Koran*, regarding which, even the pagan poet-laureates declared:

> *La Kalamul Bashar—'these are not the words of a human being.'*

Let us also not lose sight of the fact that it is at once the pride and glory of Muhammed's message, that his religion is a practical religion, a law consistent with the life of the world— for to withdraw one's hands from worldly activities is strictly forbidden, the progress of Society and participation in it is enjoined upon:

> *'to be in the world and not of it,'*

is the idea; as therein is unfolded the beauty of the creation, and divine attributes of Allah himself,—for:

> *There is a tongue in every leaf*
> *A voice in every rill,*
> *A voice that speaketh everywhere,*
> *In flood and fair, through earth and air,*
> *A voice that's never still*

And the testament of the guiding of humanity was revealed to the Prophet:

> *'The servants of the Merciful are they that walk upon the earth gently, and when the ignorant speak to them, they speak; Peace! They that spend the night in worship .... they that spend neither profusely nor niggardly .... and slay not a soul that God hath forbidden ..... and commit not fornication .... they that bear not witness to that which is false; and when they pass by vain sport, they pass it by unconcernedly ....'*

This, Muhammed left to humanity: and though the candle may have been blown out, the light remains.

Chapter 24

THE PROPHET: THE LAST PHASE

The last year of the Prophet's life and Ministry had now dawned, it was the 10th of Hijra, 632 of the Christian Calendar, for the Revelation came to him in the *Koran*:

> 'When there comes the help of Allah and the victory (of Mecca), and you see men entering the religion of Allah in companies; then celebrate the praise of your Lord, and ask His forgiveness, surely He is oft-returning (to mercy).'

North and south, east and west, Allah's message had been conveyed, and the whole of Arabia was now at the feet of the Prophet. His original work was finished, his mission, and Muhammed, now so forewarned about his journey to a different world, made preparations to perform the pilgrimage to Mecca as the indisputed head of the Moslem Church, the only Church that mattered in Arabia.

It was necessary to perform this pilgrimage, the last pilgrimage as it turned out to be, of Muhammed's life; for the various ceremonies which the master performed, the faithful should learn by first-hand knowledge, as well as the several injunctions and practices of the pilgrimage, a pattern which remains intact up to this day nearly fifteen hundred years after him.

With him now, more than a hundred thousand pilgrims performed the devolutions, and the rites, at Mecca and the regions encompassing it.

MUHAMMED: THE PROPHET

In the sun-smitten plains and hills at Arafa a concourse of humanity awaited his final sermon. From his camel he called the faithful to hear him:

> *'All the practices of paganism are now trampled under my feet,'* he lifted his voice, *'the Arab and non-Arab are equal; Adam was the father of all, and Adam was built of earth.*
>
> *The Moslems are brothers, equal in status; give the same food and dress to your slaves as you yourself use.*
>
> *None shall remember and carry on the blood feuds of yore;*
>
> *All that sum which was charged as interest on loans is condemned and unlawful;*
>
> *Fear God in your treatment towards women, for the right of women is just as great upon you as your right upon women.*
>
> *I leave the Book, the Koran for you; hold fast to it or you shall go astray;*
>
> *Give the due to whom due is to be given in heritage;*
>
> *Adultery should be punished by stoning the person;*
>
> *A son who disavows his father is accursed;*
>
> *Pay your debts; a loaned article is to be returned; the guarantor is to be held responsible for what he guarantees.'*

Then he paused, and asked, what would they say to God about him if that enquiry were made.

All replied that they shall attest that Muhammed had conveyed Allah's commands to them; the Prophet held up his finger:

> *'O! Allah, be a witness to what they have said,'*

he concluded.

THE PROPHET: THE LAST PHASE

After this long sermon, other shorter addresses were given by the Prophet during this, his last pilgrimage; as, for instance, when saying good-bye to the faithful, he said:

> *'Learn all you require regarding the pilgrimage from me, for this is probably my last pilgrimage.*
>
> *Do not adopt your pre-Islamic habits, and begin to strike at each other's necks after I go; for you will have to face Allah one day who shall require you to answer for your sins.*
>
> *The man who commits a sin, he alone is responsible for it, not the son for his father, and a father for the deeds of his son.*
>
> *Regarding the government, let me emphasise:'*

added the Prophet, intending to kill the demon of colour and race prejudice,

> *'Let me say that even if the blackest of all slaves is your officer or ruler, and he conducts your affairs according to the Book of God, then obey him.*
>
> *Five times daily you should pray,*
> *keep the fast during the month of fasting,*
> *and obey the Commandments,*
> *so that you may be the accepted ones.'*

Then again, he asked whether he had conveyed God's message, and, receiving a reply in the affirmative, called to Allah to be a witness to it: after that he enjoined upon those present to convey his words to those who were not present there at the moment.

So the farewell pilgrimage ended, and the Prophet was once again in Medina.

After the pilgrimage, in the 11th year of Hijra, A.D. 632, the physical frailty of Muhammed was making itself felt. The poison given to him at Khaiber was again distressing the Prophet; and yet, even within a few days of his death, he continued to lead the faithful in prayer.

Having said good-bye to his flock at Mecca, it was always a great thought to him that he had not prayed for the dead who had fallen at the battle of Ohud; and to that grave he now bent his steps.

There, standing beside the grave of his brave and faithful servants, he prayed, and with such earnestness that although they were now buried for eight long years, one would have believed that he was in mourning for someone who had just died.

On the 18th or 19th of the Moslem month of Safar, 11th Hijra, the Prophet went to the graveyards of the Moslems, and felt somewhat indisposed upon his return.

For five days his illness was hardly noticed, but on the sixth day he was decidedly worse, and stayed in the house of his wife Ayesha—indeed, he had become so weak that he could hardly walk, for Ali and Abbas had to help him to the harem.

Repeatedly now, he endeavoured to go to the mosque in order to lead the prayer, and just as frequently fainted, till Abu Bakr was commanded to take his place at the head of the faithful at worship. The illness took a serious turn: and he asked for paper and a pen to have his wishes recorded, the first being that no pagans should be allowed quarter in Arabia, the other that the envoy of foreign nations should be received with the same respect and should be given the same hospitality as was accorded to them during his time.

The third wish could not be recorded: but over and over again he repeated:

THE PROPHET: THE LAST PHASE

> *'hold to the Koran, consider it your way to righteousness, goodwill and peace . . .'*

Again and again he said that those are accursed who worshipped the graves of their prophets, as the last injunction was that in the religion of Islam, nothing is worthy of worship save the One God: and that the Prophet was just one like unto them, a mere man, a son of Adam, made of clay and no part of divinity; though a messenger of Allah's commandments. He was anxious that men should not fall to the error of grave worship.

The morning on which Muhammed was to die, he pulled aside the curtain of his apartment, and watched the worshippers at the prayer of the dawn, bending and swaying to the Allah Whose words he had come to announce; and the Prophet felt satisfied, his life work had been fulfilled, what more does any man wish for, what more can any man have?

Thenceforward he began to sink rapidly, in the afternoon any moment appeared to be his last, he recited:

> *'there is now none so great a friend as He,'*

and with this on his lips the Prophet of Allah died.

Men could not believe that such a personality was just as frail as any man in the face of death, none thought him really dead: a man with such a power over the hearts of men could not, would not bow to death, but death in Islam is considered a call, a command of One who has made all, and His call, when it comes, is to be obeyed. To this call, who would the more readily respond than the Messenger of God himself?

To a bewildered people; Abu Bakr announced the sad news, and emphasised the fact that the Prophet was a human being subject to the laws of life and death like any earthborn, and that he had considered himself as such, a Prophet though he undoubtedly was.

MUHAMMED: THE PROPHET

The dead body was washed by Ali and others in the small room where he died in Ayesha's house.

They lowered him in his grave: thus the spirit of the great Prophet took flight to the *'Blessed companionship on high'* on the 1st of Rabil, about the 28th May, 632 of the Christian era.

Abu Bakr, one of four of his great Companions was elected as the leader of the Faithful: the other three *Khulafar Rashidin* or the Commander of the Faithful, after Abu Bakr, were Omar, Osman, and Ali.

'From Him we come and to Him we return.'

Chapter 25

THE CARDINAL PRACTICES OF ISLAM

The four cardinal practices of the Moslem religion are Prayer, Charity, Pilgrimage and Fasting.

Whereas the Semitic precursors of Islam possessed no definite formulae for intercession, Muhammed was the first of the race to demonstrate the value of prayer as a means of moral elevation and purification of heart. As the *Koran* has it:

> *'Rehearse that which hath been revealed unto thee of the Book, and be constant at prayer, for prayer preserveth from crimes and from that which is blameable; and the remembering of God is surely a most sacred duty.'*

As even a non-Moslem scholar has said, the temples of Islam are not made with hands, and its ceremonies can be performed anywhere upon God's earth.

At home or abroad, the Moslem, at the prescribed hour, approaches his Maker in brief supplication. Prayer is not a matter for the intervention of priests, but for each individual human spirit. The Islamic concept of prayer embraces supplication five times a day, and, without understanding, is held to be of no avail.

Certain rites and ceremonies accompany the due observance of prayer, yet these are all regarded as subsidiary to piety and contriteness of heart.

Cleanliness is a necessary preliminary to communing with Allah, hence the rites of lustration, yet mere physical purity is not held as implying true devotion.

He who prays turns his face toward Mecca as being the Centre where the Faith had its birth.

Still, Moslem prayer possesses its own peculiar symbolism. Among the various gesticulations, motions and signs which a Moslem makes when praying, several of the more outstanding may be noted:

In the first place he raises the hands and touches the lobes of the ears, then folds the hands across the abdomen or lets them drop by the sides. This implies that the worshipper raises his hands from worldly affairs, and presents himself as a slave of Allah, the folding of the hands representing a slave's attitude.

Even to-day in Oriental Court circles, ministers and envoys adopt this attitude before the ruler, and at durbars, the highest officials fold their arms in the presence of Kings.

In the second phase of prayer, the Moslem worshipper stands and directs his gaze on the ground, to signify that he has been moulded from the earth to which he shall return.

He recites the prayer of thanksgiving to Allah.

Whilst reciting this, the attitude of mind prescribed is one of humility before one's Creator.

The supplicant then bends at right angles from the waist and recites the praises of Allah.

Then he prostrates himself and touches the ground with his forehead and recites the formula praising God.

The whole physical intention is opposite to that displayed by a man who stands erect, throwing back his body, his chest thrust forward; which is the attitude of defiance, the other being the idea to bend so definitely that the impression of humility is conveyed.

Charity is a marked feature of the Islamic faith.

THE CARDINAL PRACTICES OF ISLAM

By Moslem law, everyone who can afford it is bound to contribute part of his possessions for the upkeep of the poor of the community.

This was usually one part in forty, or two and a half percent of all goods or profits on trade or business. But alms are due only when the property amounts to a certain value and has been in the possession of the owner for at least a year, nor, it is noticeable, are any alms due from cattle.

At the end of the month of Ramadan, the month of fasting and on the day of Id-ul-Fitr, which celebrates the conclusion of the Moslem period of fasting, the head of the family has to give away in alms a measure of wheat, barley, dates, raisins, rice, or any other grain, or the value of the same, for himself and for every member of his family and for each guest who breaks his fast or sleeps in his dwelling during the month.

Those who receive the alms are specially indicated by the practice of the Prophet himself.

They are the indigent, or beggars, those who help in the collection and distribution of the alms, slaves desirous of buying their freedom who have not the wherewithal to do so, debtors who cannot pay their debts, a particularly merciful dispensation. Pilgrims and strangers were also included among those in receipt of alms.

General charity is also inculcated by the *Koran* in terms the most pressing.

Whereas fasting among most of the nations of antiquity was a matter more of penitence than abstinence or mortification, the institution of fasting in Islam has the definite object of encouraging spirituality through self-denial.

Useless and unnecessary asceticism or mortification of the flesh is severely forbidden, the general intention being rather a chastening of the spirit by imposing a restraint upon the body.

MUHAMMED: THE PROPHET

Fasting is not permitted to the sick, the weakly, the pilgrim, the student or the soldier, or to women in poor health.

The rule as to fasting, given in the *Koran*, is as follows:

> *'O ye that have believed, a fast is ordained to you, that ye may practise piety, a fast of a computed number of days. But he among you who shall be ailing, or on a journey, shall fast an equal number of other days. And they that are able to keep it and do not, shall make atonement by maintaining a poor man. But if ye fast, it will be better for you if ye comprehend. God willeth that which is easy for you.'*

It may perhaps be said that the idea of pilgrimage was incorporated, in the Moslem religion, with the very particular object of bringing together Moslems from all parts of the world at one definite centre.

The Prophet recognised that there were some annual reunions not prescribed, that the more distant Moslem communities might readily fall into sectarianism and schismatic tendencies, and, as this was to be avoided at all costs, the *Koran* emphasised and instituted the yearly pilgrimage to the shrine of the Kaaba.

This wise provision has done more than any other to cultivate among the various Moslem sects and nationalities a spirit of general brotherhood.

At Mecca, men foregather from all the ends of the Moslem earth, and, in a spirit of the utmost piety, behold those scenes where were enacted the drama of the Prophet's early struggles and his latter triumph, and consider among these sacred surroundings, the institutions which he gave to humanity in his inspired words.

Each year, in the religious capital of Islam, is relumed the spark of that perfervid piety which glows in the hearts of the Moslems.

THE CARDINAL PRACTICES OF ISLAM

Even now, after more than a thousand years of Islamic history, many caravans from Jeddah journey Meccaward.

With head shaven and wearing only one white sheet as the pilgrim's costume, the pilgrim nestles down in his mat-covered litter which is tied on the back of his camel, the rocking movement to and fro of the litter keeping time with the recitation of the names of Allah.

'I am in Thy Presence, O, the Mighty,'

one prays and the tongue seems to cling to the roof of one's mouth with thirst, but imbued with an intense feeling of religious fervour, the pilgrim continues:

'lead me in Thine own way, O, Allah, as I approach Thy Throne'

and the ship of the desert moves on with his fellows, munching all the time, quite oblivious to the scorching heat that beats upon the brown rocks, painting everything now violet, now red, now grey.

An indescribable feeling comes upon the pilgrim on seeing the two whitewashed pillars which stand some three miles outside the city of Mecca, to mark the inviolable sanctuary of Islam, within which no blood must be shed; and all of a sudden, in the lap of encircling blown-grey hills, appears Mecca.

Its buildings stand in the midst of a distant violet haze, and a huge cry of prayer from the thousands of the faithful lifts to the skies.

Then they plunge into silence, a silence of reverence; some prostrating, others kneeling and lifting their tear-dimmed eyes to the city towards which they have prayed five times a day all their lives, as their ancestors had done for over a thousand years of Islamic history.

MUHAMMED: THE PROPHET

Wearing the regulation costume, they wait in the sullen heat while the sun beats down on their shaven head, till room is found to approach the holy precincts.

Thousands of pilgrims pace the Harem-Sharief, or the Great Mosque, waiting to kiss the mystic Black Stone, which, set in silver, is built in a wall of a small room covered by the Carpet.

Around this stucture a white marble floor is laid, on which the faithful walk as they encircle the Kaaba seven times on entering the Mosque.

In the midst of this vast quadrangle of some 280 paces long and eighty paces broad, surrounded as it is by the double arches of the colonnades, stands the Kaaba, where the bending and swaying of the worshippers, the loud recitations of the faithful as they face the heart of the Mosque or cling to the curtains of the mystic Kaaba, appears to the pilgrim a world of its own.

For ten days or so our world-congregation is engaged in prayer in Mecca. From early morning till late at night there is nothing but one round of prayer and meditation. There is no lighter side to the life in Mecca.

From the point of view of strict Islamic injunction there should be nothing but that spirit in the city, because this exclusiveness of the atmosphere is considered to bring out the real essence of the faith, the more so to its follower in contrast to what he might have used in other countries prior to his coming to the pilgrimage.

Only in the evenings, when the heat of the sun abates a little, yet the rocks are warm with the day's heat, can one walk in the many covered bazaars and examine those wonderful silks and beads that are made in and around Mecca; or climb up the adjoining hills, particularly when the moon rises; then one sees Mecca lying in the hollow as a fairyland of silver, solemn, still,

THE CARDINAL PRACTICES OF ISLAM

mysterious; glowing with no electric lights but tallow candles paling away in the distance. The scene robs one of the fatigue of that stiff climb.

Then, many more religious ceremonies claim the attention of the faithful to the termination of the pilgrimage.

And in the gloaming, which quickly is swallowed up by the darkness of the desert, the pilgrim caravan moves back to the shore.

Men and women, all pilgrims, appear to be dazed, they seem to drop suddenly into a vacuum completely cut off from all life of moving humanity.

A joy fills their hearts for having performed the holiest action of Islamic religion. New feelings thrill their minds, and, as the moon hangs like a scimitar over rocky defiles, a thin streak on the pale face of the limitless sands is the pilgrim caravan, as that moving thread of life treks in and out of the desert hills to the shores of the Red Sea at the close of the pilgrimage.

It must not be imagined, as unhappily it too often is, that the pilgrimage to Mecca is undertaken by Moslems because of their own personal desire to gain reflected glory from a journey to the sacred precincts, for before he is deemed worthy of pilgrimage, a Moslem must have proved to his co-religionists that he is fitted for such an honour.

Several conditions are laid down which are well recognised throughout Islam as being essential to the character of a pilgrim.

He must be a man of ripe judgement and intelligence, he must undertake the journey of his own free will. He should possess sufficient means to carry him in comfort to Mecca and to pay for his subsistence there, and he must leave sufficient wherewithal to support his family during his absence.

Again, the journey must be practicable, which means that he may be placed in some part of the world from whence he may find it too difficult to make his way to the Holy City.

From these considerations, the wise and spiritual character of Islamic religious law may readily be gathered, as will the wonderful adaptability of its precepts to all ages and nations, its reasonable and logical nature, and its unfriendliness to anything that savours of the mysterious, or of sentimental ignorance.

It is indeed a most coherent body of doctrine dealing with primal truth—a corpus of religious law drawn from the natural instinct of humanity toward belief in the Divine.

Thus, it is in accordance not only with the earliest faith of Man, but with his later strivings for enlightenment.

It is, indeed, not only a link between the Old world-religion and the New, but, through its natural qualities, it constitutes a basic indication of true and unadulterated faith throughout the ages.

It may indeed be said to be the world's most characteristic effort towards the formation of a religion in which all men may find agreement. In its straightforward teachings, there is nothing of dubiety. Its tenets are capable of expansion in the light of modern development, its charity is unstrained, and it cannot be perverted unless by ignorance or bigotry.

The fundamental nature of Islam is well illustrated by its agreement with those doctrines which have, at different periods of the world's history, governed human conduct.

It lays down the belief that men will be judged by their works alone, that omnipotent Providence is loving and merciful, and that patience and resignation are essential to the loyal man.

It inspires meticulous reference to conscience, a scrupulous study of motive, and a strict reliance upon the assistance of God in all human affairs.

THE CARDINAL PRACTICES OF ISLAM

No religion has so well gauged human character, or is so practically designed to instruct its weakness, and this is in itself perhaps the best criterion of the Moslem faith—in that it supplies a certain guide to conduct in the affairs of everyday life, inculcating a large charity, self-denial and a spirit of mercifulness.

Nor, although rational in the extreme, is it lacking in the most lofty idealism.

Nevertheless it deals with the real and the actual, its strict intention being the elevation of humanity to the ideals of perfection. In so doing, it realises that the nature of man is frail and it seeks to refine him from his imperfection by the inculcation of brotherliness, forgiveness and benevolence.

Particularly does the doctrine of Islam trend to a state of human benevolence apart from false sentiment. It must be an active principle of life.

The Moslem is taught to pardon his enemies and to refrain from strife, to deal with all men justly, to glory in right-doing, right-thinking, and right-speaking, and to regard all men as equal in the sight of God.

Islam is indeed a path to be trodden, a life to be lived, and however its ancient ideals may have become shadowed or occluded, by unworthy ones, like those of other religions, for instance by the mists of time and controversy, they still remain a clear and inspired digest and commandment as to the manner in which man should deal with his fellow man.

It has been well said that an approach to the All-Perfect is the essential principle of Islam.

The charge so often brought against Islam, that it is narrow in its prohibitions and commandments, might be brought against any of the higher types of Religion, and such a charge fails miserably when it is recalled that unless a definite and well-defined path be followed, and too wide an interpretation be eschewed, the entire spirit of religion is stultified and rendered nugatory.

Moral ideas, unless expressed in positive form, rendered precise, and of definite sanction, are obviously useless to men in any state of society: barbarous or civilised.

It is not the higher ethics of a faith which appeals so much to human sentiment, when all is said, as those provisions which affect the daily lives of individuals.

And indeed, it is only in virtue of the strictest accordance of the laws and rules of a faith with common morality, that it can hope, through its professors, to rise to the heights of spiritual excellence.

That the seed of spirituality must be implanted in soil of pious everyday duty was perceived by the Prophet more keenly than by any great religious teacher in the history of man.

Chapter 26

SLAVERY AND MARRIAGE IN ISLAM

Let us now give some consideration to the question of personal and individual right in the sphere of Islamic Law.

Opinion alien to it has invariably, but ignorantly, pretended to discover in the legal code of Islam a callous indifference to the rights of the individual, and the jurists of systems unfriendly to Islam have pointed triumphantly to the position of slaves and women among the followers of the Prophet.

But those who are deeply acquainted with Moslem law are well aware that its critics could scarcely have selected for their attack a more just and reasonable set of legal maxims than those which deal with the position of the slave or the woman in the Moslem code.

In the first place, slavery is by no means restricted to the Moslem world, in which nowadays it is so extremely rare as to be confined only to peoples of the lowest cultus in human advancement.

It should be particularly borne in mind by Christian apologists that their own creed raised no protest against slavery, and defined no rule for its abolition. In short, none of the older religions did so, and in this respect none can cast a stone at the other.

Indeed, Christianity enjoined on the slave a submissive character in accordance with that spirit of humility which inspires its earliest attitude to social affairs in general.

MUHAMMED: THE PROPHET

But the equality which Islam almost immediately professed on its institution, soon became a disintegrating force, striking at the roots of serfdom.

Its insistence that all men, without distinction of race or colour, are equal in the sight of God, was among the first principles of human freedom to take root in any country, and it was only the most ancient institution of chattel-hood among the nations which surrounded the early Moslems which prevented it from being swept away entirely in Muhammed's own time. This, in the circumstances, however, could scarcely have been expected, nevertheless the precept stood and still stands.

On countless occasions the Prophet entreated his co-religionists to free slaves, pointing out to them how acceptable was the act to Providence.

One of the penalties which he laid upon sinners was the manumission of slaves, and he laid it down that slaves should be permitted to purchase their freedom by an accumulation of their wages, even stipulating that to gain sufficient means for this purpose they should enjoy a temporary freedom, or that in particular cases, sums should be advanced from public funds to purchase their liberty. Nor were their masters permitted in any way to interfere with such arrangements.

Again, the whole trend of the Islamic system as expressed by Muhammed is most favourable to the good treatment of slaves.

> '*As to your slaves,*'

says the *Koran*,

> '*see that ye feed them as ye feed yourselves, and clothe them as ye clothe yourselves.*'

Slaves are indeed bracketed along with one's relatives, with

SLAVERY AND MARRIAGE IN ISLAM

one's neighbours and fellow-pilgrims, as those who have a special claim to the most considerate treatment.

Furthermore, a misuse of personal power over a slave was regarded as a serious crime which would be avenged by Providence.

Indeed the whole chronicle of Islamic history is eloquent of the fact that slavery among believers was not in any sense comparable to serfdom elsewhere, but was to a great extent merely nominal, and all the evidence points to the fact that the so-called slave in Islamic society was merely a humble member of the family rather than a human chattel.

Fugitive slaves, on reaching Islamic territory, were at once given their liberty. The child of a free man and a slave woman was born free among the ancient Moslems while his mother regained her liberty at the death of her husband.

The amount of work, also, which a slave might perform was carefully graded, and slaves were never addressed as such, but as *'young man'* or *'young woman.'* Nor was it permitted that slaves who were relatives should be separated from one another.

Islamic history is full of illustrations of the manner in which slaves might rise to high positions of trust or government.

Zaid, formerly a slave of the Prophet, became a General, and the founder of the Moslem Empire in India, Kutb ud-din, King of Delhi, had been a slave. Moslem slaves have risen to royal power as no Christian serf has ever done.

Captives taken in war were held in bondage until ransomed, but slave-hunting and slave-dealing were utterly condemned, the slave-dealer being regarded as an outcast.

If, anywhere in Islam, slavery has flourished, it is in direct contravention to the injunctions of the Prophet.

MUHAMMED: THE PROPHET

Also, the position of women in Islam has given rise to the most extraordinary misapprehensions among non-Islamic writers and thinkers.

Among all the ancient nations of the East, polygamy was a recognised institution.

In times past, constant war kept down the male population and the only manner in which it was possible to provide for a preponderating number of women was by marrying several of them to one husband. The royal acceptance of the custom, too, gave it a popular sanction. Even among the ancient Greeks, polygamy was common, and the married woman was more or less a chattel.

It is a common and an ignorant error among the critics of Islam to believe that the Prophet adopted polygamy or in any way legalised it.

Many non-Moslem writers seem to labour under the impression that Muhammed actually introduced polygamy. The folly of such a statement is extreme.

The real truth is that the founder of the Islamic religion found polygamy practised, not only among his own people, but among the surrounding nations which environed them.

Indeed, the immorality which prevailed among the Arab and Persian peoples in the days of the Prophet's youth was so rampant that no law of marriage was recognised.

This state of things the Prophet set himself to alter fundamentally, and that he succeeded in doing so is agreed upon by all students of Islamic Law.

As an example of his reforms, he found that a man's wives might be inherited by his son.

This condition he absolutely forbade, as he did that other abominable practice of his Arab fellow-countrymen, who were

SLAVERY AND MARRIAGE IN ISLAM

prone to destroy their female children at birth, and which he prohibited under the severest penalties.

The position of woman during Muhammed's youth was indeed so utterly abject that it is difficult for any modern person to comprehend it. She was indeed regarded as a necessary evil, and in some cases even as a fiend from Eblis, introduced into the world as the spirit of evil for the torment of mankind.

This view the Prophet set himself deliberately to combat.

One of the essential teachings of his creed was respect for women. He prohibited the custom of temporary marriage, and secured to women legal rights and privileges which they had not hitherto possessed.

So far as the holding of property was concerned he placed them on an equal footing with men.

He limited the number of wives a man might take to four, but it is too frequently forgotten that that particular ordinance was accompanied by a proviso which declares that if a man cannot deal equitably and justly with all of these, he shall marry only one.

The word *'equitably'* here applies to affection as well as to the gift of worldly goods, and, as this is a moral impossibility, it must be obvious that the Prophet's prescription has actually the character of a prohibition, in which light, indeed, it is regarded by all the great doctors of Islamic Law.

The principles of the Prophet as regards the relationship between the sexes, were, indeed, having regard to the period in which he lived, of a most sweeping and fundamental nature, and modem Islamic practice, realising this, has come to abhor polygamy, which is now regarded as an institution opposed to the teachings of the Prophet.

MUHAMMED: THE PROPHET

Confusion, too, has arisen through the writings of later Islamic scholiasts, who, to please capricious rulers, have defined the Prophet's law according to their vicious tastes, putting their own interpretations upon the simple fact.

As regards the whole question, Islam is indeed going through precisely the same phase as did the nations of the West. But the feeling against polygamy, as a social vice at least, is steadily growing among the more advanced Moslem communities. In Persia, according to a good authority, only two percent of the population, and in India only five percent, are polygamous.

The oft-repeated statement that the Prophet himself was a convinced polygamist is capable of absolute disproof.

Until the fifty-first year of his age he had but one wife, Khadija, and it was only on her death that he took any others.

These subsequent marriages, in almost every particular instance, were dictated by strict political necessity and tribal jealousy, and the statement that Muhammed was a libertine is reduced by the proofs of history to an absurd fiction.

Again and again did the Prophet do his utmost to evade such marriages, but popular opinion was so powerfully in their favour that he might not escape them without courting the most serious disaster to the whole superstructure and system of Law and Religion which he had so laboriously striven to raise.

People who revere the memories of the great Hebrew patriarchs, polygamists one and all, should at least bear in mind the historic value and significance of the Prophet's several alliances, and consider how much he was hampered by the spirit of his time.

He could not efface existing social institutions, and as it has been well said, he did his best to implant in the hearts of his followers,

> 'principles which would, when the time was ripe for it'

work out the abolition of temporal necessities.

As regards divorce in Islam, Muhammed was among the first to place this on a fair and reasonable basis.

Before his time, the power of divorce among the Arabs was unlimited. This evil the Prophet set himself to uproot, saying that nothing more displeased God than divorce. He even allowed, to divorced people,

> *'three distinct and separate periods within which they might endeavour to become reconciled and resume their conjugal relationship,'*

and advised settlement by means of arbiters between the parties.

He restrained the power of divorce possessed by the husband, and gave to the wife the right of obtaining a separation on reasonable grounds. To him:

> *'divorce was the most detestable before God of all permitted things, destroying the marriage state and interfering with the proper upbringing of children.'*

As regards union with female slaves, the Prophet permitted this through marriage alone, denouncing any other system of union and indeed forbidding it.

So far as the seclusion of females is concerned, this provision was directed with the specific intention of striking a blow at the awful immorality which prevailed in his own times.

But there is nothing in Islamic law which tends to the perpetuation of the custom. Indeed the females of the Prophet's own household enjoyed the greatest liberty.

Many historians of insight have advanced the theory which is, indeed, no theory at all, but a well established truth, that the spirit of chivalry, far from having its inception on European

MUHAMMED: THE PROPHET

soil, was in fact introduced by the Islamic Moors of Spain—a statement which all students of early Spanish Literature will find in agreement with their researches.

The Wars of the Crusades, also, by bringing Europeans into touch with Islamic refinement, did much to quicken the process; and no unprejudiced European writer or thinker will honestly admit that the Islamic system lowered the status of womankind.

It was only the day before yesterday that a married woman in England possessed no rights independently of her husband, whereas this privilege has been enjoyed by Moslem women for centuries.

Chapter 27

THE INTERNATIONAL SPIRIT OF ISLAM

The existence of the Islamic religion as a practical medium for humanist and international relationship and development has not received the consideration it merits.

The world's thinkers and publicists have failed to recognize those of its tenets which trend toward international and fraternal relationships, and profess to see in it nothing more than an antiquated system of theism and rigid legal dogma having no tendency whatever to modern ideas of internationalism.

Yet Islam was the first code actually to profess the brotherhood of man, and it still remains one of the most potent forces possible for achieving this great ideal in a practical manner, were it employed for the purpose.

Even at its inception the Islamic faith expressed its civilising and fraternal sentiments by checking the pagan licentiousness of the pre-Islamic Arabs, and altering the tribal habits of the vice-ridden, warring and scattered clans of Arabia.

Muhammed was, indeed, pre-eminently a practical prophet, who inculcated in his followers a profound feeling for peace, nor are any of the campaigns in which they were subsequently engaged traceable to his personal influence. He made war on none, and on numerous occasions expressed abhorrence of armed strife.

So it is both inaccurate and misleading to state that the

MUHAMMED: THE PROPHET

Islamic faith was spread by the sword or by conquest.

Any wars in which its religionists were engaged during the lifetime of the Prophet were deliberately forced upon them for sectarian purposes, as a faithful study of history reveals.

The cardinal spirit of the Prophet's mission was that he was the first great religious leader to preach the equality of man.

He laid it down that all Moslems were brothers before the eyes of Allah, with no distinction of rank or wealth. Nor is race any barrier to absolute religious equality among Moslems.

Indeed the primary and lasting power of the Prophet's mission is that he led men out of the narrow grooves of tribalism and nationalism to the wider vistas of internationalism, which he regarded as a powerful instrument for world peace.

What it has taken the Christian West nearly two thousand years to recognise, as evinced in one degree or another by the ideal of the League of Nations or even in the Communism of Russia, was already expressed by Islam nearly fifteen hundred years ago and practised in the maintenance of peace between the Islamic peoples.

Any man, no matter of what racial origin, who becomes a Moslem, at once breaks down the racial barriers betwixt himself and all other Moslems.

Whether he be a Chinese, a Negro, an Indian, an Afghan or an Arab, he is no longer regarded by his brother Moslems as a member of that race, but as a Moslem pure and simple.

It was, indeed, this specifically human appeal which Muhammed regarded as among the most powerful civilising agencies associated with his ideal.

Nor has personal rank or social condition any sanction in the Moslem world, so far as religious equality is concerned.

In the mosque, a beggar and a king may stand at prayer in

THE INTERNATIONAL SPIRIT OF ISLAM

the same row without offence. The house of prayer is free to all at any time, and is sacrosanct in that a man may take refuge there without fear of being injured by his enemy within its precincts.

Moreover, in the Islamic Church, one does not pay for accommodation, as in other religious bodies. Religion in Islam is regarded as the free right of all, and is maintained by the offerings of the pious according to their own abilities.

The equality of man, therefore, was established for the first time in the history of humanity by the preaching of Islam, the tenets of which, by reference to its writings, may be discovered as enshrining the noblest ideal of human fraternalism ever excogitated—a fraternalism as practical in action as it is beautiful in essence.

Is it not then possible for the world to discern in Islam an agency for the furtherance of that spirit of Intentional amity which is the one hope of humanity?

Is it not eloquent of that very essence of Internationalism which good men of all races perceive must be the grand human aim, if peace and prosperity are to be achieved at last in a weary and strife-sodden world? To seek for such a spirit in the writings of Islam is to discover expressions of the most lofty international ideals on nearly every page.

Who can be in doubt that a perverted sense of nationalism must in the end lead its protagonists to war?

Nationalism unchecked is as much a disease as a violent fever which ends in mental instability; it is an intoxication rushing through the national bloodstream which cannot but eventuate in collision with some neighbouring community similarly afflicted with racial pride.

But from the beginning Islam was regarded, not only by its founder, but by his contemporaries, as a new democracy which held out hope of international accord to all the races of the world.

That it has been stigmatized as a code propagated and upheld by the sword is a profound misreading of history. The wars of the Moslems were inspired almost wholly by the necessity for self-preservation, and had they not thus defended themselves they would speedily have been decimated by relentless enemies.

But Muhammed's ideal of internationalism was founded on the basis that nations, like individuals, must recognise a standard of responsibility and honour.

There cannot, indeed, be one standard for the individual and another for the nation, for as individuals go to compose a nation, so nations compose humanity, and their obligations to one another cannot differ in essence from those laid down for the proper performance of the personal code of good faith.

The spirit of Islam is, in a word, opposed to racial or national isolation and exclusiveness. No creed so well or so charitably insists upon the principles of racial equality.

> 'Islam,' says Hallam, 'offered its religion, but never enforced it; and the acceptance of that religion conferred co-equal rights with the conquering body, and emancipated the vanquished States from the conditions which every conqueror, since the world existed, up to the period of Muhammed, had invariably imposed.'

Wherever there was Moslem conquest, a mild and pacific rule assuredly followed.

In Spain, the native races were governed with liberality and goodwill, were permitted to retain their own religion, and in many cases to administer their own laws.

The enlightened rule of the Islamic Moors in the peninsula

THE INTERNATIONAL SPIRIT OF ISLAM

is perhaps the best illustration of the truth that the Moslem code is the most tolerant among the world's legal institutions, and is therefore the best fitted to encourage that spirit of internationalism for which mankind so pathetically longs.

The present position of the world reveals that nationalism, so far from being a beneficent influence, is a very mixed good indeed.

More than ever, since World War I, have national propensities been exacerbated and aggravated, and international hatreds incurred. The utter failure of religion to cope with an orgulous racial or national outlook is proven to all men.

When it is recalled that something more than mere good feeling and lip-service is essential to a better international standard, when it is remembered that the modern institutions, which are based on the principle of mere international brotherhood, have egregiously failed of their purpose, it becomes manifest that something more spiritual than mere fraternalism is essential if the gulfs which separate nations and races are ever to be bridged.

For international fraternalism must have a spiritual sanction to be successful in its aims, and this sentiment is nowhere better revealed than in the traditions and writings of the Moslem world, which lays peculiar stress upon the brotherhood of man and supplies the necessary religious and altruistic precepts for its successful application.

Just as Islam makes the way plain for good relationships between individuals, so does it outline the methods by which nations or races can enter into bonds of world-wide fraternity. Indeed that which it posits regarding personal amity is to be regarded as having also international implications.

The first note of international accord struck by the Prophet is to be found in the charter which he granted to the Jews and

MUHAMMED: THE PROPHET

the message he sent to the Christians of Najran. The latter runs as follows:

> 'To the Christians of Najran and the neighbouring territories, the security of God and the pledge of His Prophet are extended for their lives, their religion, and their property—to the present as well as the absent and others besides;
>
> there shall be no interference with the practice of their faith or their observances; nor any change in their rights or privileges;
>
> no bishop shall be removed from his bishopric; nor any monk from his monastery, nor any priest from his priesthood,
>
> and they shall continue to enjoy everything great and small as heretofore;
>
> no image or cross shall be destroyed;
>
> they shall not oppress or be oppressed;
>
> they shall not practise the rights of blood-vengeance as in the Days of Ignorance;
>
> no tithes shall be levied from them, nor shall they be required to furnish provisions for the troops.'

Nowhere in Moslem territory have non-Moslem subjects been precluded from building new places of worship, unless in districts exclusively inhabited by Moslems.

Indeed, in the reign of Mâmûn there were no less than eleven thousand Christian churches in Moslem lands, while Christians, Jews and representatives of other Faiths were included in his Council of Government.

After the conquest of Egypt, the Caliph Omar preserved intact the property of the Christian Churches and continued

THE INTERNATIONAL SPIRIT OF ISLAM

the allowances made by the former Government for the support of the priests.

Illustrations, indeed, abound that wherever the faith of Islam is to be found the feeling of internationalism is strong.

So long as the central doctrine of the Unity of God is recognised and accepted, there is general equality in the eye of the law, which in itself is a code simple—but capable of the greatest development—flexible, and based on a just appreciation of human rights and duty.

Ancient Moslem law stands in sharp contradistinction to that of Feudalism, not only as regards its paternal spirit, but in the latitude it allowed in the relationships between peoples.

The Feudal system nourished a narrow nationalism, which even descended into tribalism on occasion, which viewed its neighbours with a jealous eye and existed on warfare.

And just as nationalism in modern times, in far too many instances, is chauvinistic in spirit and prone to the retention of deep gulfs between the peoples of the world, so is Islam inspired by a freedom of intercourse among peoples.

Throughout the Moslem world the son of Islam may travel unquestioned, assured of brotherhood and hospitality wherever his affairs may take him.

Is not this the spirit of the true internationalism, and can the world today exhibit any parallel with the free and generous intercourse by which Islam has already established a bond among its peoples which no other faith has so far been able to establish?

Those who desire to see the world-wide acceptance of a fraternal internationalism might well direct their closest attention to the methods by which the code and principles of the Prophet established it long ago, in those lands where it still remains unbroken in its purpose.

Chapter 28

THE SPIRIT OF ISLAMIC IDEALS

Perhaps no part of the Islamic ideal is so greatly misunderstood as the particular spirit which underlies and goes to inspire it.

Broadly speaking, it may be asserted that the cardinal truth regarding the spirit of Islamic thought is the sense of unity which it emphasises. This, of course, arises out of the idea of the oneness of Allah, His essential unity, the integral nature of His being.

Allah, according to Moslem belief, was not begotten, was not united in marriage, nor had He any progeny.

He is unique, nor does anything stand between Him and that humanity which is His creation.

This conception of unity is found as a natural sequence in every department of the Islamic religion and polity.

If, for example, we seek for it in the idea of worship we discover it in full measure. Five times a day the world of Islam, wherever it may be situated, addresses itself in prayer to its Creator.

Thus when one Moslem is praying at dawn, at afternoon, at late afternoon, at sunset or at night, he is aware that every Moslem is doing precisely the same, whether it be in China, in India, in Afghanistan, in Arabia or in England. Moreover, he is observing the same particular motions and is reciting his devotions in Arabic, whatever his mother tongue.

MUHAMMED: THE PROPHET

There is thus a universal language in use among Moslems, and by praying at one and the same hour they establish a universality of time. A unity of worship is also respected, and this is associated with a consensus of spiritual thought and impulse.

At the hour of prayer, too, each and every Moslem faces Mecca, so that all the circumstances of prayer embrace that ideal of totality which springs from the belief in one God.

The centralisation of the Moslem world in Mecca, where all races of whatever colour and language tread in pilgrimage, brings about, furthermore, a universality of social thought.

From Mecca men return to practically every part of the world, carrying with them those ideals of brotherhood which transcend race and language and which compose a tremendous force for the quickening of the belief in social equality. Five times a day, master and servant stand side by side in prayer, and this alone suffices to quicken a sense of fraternity unknown in Western society.

These considerations are jointly and severally indications of two express ideals, the oneness of God and the oneness of humanity, for God is one, and so are His creatures. What other system of thought has so definitely established an ideal so expressive of unity?

It is often rashly stated that the nature of the Islamic religion is highly dogmatic, that its institutes are hedged round by hard and fast laws almost of the nature of taboos.

The folly of such a statement is extreme. Dogma signifies unswerving belief without question in the tenets of a religion, and non-Moslems have mistakenly regarded as dogma many Islamic beliefs which are actually not of the nature of dogma at all.

For example, they state that the belief in the existence and

THE SPIRIT OF ISLAMIC IDEALS

the unity of God and in the prophethood of Muhammed and his finality, the trust in an existence after death and in other similar questions, are of the nature of pure dogma. Let us examine these and see if such be the case.

Take, for example, the belief in God.

This is by no means dogmatic, for the whole consensus of intellectual opinion throughout the ages is in favour of the belief in the existence of God or of a First Force. The great majority of thinkers of the first rank are also agreed that the chief attribute of God is unity. Belief in the deity is, indeed, a rational proposition acknowledged by a majority of men in all ages, nor does Islam present this belief as dogma, it merely agrees with the opinion of humanity that the existence of God is proven by instinctive feeling.

So far as the belief in the prophethood of Muhammed is concerned, it will readily be admitted that in all ages and in all countries, prophets and teachers have arisen as guides and torch-bearers to mankind.

Muhammed was not egregious in this respect, and if his prophethood be regarded as implying a dogmatic belief, this must in reason be posited of all other prophets who have ever appeared. Why belief in the abilities of Muhammed as a prophet should be particularly selected as an evidence of the dogmatic character of the Islamic faith, it would indeed be hard to guess.

Nor is the statement of his infallibility more extreme or dogmatic than that concerning the prophets of any other religion. It is certainly laid down that divine revelation terminated with him, because his preaching struck at the very root of ancient superstition, and especially at those gross fetishistic beliefs which personalised the forces of nature.

The sacred writings, revealed through his agency, demonstrate in a practical manner the absurdity of the worship

MUHAMMED: THE PROPHET

of Fire, of the Sun, Moon and Stars, of the Wind, of fetish stones and of the elements of nature.

At the time of the advent of the Prophet, the people of Arabia still persisted in those polytheistic beliefs which the Semitic races had respected for countless centuries, and just as the theistic and unitarian theology of the Hebrew prophets was forcibly addressed to the destruction of the gross superstitions developed by the early and faulty reasoning of man, so Muhammed, in his day, witnessing the degradation to which these beliefs and practices gave rise, boldly denounced their use, and in the course of time, succeeded in extirpating them entirely.

The consequence of this was that men's minds received a fresh impetus towards liberty of thought. Hitherto this had been repressed by the notion that the forces of Nature were in themselves sacred, and must not be brought to the use of man.

For the first time, therefore, these processes of thought were released, which gave man free play with natural forces and which eventuated in the institution of modern Science, with all its liberal opinions as to the utilisation of natural forces wherever they were to be encountered.

It was the destruction by the Prophet of the fear of elemental force, of the superstitions that lay behind the belief in the potency of inanimate things, that in the first place made it possible for men to explore the potentialities of nature.

Before his time, the mere fact that they worshipped these forces and were thus afraid to examine or harness them on behalf of humanity, had made a scientific attitude impossible.

Within the following generation, not one but many schools of scientific effort in thought, in chemistry and in early engineering, arose in various parts of the Islamic world. One has only to point to the extraordinary genius of the Arab and

THE SPIRIT OF ISLAMIC IDEALS

Moorish schools of chemistry, upon which all modern chemical endeavour has been founded, to prove that this was so.

Indeed, it is not too much to say that had it not been for the liberal and modern outlook of the Prophet, the position of Science today would certainly be many generations behind.

The false taboo broken, men at once addressed themselves to the study of the physical nature of those elements they had previously adored, and in so doing unloosed possibilities and marvels beside which the ancient magic supposed to be resident in the subjects of their studies paled into insignificance.

If nothing else suffices to prove the finality of Muhammed's prophethood, the inspiration which he thus set free would demonstrate its divine quality, nor is this of which we speak in any way related to dogma, justified as it is by science.

It is, however, still more irrational to regard the Prophet's belief in the life hereafter as of the nature of a dogma.

More than ever does man now believe in a continuance of life beyond the grave. Man is the outcome of a long and special development, and it is scarcely conceivable that the brief period of his existence on this earth should be other than a preparation for another and fuller life.

The separate existence of spirit is generally acquiesced in today by men of all faiths, and these will readily agree with the Prophet's attitude to this great question.

But it is not so generally understood that Muhammed, more than any other teacher, laid particular stress on the more precise character of the after-life, especially with regard to its atmosphere and conditions.

The idea that he regarded it as a mere sensuous Paradise has, of course, arisen out of the exaggerated notions of later non-Moslem scholiasts and commentators, from whom Islam

MUHAMMED: THE PROPHET

has suffered, as have other religions. But an examination of his inspired revelation will provide a very different picture of the after-life from that which is entertained by popular supposition. If the antagonist of Islam condemn it because it necessitates a belief in Eternity, then he must at the same time condemn the belief of millions of non-Moslems.

A point worthy of note regarding the Prophet is the veiled character of his personality.

This extraordinary man who changed the course of human history, how much is actually known about him?

He was not divine, no divine birth was claimed for him. But he certainly possessed the divine right of personality in the worldly sense of the term. The phrase *'Divine Right of Kings'* describes the significance of the term in this respect.

Kingship has usually rested upon three bases: armed force, wealth and segregation from the public.

The army always established the power of the king, money supported it and rendered him popular, but undoubtedly the most potent instrument for creating an atmosphere of divine right is personality.

Legends were woven around the name of king until, to the minds of the people, he appeared almost as a god. He was unapproachable, he did not mix with the people, the mass-mind conjured up legends regarding him until he appeared remote and dwelling in an almost non-human sphere.

But when the Prophet began his mission he was destitute of any of those advantages.

He had no armed forces behind him, the people were hostile to him, he was without means and, so far from being remote from the public, they could have access to him at any time, for Muhammed had practically no private life.

THE SPIRIT OF ISLAMIC IDEALS

In this, he was unlike most Oriental kings and potentates, who at that period were seldom seen in public.

It was, indeed, the open book of his personality which made him so popular as a ruler and which permitted him to alter the relationships between monarch and subject.

Muhammed indulged in no supernatural manifestations, he lived a plain and simple life, a poor man's life indeed; he never flinched from practical work, he fought like a common soldier in the ranks, bought and sold goods like an ordinary tradesman, mixed with people of every kind and made no difference between persons as regards condition of birth, or wealth.

At length, by this means, the whole of Arabia lay at his feet and gave allegiance to one God.

The old idea of the peculiar sanctity of prophets and leaders was broken forever so far as the Islamic religion was concerned, for Muhammed showed that the part of the true leader is to identify himself with those he leads and not to appear as on a different plane from them.

If this liberal attitude was not carried out by later Islamic rulers, it was certainly not the fault of the Prophet, nor was it due to the weakness of the lesson which he had bequeathed to them—a lesson which might well be taken to heart by all governors of men, wherever their lot be cast.

On his death-bed, and when too feeble to join his followers in the worship of Allah in the Mosque at Medina, he faced his end cheerfully.

'My mission is fulfilled, praise be to Allah,'

he said, lowering the curtain of his cell that looked toward the mosque.

Pagan Arabia had been redeemed to the eternal glory of this wondrous man, who, single-handed, aproached the gigantic task of changing a world, and succeeded in changing it to his own virtuous desire.

The great triumph of Muhammed was that he brought the idea of the unity of God back to a world which had practically forgotten it, and in a certain sense had never realised it.

As is well known to the students of Comparative Religion, modern researches have established the truth of the hypothesis that primitive man, wherever he is to be found today, naturally believes in the existence of a great God or Allfather, who looms behind the dark superstitions which form the religion of the savage.

Doubtless behind the fantastic beliefs of the pagan Arabians this ideal of a single great deity was to be found obscured by broken mythologies and gross fancies, and, indeed, we are assured that their Semitic brethren in Palestine and elsewhere had long entertained a similar doctrine.

But the struggle for the supremacy of that belief was a prolonged one, covering nearly 2,500 years of time.

The Jahvists of Palestine certainly made the earliest essays in monotheism, but the deity whom they placed above all others was simply a form of a rather localised wind-god, and not even the most strict among Jewish or Christian doctrinists would now agree that this early form in any way resembles the later conceptions of deity recognised by their faiths.

It was, indeed, reserved for Muhammed to give to the world the first conception of God as a being of justice and mercy, not associated with any particular mythology, race or nation, and not favouring any particular people.

This, indeed, had been the curse of the older religions: but when they conceived the idea of a great God he was usually regarded in the light of a national leader, a god of battles, whose chief desire was the triumph of his worshippers over their neighbours.

THE SPIRIT OF ISLAMIC IDEALS

This tribal idea of God, Muhammed discarded entirely, substituting for it belief in the idea of a world deity, a god to whom the peoples of all the earth were equal.

Out of this conception of godhead, there could not but emerge a much more liberal spirit of tolerance.

When the people of Islam conquered a province, and that province accepted their faith, its inhabitants at once became their equals. This is, indeed, the secret of the ready acceptance of the Islamic faith even today, by millions of people in Africa and Asia.

Christian missionaries and other observers frequently express great surprise to see the manner in which mere Mohammedan merchants succeed in converting pagan peoples in these continents, where they, with all their experience and equipment, have failed; but the reason for their success is to be discovered in the circumstance that the son of Islam adopts an attitude of fraternalism which the European Christian is loath to affect.

While his religion may dictate to the Christian the necessity for brotherhood, his racial inhibitions and traditions make it almost impossible for him to carry it out, but this in no wise restrains the Moslem.

Unity is, therefore, both the nucleus and the aim of the Islamic faith and polity. A unity which springs from a belief in the oneness of the Creator, and which spreads out to and inspires everything in creation.

From this idea of oneness, every belief in the Islamic faith has its rise and sanction; there is one God, one Prophet, one faith, one law, one status for mankind.

The beautiful and simple perfectness of the scheme is the best proof that it emanated from a divine source, and was directed by a personality who has changed human history.

MUHAMMED: THE PROPHET

INDEX

A

Aais 199
Aas Bin Waal Sahmi 114
Abbas 63, 64, 65, 84, 113, 139, 140, 224, 244
Abdu Manaf 61
Abdud-Dar 61, 62
Abdul Muttalib (Shayba) 62-76, 78, 83-85, 139, 225
Abdullah, father of Prophet 63, 65-69, 78, 83, 85, 95-96 119, 148, 160, 170, 174, 177, 188
Abdullah Bin Abialhumsa 95
Abdullah Bin Anees 179
Abdullah Bin Hazafa 209
Abdullah Bin Jahsh 170
Abdullah Bin Ubay 166
Abdur Rahman Bin Auf 107, 156
Abdus Shams 61, 62
Abi Wakkas 107
Abra or Abraha al Arsham 45, 47, 49, 50, 51, 52, 53, 55, 57, 66, 70-76, 78, 116, 130, 131, 161, 163, 196, 220, 222, 229
Abraham / Ibrahim 47, 49, 51-53, 55, 57, 75, 76, 78, 108, 130, 131, 161-163, 196, 220, 222, 229
Abu Ayub Ansari 154
Abu Bakr 63, 107, 113, 142, 143, 144, 146-147, 215, 229, 231, 244-246
Abu Bara Kalabi 179
Abu Dar, dynasty 176

Abu Daud, traditionist 185
Abu Fakiya 121
Abu Jahl 114, 121, 143-145, 174
Abu Jundal, son of Suhail 198,199
Abu Lahab (Abdul Uzza) 65, 114, 115
Abu Qubay, Meccan peak 216
Abu Sufyan (Bin Hurb) 63, 64, 114, 169, 175, 177-178, 186, 207, 220, 226
Abu Sulma 179
Abu Talha 156
Abu Talib 64, 65, 84-87, 90, 95, 97, 99, 108, 110, 114, 118-120, 123, 127, 139
Abu Zeitun, historian 38
Abul Hasham 140
Abwa 83
Abwal Hasheem 141
Abyssinia 122, 125, 206, 210
Adal, clan 180
Adam 130, 222, 242
Aday, family 113
Aden 45
Adnan 59, 78-79
Ahram, pilgrim costume 216
Al Aqsa 130
Al-Ahsa 44, 283
Al-Amin, the righteous 108, 283
Al Bara 141
Al-Isra, the nocturnal journey 129
Al-Miraj, the Ascension 127, 129

278

INDEX

Alms, giving & receiving 249
Ali (Bin Abu Talib) 6, 36, 41, 47, 59, 60, 63, 107, 108, 110, 42, 144-146, 173, 176, 217, 203, 229, 231, 244-246
Amalika 46, 47
Amina, mother of Prophet 78-85
Amir Ali, scholar 6, 47, 59-61, 63, 128, 178, 224, 226
Ammarah Bin Walid 119, 120
Amna 69
Amru Bin Aas 124
Amru Bin Uof 150, 153
Amru Omayah 179
Ansar or helpers 141-143, 147, 149, 150, 153, 155, 156, 167, 171, 185
Aqaba 137-139, 141
Arab ul Aariba 45, 46
Arab ul Baidah 45
Arab ul-Mustaariba 45
Arafa 242
Armistice between Moslems and Qureish 156-157
Arqum 107
Arzaqi, historian 55
Ashora, respecting fast of 185
Asia Minor 116
Asir 44, 46
Assad Bin Muaz 192
Astra-worshippers 45
Atba Bin Aseed 199-200
Auf, family 107
Aus, tribe 138-141, 157
Ayesha 129, 231, 233, 234, 244
Azlam, divining arrows 64

B

Badr, battle of 170-176, 184
Badu 236
Bahira, Christian monk, 87-90, 97

Bahrein 227
Bakka or Mecca 55
Bani Aad 46
Bani Abed-Dar 92
Bani Adiyy-bin-Kab 92
Bani Hashim 115, 126
Bani Jadis 46
Bani Khuzaa 59
Bani Sad 82
Bani Thamud 46
Banu-Amalika 46
Banu Amru 153
Banu Bukr 219
Banu-Jurhum 46, 59
Banu Kohtun 46, 113
Banu Omayah 82, 85, 107, 113, 115
Basra 43, 238
Bedouins 81-83, 166, 167, 178, 189, 201, 224
Bilal 195, 196, 212, 221, 235
Bin Ibrahim, (Suliman), historian 6, 88, 97-98, 129, 138
Bin Zarara 141
Black Stone (also Kaaba) 57, 59, 91-92, 161, 215, 252
Bokhari, traditionist 79, 96, 109, 119, 147, 150, 202
Buddhist 25
Buraq 130

C

Caesars 43
Camel, sacrifice of 40, 83
Camel, ship of the desert 251
Cave of Hira 99-100, 104-105
Cave-dwellers 46
Chalcedon 116
Chaldaeans 44
Charity, see Zakat
Chosroes 43, 116, 209, 210

Christ 46, 59, 124
Crusades 264

D

Dadd, idol 36
Damascus 97, 116, 225
Dancing girls 17, 171
Dark Ages 11, 20, 24
Day of Judgement 31
Days of Ignorance 270
Deuteronomy, Book of 192
Devolution 132, 241
Dhirar 65
Dhu Nafar 70, 71
Dhul Khalasa, idol 15
Dimensions of Mecca 56
Divinity of Jesus 124-125
Divorce 262-263
Diyat, magistracy 63, 285
Domatul Jindal 36

E

Egypt 116, 206
Elephants, Abyssinian siege (see Sura) 70
Epopts 25
Expansion of Islam 205-211, 227

F

Faid Qutan 178
Famine during warfare 187-191
Fasting during Ramadan 165, 249-250
Fatima 231
Fighting only when attacked 174
Fihr 59
Fijar, battle of 115
First Mosque at Quba 150

G

Gabriel, or Jibrail 104, 129
Gambling 90, 166
Genesis, Book of 51
Ghassan 225
Ghurta 179
God or Allah 5, 22, 23, 27-29, 35, 50, 52, 68, 72, 73, 75-78, 89, 103, 105, 106, 109, 110, 115, 119, 120, 123-125, 127, 128, 132, 135, 137, 143, 144, 148, 150, 161, 162, 167, 177, 178, 180, 187, 192, 196, 207, 208, 210, 211, 217, 221, 222, 230, 236, 238, 239, 242, 243, 245, 247, 248, 250, 255, 258, 263, 270, 271, 274, 275, 279-281
Gods, pagan 16, 18, 36-39, 40, 56, 136, 170, 278,
Grave worship 245
Grote, historian 193
Greece 14, 206

H

Haaris Bin Abayhala, first martyr 110-111
Haars Bin Qays 113
Hadhramut 55
Hagar 50, 51, 215
Harab 85
Harrés 180
Haj, or pilgrimage 53
Halima Saida 82, 83
Hamitic colonies 45
Hamasa, pre-Islamic epic 32
Hamza 65, 126, 173, 176, 177
Harith, son of Qais 65
Hashim 62
Hashim, family of 62, 63, 64, 78, 84, 95, 108, 113-115, 117, 126-127
Hasan 231

INDEX

Hassan, son of Kaab 64
Hauris Bin Amir 210
Heraclius (Harqoul) 206-208
Hijaba, guardianship of keys 63
Hijaz 44, 59, 60, 74, 97
Hijra (emigration, flight, exile) 122, 133, 135-151, 150, 213
Hindu 25
Hira 56, 99, 100, 104, 105, 149
Hobal, idol 36, 38, 56, 68, 69, 83, 136, 171, 177
Hodada 45
Holy Ghost 88, 89
Howazin, tribe 82, 223
Hozah Bin Ali 210
Hudaibiyya 195-200, 213, 214, 219
Hunain, battle of 223-228
Hurs Bin Amir 113
Husain 231
Hypocrites 160, 185

I

Ibn Abi Shayba, historian 215
Ibn Hisham, historian 6, 100, 106, 122, 125, 185, 225
Ibn Ishaq, historian 69, 83
Ibn Nadim, historian 55
Ibn Saad 121
Ibnul Athir, historian 226
Id-ul-Fitr 249
Idolatry 56, 75, 109
Idris 130
Ikhlaqay, or courtliness 123
Imam 165
Imam Malik, traditionist 52
Imra ul-Qais, pre-islamic poet 11, 15, 19, 38
Initiation 23-29
Injunction of five daily prayers 131, 155
Injunctions, islamic 165-168, 212

Iraq 44
Isbabol Nuzool, historian 184
Isaac 50, 51, 52
Isa Ibn Talha, historian 215
Istibza or Niyoga 41
Ishmael 49, 50, 51, 52, 53, 55, 59, 78, 79, 161, 196, 215
Isiah, Book of 101
Islam, meaning of 168
Islamic Law 256-264
Islamic thought 272-282
Ishmaelites 47, 49, 60, 75, 79

J

Jabel Soor 145
Jabul Haroon 87
Jafar 122-124, 125, 210-212
Jahl 65
Jahvists 280
Jazam 225
Jerusalem 43, 108, 115, 116, 128, 130, 131, 132, 133, 135, 154, 160, 163, 206
Jesus 52, 77, 88, 89, 100, 124 124, 125, 127, 130, 131, 141
Jews 97, 137, 157, 160, 163, 183, 185, 187, 201, 204, 228, 270
Johnson, historian 103
John, Book of 88
Judges, Book of 52, 53
Justinian 16, 233

K

Kaaba, Meccan shrine 17-20, 36, 37, 47, 49, 52, 56, 57, 59-63, 67, 68, 70, 72, 76, 91, 110, 113, 115, 126, 132, 136, 142, 161, 166, 196, 214, 216, 217, 221, 222, 226, 229, 250, 252
Kab Ibn Malik, historian 138-140
Kabaat Mecca, see Kaaba

Kalab, clan 179
Khabeeb, martyr 180-181
Khadija 96, 97, 99, 104, 105, 107, 127, 231, 262
Khaiber 185, 186, 201-204, 206, 228, 244
Khaimmeh, council chamber 64
Khalid Ibn Walid, cavalry commander 64, 177, 205, 212, 220, 221
Khalifa or Caliph, function of 122
Khayyam 20, 23
Khazraj, tribe 137-141, 157
Khazina, public finances 64
Khidash 33
Khizaah, tribe, 219
Khowalid, pagan chieftan 178
Khozar al Ahmar 46
Khrusra Parviz 206
Kidah, or pointless arrow 41
Kinena, tribe 175
King David 193
Kohtun, see Banu Kohtun 45, 46
Koran 104, 116-117, 123, 124, 133, 135-137, 140, 143, 151, 156, 160-163, 165, 166, 174, 194, 197, 204, 206, 212, 216, 229, 232, 239, 241, 242, 244, 247, 249, 250, 258
Kurzur Bin Jabar, camel thief 169
Kuzaites 59

L

Lagham 225
Lane Poole, historian 193
Last day 236
Lat, idol 16, 36, 88
Law of Moses 183, 192
Lebanon 85
Liwa, or standard 61-63
Lustration 247

M

Maad 59
Maghaz 222
Mahmud Pasha Falki 78
Mahra 227
Maisarah 97, 98
Makhzoom, family 113
Mâmûn 270
Marva, see Moreh
Maulana Shibli Nomani, scholar 6
Mawahib Ladunyah, historian 126
Mecca 15, 16, 23, 24, 36, 37, 44, 47, 49, 52, 53, 55, 56, 59, 60, 63, 65, 66, 69, 70, 71-75, 77, 81, 83, 84, 85-90, 95-99, 100, 105, 107, 113, 115-120, 122, 123, 125, 126, 128, 130-138, 142-145, 147, 149, 150, 154-156, 159, 160-163, 165, 166, 169-173, 175, 177, 178, 180, 184, 185, 191, 193, 195-201, 205, 207, 211, 213-217, 219-223, 229, 238, 241, 244, 248, 250-253, 274
Medina (Yasrib) 37, 38, 44, 83, 133, 137, 138, 141-144, 147, 148, 150, 154-160, 166-175, 178, 179, 181, 183-185, 189, 191-195, 197, 199, 201-202, 205, 206, 209-214, 217, 219, 220-222, 225, 227-229, 234, 236, 238, 243, 279
Meghass-ibn-Amr 47
Midyan 52
Minat, idol 16, 36, 37
Muezzin, call to prayer 165, 221
Mohammed Ali, historian 36, 41, 74, 116, 157
Momerie, historian 127-128
Moreh or Marya, Moriah, Moarya Marveh, Marwah 52, 216, 217

INDEX

Moses, Prophet & Law of 105, 123, 130, 131, 183, 184, 192, 204
Mount of Light (Hira) 99-100
Muallaqat 19, 20, 23, 34
Muir, Sir Edward, historian 42, 55, 216
Mukawwim 65
Munsoor Bin Akramah 126
Musoodi 55
Musab ibn Umr 138
Muslim, traditionist 49, 96
Mutah 210, 212
Muttalib 62

N

Naam, Khaiber fort 203
Nabi, Mosque of 154
Nabighah, historian 74
Nadwa, or national assembly 60, 61, 64, 214
Nadheer, jewish clan 183, 185
Nadhir 185
Nasim, or zephyr of Nejd 45
Nazir, jewish clan 157
Najibs, or deputies 140, 141
Najran 15, 270
Nakhla 170
Negus 122, 123, 124, 125, 206, 210
Nejd 44, 45, 59, 179
Noful, family 113, 219

O

Obayda, swordsman 173
Ohud, battle 175-178, 202, 205, 244
Old Testament 50, 193
Om Aman 83
Oman 45, 227
Omar bin Khattab 63, 113, 126, 174, 176-177, 115, 231, 232, 246, 270
Omar Bin Khattab 113
One Maad 59
Oracles 41, 69
Osman 63, 107, 122, 246
Osman Bin Talha 113
Otla Bin Rabiyah 114
Otwa 225
Outnumbering of Moslem forces 171, 176, 186, 210-211, 225

P

Pacts with Jewish tribes as basis for Islamic State, 141, 157-158, 184, 185, 187
Pact, disregard of 184,
Pact, denunciation of 187
Paradise 130, 141
Persian Empire, Persia 117, 206
Pentateuch 50
Pilgrimage 250-251, 253
Pledges, religious basis of 230,
Practicality, emphasis on 236
Prayer, form of, in mosque 165, 248
Prayer, inward meaning of 167, 247
Prayer toward Meccan Qibla 160-161, 248
Pre-Islamic worship 162, 163, 172, 243, 265
Property, return of 145-146
Preaching 107, 108, 110, 115
Ptolemy 55

Q

Qadid 37
Qamoos, Khaiber fort 203
Qainuqa, Jewish clan 157
Qais 64
Qarah, clan 180

Qariteh, Jewish clan 183
Qasida 19, 20
Qays b. al-Khatun 32, 33
Qibla or shrine of Mecca 161-163
Qinqah, Jewish clan 183, 185
Qossay 56, 59-64
Qossay Bin Kullab 55
Quba, first mosque 150
Qureish 19, 36, 56, 57, 60-65, 67, 70, 71-73, 75, 76, 77, 83, 84, 89, 90, 91, 95, 105, 107-110, 113-122, 125-127, 135-138, 141-147, 160, 166, 167, 169-178, 180-189, 191, 192, 196-200, 205-207, 211, 212, 214, 217, 219-222 227, 238
Quraiza, Jewish clan 157, 183
Qutan 178

R

Rabeayta Bin Harsa 37
Rain-making, cult of 38
Ramadan 104, 165, 220, 249
Razaqi 69
Red Sea 43, 44, 45, 55, 136, 210, 227, 253
Revelation 27, 104, 108, 166, 168, 197, 241, 275, 278
Rifada, poor-tax 61-64
Romans 116, 210, 211, 227
Rome 14, 82, 225
Roum 208
Rubi-el-Khali 44
Rumi 20, 200

S

Saad 107, 187
Saad Bin Maaz 161
Saad Brothers 187
Saad, son of Abi Wakkas 107
Sacrifice 52, 54

Saey, rite of pilgrimage 53, 216
Safa 107-109, 216, 217, 222
Safawan 64
Salma 62
Samuel 100
Sanaa 70
Sarah 50, 51, 52
Seal of Prophethood 90, 96
Sennacherib 74
Shaddad 46
Shahabraz 116
Sharjeel Bin Umru 210
Shibli, historian 124
Shima 82
Shrine of Idols 16
Sifarath, legation of state 63
Sikaya, intendance of sacred well 63
Simeyah 121
Siraqa 148-149
Slaves, freeing & treatment of 258-259
Soothsayers 16
Sowaa, idol 36
Stone deities, worship of 38, 136, 221, 226
Storytellers 16
Sufyan Bin Khalid 179-180
Sufyan Bin Omayah 113
Suhail 197-199
Sukhra 130
Sulman 212
Suliman Bin Ibrahim 97
Sura Al Haq 49
Sura Al Imran 55
Sura Ar Rum 117
Sura Baqarah 49
Sura Barat 229
Sura of Maryam 123
Sura of the Elephants 70, 75
Syria 90, 97, 116, 210

INDEX

T

Tabala 15
Tabiri, biographer of Prophet 71, 73, 75, 78, 79, 210, 224
Tabuk, expedition 225, 229
Tafsir-i-Kabir 55
Taif 36, 66, 135, 223-226
Talha, Pagan standard-bearer 176 178
Tameen, family 113
Taqwa, mosque 151
Tayyi, pre-Islamic poet 34
Temple of Mecca 130, 131, 132
Temple of Solomon 52
Tihama, tribe 175
Tirmizi, traditionist 96
Thebaid 46
Treatment of prisoners 174
Torah 51, 163, 193, 204
Toyaba 78, 81
Tree of Eternity 131
Trench warfare 186
Trinity 75, 124

U

Ukaz, fair of 15, 16
Umru Bin Lahi 37
Unays 71
Unity, divine concept of, 24, 29, 42, 75, 122-123, 137, 159, 160-162, 208, 221, 230, 245, 271, 273-275, 280, 281
Utba, swordsman 172
Uza, idol 16, 36, 289

V

Von Kremer, historian 217

W

Wahb Bin Abdul Manaf 69

Wahiyah Kulbi 206
Walid Bin Mogheera 113, 114
Waqidi 69, 290
Waraqa Ben Noful, sage 105, 106
Wine-bibbing 17, 18, 90, 136
Wise Men of the East 77
Women in battle 177, 202
Women, treatment of 260-264
Worship, form of 155

Y

Yaghwas, idol 36
Yakhzam, son of Marra, house of 64
Yamama 44
Yaqut Humwi, historian 55
Yasrib 137, 138, 139, 140, 142, 143
Yathrab or Medina 44
Yawaq, idol 36
Yazid Bin Rabiyatul 113
Yemen 36, 44-47, 55, 59, 62, 65, 69, 73, 97, 116, 136, 209, 227, 238
Yemenite invasion 70, 74, 77, 115

Z

Zaid 107, 154, 180, 211, 212, 259
Zainub 231
Zakat or Charity 166, 249, 255
Zanerah 121
Zam Zam 61-63, 84, 129, 215
Zubair 65, 107, 125
Zuhra, tribe 69
Zulmajaz 223